GYPSY MUSIC

IN EUROPEAN

CULTURE

ANNA G. PIOTROWSKA

Translated by Guy R. Torr

Gypsy Music in European Culture

FROM THE LATE

EIGHTEENTH

TO THE EARLY

TWENTIETH CENTURIES

Northeastern University Press | Boston

Northeastern University Press
An imprint of University Press of New England
www.upne.com
© 2013 Northeastern University
All rights reserved
Manufactured in the United States of America
Designed by Mindy Basinger Hill
Typeset in Arno Pro

 NARODOWY PROGRAM
ROZWOJU HUMANISTYKI

This publication was financed with the support of money from the
"Narodowy Program Rozwoju Humanistyki" funded by the Polish
Ministry of Science and Higher Education in the years 2011–2014.

University Press of New England is a member of the
Green Press Initiative. The paper used in this book meets their
minimum requirement for recycled paper.

Library of Congress Cataloging-in-Publication Data

Piotrowska, Anna G.
Gypsy music in European culture : from the late eighteenth to the early
twentieth centuries / Anna G. Piotrowska ; translated by Guy R. Torr.
        pages   cm
Includes bibliographical references and index.
ISBN 978-1-55553-836-1 (cloth : alk. paper) —
ISBN 978-1-55553-837-8 (pbk. : alk. paper) —
ISBN 978-1-55553-838-5 (ebook)
1. Romanies—Music—History and criticism. 2. Music—Europe—
Romani influences. I. Torr, Guy Russell, translator. II. Title.
ML3580.P54 2013
781.62'91497—dc23   2013030197

5   4   3   2   1

Contents

GYPSY MUSIC

IN EUROPEAN

CULTURE

Prologue

The figure of the Gypsy musician—from the end of the eighteenth century onward—has aroused notable interest, similar to that drawn by the myth of Orpheus since the Renaissance. Within the framework of constructing an image of idealized Gypsy music both in literature and within musical works, the Gypsy musician has been considered the embodiment of the inspired creator, possessing the specific features of the sensitive romantic artist. He was seductive while at the same time free and rebellious, and his separateness from bourgeois society was strongly emphasized. Hence, within the common consciousness, the music he performed was bestowed with similar traits. The idealized concept of Gypsy music, only loosely related to the musical practices of real Romanies, fulfilled the romantic hankering after exotic, charming, and highly emotional music. At the beginning of the twentieth century, together with a new approach to the research of music—stimulated by, among other things, radical nationalistic ideology and the academic development of ethnomusicology, with its own methodology—the attitude to the problem of so-called Gypsy music changed. Accepted became the nonuniformity of the musical practices present—differentiated by sociologists and anthropologists—among Romany groups. As a consequence of such an approach, while talking of "Gypsy music" or "music by Gypsies," I refer to the idealized representation propagated by literature and musical works created during the nineteenth and beginning of the twentieth centuries, reserving the term "Romany music" as an integral element of Romany social culture. Indeed, Gypsy music, as this book presents it, was not necessarily performed by musicians of Romany descent.

The new research perspectives put forth by ethnomusicology would turn the ideological legacy of seeing Gypsy music as a single conglomeration of varied styles into an anachronism. From the very beginning of the twentieth century, the romantic approach to questions relating to the Romany was reevaluated, starting with the variety of styles representative of Romany music derived from various groups. In concentrating on research into the music of concrete Romany groups within a broader perspective of ethnic minorities, ethnomusicologists consciously distanced themselves from an understanding of Gypsy music as a monolith, defining such a perception as the legacy of "the great romantic tradition" (Kertész-Wilkinson 2005, 779–822). Numerous articles written in this spirit are published in specialist journals covering both musicology and Romany studies, and entire monographs are devoted to the music of the Hungarian or Spanish Romany (Washabaugh 1996; Leblon 2003). In the twenty-first century, specialized articles reflecting the paradigm shift on Romany music appeared in lexicons and encyclopedias, including *The New Grove Dictionary*, by Irén Kertész-Wilkinson (2001, 613–620), Ursula Hemetek's *Die Musik in Geschichte und Gegenwart* (2003, 443–457), and an interesting piece on comprehending national contexts presented by Carol Silverman in the *Garland Encyclopedia of World Music* (Silverman 2000, 270–93).

Whatever the developments, the attitude of many musicologists toward the issue of Gypsy music has often remained ambivalent. Particularly in the last century, this was manifested in the absence of entries on the subject in prestigious encyclopedias, or else its treatment in a "nineteenth-century way," involving the mere duplication of certain, usually a priori, viewpoints. In the entry for "Gypsy Music" in the *Harvard Dictionary of Music,* Willi Apel writes provocatively, "Whether the Gypsies ever possessed a musical tradition of their own is a matter of doubt" (1974, 364). Somewhat less disdainful, though similar in effect, are the objections formulated in *Riemann Musiklexikon,* whose author posits, "In what area the Gypsies possessed an original way of making music has not been explained" (F. B. 1967, 1078).

Aside from these emphases on the existence, or character, of a Romany musical tradition, only a very few researchers have touched on the subject of European professional musicians who drew, for their own art, on their romanticized vision of music-making attributed to Gypsies. Such material was usually conceived as a supplement to collected works on either Romany music (Baumann 2000, 393–443) or the question of local color in nineteenth-century music (Angermüller 1976, 131–58). The authors of these publications rarely asked about the means by which works inspired by Romany heroes and the music linked with them existed within European culture, focusing rather on a quantitative count and panoramic presentation of works created in modern Europe as a result of admiration of Gypsy culture.

This shortage of works accounting for the multidimensional presence of Gypsy music in the European tradition is a direct inspiration for my research. Also formative has been the lack of critical analysis on how the discourse was created—that which influenced not only intellectuals and academics but also public opinion and the very composers themselves who succumbed to and reproduced conventionalized thought schemes in relation to Gypsy music. In seeking to fill this scholarly gap, I have sought to isolate models for the litera-ture's forming of a discourse as well as to trace the influence of this discourse on compositional works.

In sketching a broad picture of the phenomenon, my research analyzes ma-terials of a dual type: on the one hand, written sources such as statements, declarations, monographs, and articles dealing with notions of Gypsy music, while on the other, the scores of selected musical works that were produced as a result of a fascination with Gypsy culture.

While selecting musical material, I considered the nonsonic components that affect the production and reception of music as well as specific works' intended use (Piotrowski 1984, 24). The compositions chosen were divided into stage works (operas, operettas, ballets) and nonstage works, and those with texts (songs) and those without (instrumental pieces).

The period covered—from the end of the eighteenth century to the early twentieth century (with the end date extending as far as 1950 and sometimes beyond)—is important for an understanding of Gypsy culture and music. The period's beginning corresponds with the publication of cutting-edge books on the Gypsy question in Europe (Willems 1997, 22–92), and its end is marked by a paradigm change that brought, among other things, a postmodernist conception of Gypsy music within the framework of a phenomenon ultimately deemed *world music* (Kajanova and Zaborska 2007, 217–45).

The conceptualization of the phenomenon of Gypsy music in European cul-ture proposed here concerns itself as much with the discourse on Gypsy music presented against various sociological, historical, and political conditions as it does against questions of particular works devised under the inspiration of ideal-ized Gypsy culture. Research into the network of connections occurring among works on Gypsy music and compositions allows for the deconstruction of the types of discourse accompanying Gypsy music, with a particular split between assimilative and nonassimilative approaches, which will be explicated shortly. These two codes, which often intermingle, were to fundamentally influence the composers who—through both their works and their statements—entered into the discourse, not only indirectly preserving it but also propagating its essen-tializing characteristics. The feedback between the discourse on Gypsy music and actual musical works with Gypsy connotations (most frequently through the choice of title or the selection of protagonists) reinforced the conventionalized image of the Gypsy, and particularly of the Gypsy musician, resulting in an ossification of the very stereotype of Gypsy music and the Gypsy musician, as well as influencing the discourse on Gypsy music and Gypsy culture.

The Shaping of the Topos of Gypsy Music

The deeply rooted notion within the European consciousness as to the musicality of the Gypsies was touched on by early researchers. Those academics were, however, primarily interested in the study of Gypsy origin and language. Among those to mention Gypsy music-making was Heinrich Grellmann (1756–1804), in the work *Die Zigeuner,* published in Göttingen in 1783, which not only established the substructure for the subsequent, more penetrating research but also—having been translated into other languages—constituted the main source of knowledge on Gypsies at the beginning of the nineteenth century.

Whatever the impact of Grellmann's work, sources on the Gypsies' musical tradition can be found many centuries earlier. Among the oldest of these is the Arabic chronicle of Hamza Ispahani, dating to about 950. The text mentions the tribe of Zott, imprecisely designating all who had arrived in the Persian kingdom from the Indus River valley, including possibly the Romany (Fraser 2005, 33). The author cites a tale of people settled from India, throwing light on their musical traditions: apparently under the rule of the Persian monarch Bahram Gur (r. 420–438), twelve thousand musicians were brought from India. The same legend is referred to in 1010 by the poet Ferdousi, who writes of the ruler Bahram Gur, who is said to have asked his father-in-law (or possibly brother-in-law), King Senkal (Szangul), of Kannauj in northern India, to send him ten thousand musicians called Luri.

Many researchers associate the very name of the Luri people (possibly Gypsies) with the word *lute,* an instrument they presumably played. For instance, Bernard Leblon states that according to European chronicles (e.g., from Dubrovnik), the first instruments on which the Gypsies played upon arriving in Europe were lutes (Leblon 2003, 3). Jean-Paul Clébert, discussing the linkage of the Gypsies with the Luri people, refers directly to the etymology of the term *lute* from the Arabic *al oud* (meaning "of wood"). He points out similar formations in other languages, such as the Provençal *laut,* the old French *leüt,* and the German *der Laut,* and emphasizes that Gypsy musicians often called themselves *Lautari.* Moreover, within Romanian territories, the surname Lautari (with spelling variations) was widespread among Gypsy musicians (Clébert 1970, 144). For example, we have the legendary nineteenth-century Romanian Gypsy violinist

Barbu Lautaru, who enraptured Franz Liszt with his instantaneous reproductions of the most complicated melodic arrangements (Noica 1995, 49–51).

Eleventh- and twelfth-century records discuss Gypsies in Constantinople, where a name for them emerged from one of the Manichean sects—the Athinganoi, or possibly Hatsigganoi. From this etymology, the name for Romanies (i.e., Tziganes) entered into many languages, among them Slavic languages. Gypsies were already noted for their talents in public performance, with records extolling their ability to tame wild animals and perform spells. Over time, the image of Gypsies as magic conjurers would be joined by associations with fortune-telling, acrobatics, and street music. Such ties accompanied Gypsies as they entered the heart of Europe.

Gypsies more than likely arrived in Central Europe before 1250, although documents verifying their presence date only from the fifteenth century. And while some stayed, most used Central Europe as a stopping point before continuing west: individual Gypsies appeared in Switzerland in 1414 and a year or so later in France. Significant numbers of Gypsies followed in their tracks, successively relocating themselves in the direction of Western Europe, escaping, among other things, the slavery that they had been subjected to in Romania. By presenting themselves as Christians on a seven-year pilgrimage, Gypsies initially enjoyed the support of the local population. During their journeys, they were protected from any dangers by guarantees of safe conduct granted by the authorities, allowing them to move freely over a given territory: letters of protection for Gypsies were issued by, among others, Sigismund, the Holy Roman Emperor, who lived from 1368 to 1437. With time, though, the intentions of Gypsies were speculated upon and the validity of these letters was questioned.

Wandering Gypsies, as we have seen, were already perceived, first and foremost, as providers of entertainment—musicians and acrobats, magicians and fortune-tellers. Gypsy women displayed a special ease at mastering local languages and used this ability in telling the future and reading people's palms. Furthermore, the Gypsies embellished their performances with stories about their dangerous, adventure-filled journeys. As confirmed by historical records, these public performances, initially together with non-Gypsy partners, were immensely popular. For instance, a troupe of Gypsy acrobats performed in Constantinople in 1321—tightrope walking, hanging from the trapeze, and showing off juggling skills (Kendrick 2004, 67). Accounts from the fifteenth and sixteenth centuries inform us of the continuation of such activities, with Gypsy acrobats and palm readers appearing, for example, in Paris around 1427. An anonymously authored 1475 play from Lucerne, Switzerland, introduced the

Gypsy palm reader in literature, and the figure would reappear in the 1521 play *Farsa das Ciganas*, by Gil Vicente of Portugal, which recounted the fate of eight Gypsy heroes (Fraser 2005, 99, 124).

In Christian Europe, the attitude toward entertainment remained ambivalent; in Gypsy performances, the combination of musical, magical, and acrobatic elements caused associations with devilish practices, though even the sixteenth-century physician and scientist Paracelsus himself acknowledged the Gypsies' magical abilities (Gilad 1999, 78). In medieval Europe, traveling musicians—both Gypsies and others—were widely perceived as purveyors of quackery and the magic tradition, constituting a potential threat to Christianity. Gypsies' dark complexion encouraged their demonization, with the color black associated with impure powers and even the devil himself (di Nola 2004, 311–12). The ambivalent situation, more generally, of secular musicians in medieval Europe may have pushed Gypsies to adopt the custom of wandering music-making. These musicians were considered classless, not afforded judicial protections, and often treated as potential murderers, robbers, and antisocial troublemakers possessing no rights whatsoever (Salmen 1983, 25). Gypsies, in traversing such a path, ensured themselves the possibility of a relatively independent lifestyle, while at the same time filling a market niche. Yet in embracing the life of the wandering musician, Gypsies strengthened stereotypes about themselves. The association of Gypsies with music-making has developed so strongly within the European consciousness that in some places today, such as Greece, the words *Gypsy* and *musician* are synonymous (Leblon 2003, 5).

As professional musicians, Romanies were hired with increasingly frequency to perform at courts, where musicians' social and ethnic origins were of almost no significance. In the fifteenth century, at the court of the prince of Ferrara in Italy, Gypsies performed on plucked string instruments (Kertész-Wilkinson 2001, 614). Among the musicians employed at the Polish royal court at Wawel Castle during the reign of Zygmunt Stary (Sigismund the Elder) can be found the name Stanislaus Czigan, who more than likely served, from 1539 to 1548, as a poorly paid *tubicinator* (a term in old Polish adapted from Latin meaning "trumpeter") (Głuszcz-Zwolińska 1988, 101). His surname and variants would have indicated Romany/Gypsy background in fifteenth- and sixteenth-century Poland (Mróz 2001, 53).

Surprisingly, the first records on the presence of Gypsies in Europe rarely dealt explicitly with their musical traditions, with little room devoted to the instruments they used. Appearing sometimes in that context, the word *cithara* (with spelling variants) referred generally to plucked string instruments. So-called Gypsy *cytharedos*, mentioned, for example, in a 1532 letter by a Hungarian hussar commander, presumably played either on a lyre, a zither, or a lute (Fraser 2005, 109). Beginning in the fifteenth century, however, such instruments were preferred to provide chordal accompaniment for four-part vocal arrangements (Chomiński and Wilkowska-Chomińska 1989, 183–185). Gypsies' skill on such instruments earned them recognition, and as professionals in France, for instance, they were often much sought-after as harpists (Leblon 2003, 4).

Toward the end of the eighteenth century—when academic research into Gypsy traditions was taking place—Gypsy musicality was taken to be the immanent trait of their culture. Grellmann, in discussing the observed instrumental abilities witnessed among Gypsies, cited the violinist Mihály Barna and Gypsy girls in general, asserting the particular predilection for music displayed by Gypsies from Spain (1810, 111). Many nineteenth-century authors reproduced this information without attribution. For example, in Poland, Ignacy Daniłowicz wrote in 1824 of how Gypsies of both sexes played at country weddings (Daniłowicz 1824, 45). Another Polish scholar Teodor Narbutt confirmed this almost to the word in his account of Gypsy virtuosity on the dulcimer and violin. Narbutt also commented on Gypsies' exceptional improvisatory and memory skills. However, especially striking in Narbutt's account—and clearly influenced by previous accounts—are the darker expressions linking Gypsy musical prowess to collusion with the devil, as this passage illustrates: "Gypsies told me that this type of improviser was seen at the court of their king, Marcinkiewicz, so perfect in deed that he was called a wizard. . . ." (Narbutt 1830, 119).

Indeed, it seems that Gypsies' public performance of music elicited two distinct social reactions. On the one hand, Gypsies were associated—as already discussed—with entertainment, with having a good time and even with debauchery; in sixteenth-century France, the acrobatic-theatrical-musical spectacles performed under an open sky by two or three conjurers dressed up "with blackened or painted faces" were considered frivolous and seen to correspond to the performers' free lifestyle (Dufour 1998, 257). On the other hand, Gypsies—by utilizing their musical talents in a relatively problem-free way—often managed to gain the trust of other social groups and even integrated with them (Fraser 2005, 200). In the eighteenth century, for example, a Gypsy violinist named Abram Wood settled with his family in Wales, and when he had managed to master the harp—the Welsh national instrument—his family was completely accepted by the local population (Sampson 1932, 56–71; Jarman and Jarman 1991, chapters 4–5).

It was in the nineteenth century that the stereotypical image of Gypsy musicians emerged. The image of a solitary Gypsy musician, presented as an alienated romantic hero, resulted in an idealized conception of the figure. Not only were Gypsy musicians themselves appreciated and valued, but also—broadly speaking—Gypsy themes started to be referenced in professional, *non*-Gypsy musical works. At the same time, the literature accompanying the rise of such musical awareness treated Gypsy music in a generalized, monolithic way. As we have seen, this situation would only change with the more discerning musicological work of the twentieth century (Awosusi 1996–1998). And in our present century, to restate an earlier point, academics have sought to achieve an even more holistic view, by looking into actual values, forms, and functions associated with the music in Romany societies (Kertész-Wilkinson 2005, 779–822).

Contemporary research into Romany music is conducted within two parallel currents: one focuses on the musical practices of particular Romany groups, and analyzes their musical traditions; the second seeks to assess Romany music as a comprehensive phenomenon. These two tracks, while not contradictory, reflect the elusive, generalized nature of the term "Gypsy," or "Romany," which refers to the collectivity of nomadic groups. Likewise, so-called Gypsy music is not monolithic: as the cultural product of diverse representatives of "Gypsies," it constitutes a conglomerate of varied musical traditions. Some groups, for instance, although settled for generations, have revived their music and developed their own idiom, as a result of intense pressures associated with acculturation. Other Romany groups, for their part, have remained migratory and have absorbed musical styles from other ethnic groups with which they have interacted. These other influences have thus played an important role in the shaping of Romany music, just as Romany music has affected the other ethnic groups that have absorbed its elements. What we might call *inter*-Romany exchange in a given geographic region has also been powerfully important in creating a musical language (Kovàlcsik 1990, 178).

Accordingly, researchers of Romany music have emphasized its intensely varied strains: from Spanish flamenco through Bulgarian wedding-reception music to the choirs of the Russian Romany and right up to the music of the Hungarian Gypsies performed for restaurant guests. Host countries have exerted strong pressures on such musicians, compelling them not only to adopt local instruments but also to often invoke motifs borrowed from the nation's folklore, giving the music a new significance and dimension. These adaptations reflect the widespread musical practice among Gypsies to preserve "the traditional musical material and customs of the dominant society" (Kertész-Wilkinson 2001, 614).

These adaptations of musical language have meant that no single, dominant style of "Gypsy music" exists, nor does a common model for musical adaptation unite all Romany groups. For instance, the music of Andalusian Gypsies is associated first and foremost with flamenco, Gypsies in Scotland have adopted the bagpipe, and Russian Gypsies have cultivated choral singing. In Central Europe, Romany boys often receive a guitar immediately after birth, while girls learn to sing from an early age. This ability to adapt and diversify explains the huge scope of the influence of Romany music—not merely in its commercial popularity among the non-Romany but also in its emotional nature and power for a variety of listeners. Carol Silverman has summed up this phenomenon in the concise claim that "Roma are powerless politically and powerful musically" (Silverman 1996, 231).

Despite such a huge array of styles and repertoires, Romany music is also widely accepted to contain certain, deeply rooted, common traits. These include the specific mode of performance—often improvisation; the high level of expressiveness—resulting from rapid changes in tempo and tempo rubato as well as the elaborate embellishment of the melody; a selection of texts—on daily life or tragedies connected with lost love or dreams of an end to discrimination. Hence, since the eighteenth century, both academics and musicians have sought an unequivocal answer to the seemingly simple question "What is Gypsy music?" But such a definition has been impossible to locate, despite the Romany people's common origin in India and common language (with many local dialects). A necessary degree of musical cohesion simply cannot be found.

Individual researchers into Romany music present various positions on its common features, with two main distinctions. The first group concentrates mostly on the musical side (including the manner of performance and the influences the music reflects) while the second group is inclined to examine extramusical factors.

Among the theories supporting the musical cohesion of Romany music, those of Lev Tcherenkov and Stéphane Laederich as well as of Michael Beckerman are characterized by a consistent internal logic. Tcherenkov and Laederich maintain that the starting point for all Romany musical styles is the music's common roots, which were "present before Roma separated into various branches" (Tcherenkov and Laederich 2004, 704). The authors then differentiate five elements constituting distinguishing features: vocality, sense of time, phraseology, harmony, and way of singing.

Beckerman approaches the situation differently, by suggesting a thorough look at the Romany musical culture. He propagated his ideas to a presumably wide readership in a *New York Times* article dated April 1, 2001 ("Music: Pushing

Gypsiness, Roma or Otherwise"), in which he proposed the equation $I + V = E$, with I representing "improvisation" as an immanent feature of most Romany musical cultures, V indicating "virtuoso" performances as expressed especially in instrumental music, and E reflecting the "emotions" stirred in the listeners, in response to the expressiveness created by the combination of improvisation and virtuoso artistry.

Another researcher, David Malvinni, interprets Beckerman's equation $I + V = E$ in terms of the mediating role the Gypsy performer plays—saturating an emotionally unmarked space with his own expression (2004, 11). The equation, although referring in principle to Romany music, may perhaps be applied in the broadest possible reading of "Gypsyness," covering not only Romany groups but also artistic bohemians.

A member of the second group, focusing on extramusical contexts, Irén Kertész-Wilkinson notes that "under the clear differentiation of Gypsy music there are hidden . . . common socio-cultural values which constitute an answer to the pressure of assimilation and the constant persecution on the part of various 'host' societies" (Kertész-Wilkinson 2001, 613). These values, she contends, constitute the chief frame of reference for the music of various Romany groups, as seen in the texts that accompany the music. Among the values found in these texts, she includes the absence of a common (even mythological) homeland, an emphasis on the possession and knowledge of one's own genealogy, an absence of economic independence resulting from the practice of freelance occupations, as well as a clear social system emphasizing the differences between the Romany and the non-Romany, together with the internal stratification of Gypsy groups. As a consequence, Kertész-Wilkinson has formulated the thesis that "European Gypsy songs display a tendency to touch on a similar thematic range and usually, although not exclusively, from a male perspective." Such themes include "personal loss, loneliness, imprisonment, family relations (especially between mother and children) and the ambiguous nature of love, but also the joys of Gypsy life, such as being together with their 'brothers,' going to a fair, selling and buying horses, as well as explicit notions of physical love, a topic that is also part of the kinaesthetic expressions of many Gypsy dances" (Kertész-Wilkinson 2001, 616). The content touched on undergoes a certain modification (both thematically and linguistically) if it is designated for external recipients and updated to match, for example, the names of known actors, references to television program, and so forth.

The Hungarian ethnomusicologist Katalin Koválcsik, for her part, points to the seeming lack of any common features among the varied musical idioms created by Romany groups. She suggests two causes for the difficulty of identifying common traits among diverse Romany groups' musical idioms: assimilation and the quick appearance of new stylistic elements (Kovalcsik 1990, 179).

In summing up the multifarious positions on the issue, Malvinni (2004, 213) proposes the following list of traits:

1. An authentic way of expressing a spiritual belonging to the Romany world
2. An expressive musical style
3. A cognitive construct, a category helping both the Romany and the non-Romany to distinguish Romany music from other forms
4. A marketing trick
5. A form having culturally specific meaning as defined in the framework of ethnomusicological research
6. An element within a movement aspiring to unify all modern Romany

Yet even as Romany music responds to and deftly incorporates other musical forms and innovations, and despite its great richness in style and performance, it remains easily identifiable within non-Romany circles with the "colorful" world of Gypsy life. The very reception of this music by the non-Romany, with the reception contoured to the receiver's specific values, results in a perception of internal cohesion, if not stylistically then ideologically. And this dynamic is confirmed by the fact that researchers from outside Romany societies are those most likely to propose answers to questions about the essence of Gypsyness (Lemon 1991, 365). The music-making by the Romany, as broadly known and as emphasized by researchers, is still the aspect of Gypsy culture that—for external observers—most commonly results in the formation of the stereotype of the Gypsy in the modern world (Stewart 1997, 181).

Part I

TWO MODELS OF DISCOURSE

ON GYPSY MUSIC

The music played by Gypsies was perceived within Europe, on the one hand, through the prism of the Gypsy question—a question burdened with the pejorative overtones of general attitudes toward Gypsies—and, on the other, according to the musical practices connected with Gypsies seen within the broader cultural conditions of modern Europe. Academic consideration of Gypsy music—beginning at the start of the nineteenth century and tied to rising interest in Romany people overall—would culminate in two models: those of assimilation and nonassimilation. These models both aimed to situate Gypsies and their music within European culture.

In the period following the French Revolution right up until the beginning of the twentieth century, the assimilative model was based on the concept of nationality propagated within the whole of Europe. As such, Gypsy music was presented as an integral component of European culture, a form that joined with local musical idioms to create national musical traditions in individual countries, especially those with high proportions of Romanies. Meanwhile, within the nonassimilative model, Gypsy music was presented as belonging to a distinct culture, whose outlook was inherently alien to European civilization. The nonassimilative model employed the concepts of exoticism (Orientalism) and race, weaving Gypsy origin, musical characteristics, and thinking on the culture of Gypsies into an interdependent web.

The popularized versions of Gypsy music that emerged from the late eighteenth century onward—performed in particular by Hungarian Romanies but also by Russian and Spanish Romanies—came about in the context of creating national cultures as opposed to the earlier abstract humanism of the eighteenth-century Classical period. Music performed by Romanies was considered a binding agent for countries of broad geographical scope, with the figure of the wandering Gypsy musician playing an especially useful role as a unifier of dispersed musical practices. Academic writings on Gypsy music of this period thus concentrate on the links between Gypsy music and the music of a given country, intertwining Gypsy with national motifs and thereby acknowledging hybrid forms. The model of assimilation bolstered the thesis that the nation was both a spiritual and a historical concept and therefore eternally ascending, whereas the concept of race was perceived as naturalistic or static.

The concept of race—as applied to Romanies, more or less interchangeable with exoticism—was used in the construction of the nonassimilation model. Indeed, race was the dominant element of secular European identity and closely connected with the idea of Europe as such. Especially beginning at the end of the nineteenth century—driven by various peoples' search for noble roots in the ancient world—it became of special importance for European history (Delanty 1995). To emphasize one's own racial purity could mean denigrating the Other, with Gypsies and their music often the casualties of academic writings having such a bent. The recognition of Romanies (as well as Jews) as representatives of a non-European but Oriental race constituted a seminal moment in the alienated stance of the researcher toward Gypsy music. The concept of "still exotic arrivals" (Ficowski 1953, 18) would persist into the twentieth century. A notion of European exceptionalism, among nineteenth-century intellectuals and others, guided such views (Sokolewicz 1974, 182). Broadly speaking, in the nineteenth century, anyone who did not fit in might be considered Other (Skarga 1973, 277); Gypsies likewise were often treated as strange, and potentially dangerous, and, as noted, possessed of a culture alien to the European. This Eurocentrism was a specific form of ethnocentrism, a mixture of ethno- and logocentricism negating unknown elements as a result of broad centralizing processes (Waldenfels 2002, 146).

The inclusion of music cultivated by Gypsies within the nonassimilative model was aimed at building the scholars' own ethnic and national self-conception. In making their arguments, they emphasized differences, presented the marginalized nature of Gypsy music, and finally sought to reduce its role in the development of Europe's musical culture. Such reactions occurred almost mechanically, naïvely, although they may have resulted from the assumptions of a conscious program. Stefan Treugutt writes that, "mistrust, aversion, even hostility in relation to others and that which is different characterizes human societies in exactly the same way as interest, wonder in relation to something foreign, the desire to emulate being last" (Treugutt 1973, 393). The inclusion of discourse on Gypsy music in a wider spectrum of exoticism was linked closely with the search for a "noble savage" as well as the attribution of the emotional layer of Gypsy music with traits associated with Oriental peoples (on the one hand sentimentalism and naïveté, on the other wildness and barbarianism).

Both the assimilation and nonassimilation models seem to have drawn their sources from the early modern belief in knowledge as the motor of progress. For centuries demonized as a result of their skin color, Eastern origins, and cultivation of their own customs, Gypsies constituted within Europe a group "pushed to the edge," as they were considered the bearers of a certain "ceremonial or mythological legacy which, in dangerously opposing those models suitable for the majority, became sorcery by dint of its antithetic relation to these models" (di Nola 2004, 231). Containment of fear of unknown practices, ones not fully identified and consequently seen as endangering European culture, was inseparable from the belief in science and the rational explanation of phenomena. Hence, the academic descriptions of Gypsy customs and music more than likely fulfilled an auxiliary function of overcoming external fear, registering itself in the process of rationalization, whose chief medium was science and the reasonable comprehension of the world—or its "disenchantment." Furthermore, science brought with it not only cognitive possibilities but also the illusion of power and control. I therefore believe that the nineteenth-century subjugation of Gypsy music took on specific traits connected with the trivialization of fear, based on the principle that "the greatest medicine is familiarity, one needs merely to become accustomed to fear in order to keep it in check" (Lepenies 1996, 45).

These two proposed models of discourse—assimilative and nonassimilative—on Gypsy music, as observed in European academic and nonacademic literature of the nineteenth and early twentieth centuries, were additionally encapsulated within a broad spectrum of interpretative possibilities, which were extremely radical in their significance.

The Idea of National Music and the Question of Gypsy Music

An awareness of ethnic identity in music arose at the moment when national ethnic cultures started to emerge from universalist Latin Europe and from within the Western Church (Bielawski 1999, 69). Examining the tradition of art music within the context of its creators' nationality constituted a dominant interpretative model that would emanate through the entire twentieth century. Diverse musical traditions would be drawn into the debate, which was rooted in politics and, in particular, hierarchies of cultural value within given nations. For example, the supremacy of German-speaking musical circles was upheld by Wagnerian attempts to revive Teutonic mythology, academic works of a musicological character overall were favored, and interest in music among amateurs was encouraged through numerous popular publications. Chiefly within the framework of German-centric musicology, scholars sought to define music outside the German scope and therefore concocted formulations of national school and national style.

Opposing the (Austro-)German-centric view on European music was the Francophone current, which sought over centuries to show its own importance. In countries such as Russia, Poland, the Czech lands, and Scandinavian countries, literature on music likewise strongly exhibited a division into dominant trends and those on the fringes. The influential twentieth-century German musicologist Carl Dahlhaus claimed that "the concept of national schools . . . implies . . . that national is an alternative to universal. The term 'national school' is a covert admission that the phenomenon it describes is peripheral" (1985, 89). The discrepancy in music between universality (classical grandeur, mastery) and nationalism (color, manners, fashion) brought an evaluatory factor, freely discussed, for example, by the German-born composer and theorist Paul Hindemith (1952, 198).

The general tendencies assimilating Gypsy traditions into the national cultures of certain European countries, integrating art and—particularly—music within a national legacy, were reflected in the inclusion of Gypsy musical themes and even more topical allusions such as stage works' titles. The Hungarian and Spanish traditions of actively incorporating Gypsy culture in the creation of national identity appeared both in literature and musical composition. The undoubtedly significant contribution of Russian Gypsies to the formation of Russian culture, for its part, is not shown so prominently in the country's professional music; rather, more marginally, its stamp is found in the Russian folk musical idiom. Hence, from a European perspective, Russian national music (already considered exotic in the eyes of Western Europe) does not use Gypsy culture in the same way as Hungarian and Spanish music does.

⋎ ⋏ ⋎ ⋏ ⋎

CHAPTER ONE

Hungarian National Music

Gypsy Musical Traditions within Hungarian Culture

Historical Background

Musicologists, ethnologists, historians, and anthropologists often express a version of the following statement: "There is hardly a country where Gypsy musicians played such an important role in the development of a national musical style . . . as was the case in Hungary" (Erdely 1983, 550). This notion was—chiefly—linked to a sense among Gypsy musicians of the Gypsy people's high standing within Hungary from early on. Gypsies had arrived in the territory around 1410 and already by 1423 the first mentions are found of letters granting them safe conduct. Documents from the mid-fifteenth century also attest to the activity of Gypsy musicians in Hungary. By the end of the seventeenth century, the tradition of associating a Gypsy with the musical profession in Hungary was already established. Contemporary documents and (later) publications devoted to Gypsies reinforced this interlinking of Gypsies and music-making. In 1783, Grellmann wrote in particular about the musical talents of Gypsies from Hungary. At the beginning of the next century, authors elsewhere in Europe, including Poland, likewise referred to the unusual talents of Hungarian Gypsy musicians (Czacki 1835, 54).

The *Zigeunerkapellen* Lineup

Hungarian Gypsies started to organize their own musical groups, known as *Zigeunerkapellen*, at the end of the eighteenth century; the lineups and repertoires of these groups reached a second stage around the mid-nineteenth century; and they arrived at a final stage in the second half of the nineteenth century.

In late eighteenth-century Hungary, Gypsies were often employed, according to firsthand accounts, as smiths. Music thus constituted a secondary occupation. Yet from the 1780s on, one increasingly comes across Gypsy musicians at folk musical celebrations. Rural non-Romany inhabitants thus slowly but surely shed the use of certain instruments, such as the bagpipe. At the same time, as Gypsies filled the role of musicians in the Hungarian countryside, they adapted their music to the expectations of the rural communities. For example, traditional Hungarian songs had not required harmony accompaniment, while the instruments used in Gypsy bands could easily provide such accompaniment. Here, a dynamic emerged in which the Gypsy musicians and local audiences would find common ground on musical arrangements and preferences. Around the same time, the bands' lineup became established, with two required instruments, a lead melody instrument (violin) and an instrument providing harmony and percussion effects (*gardon*, which was similar to the cello and often homemade). This other instrumentalist (often the spouse of the violinist) never played alone but rather always accompanied the melody instrument. Such a composition was to become the prototype for the later, celebrated Gypsy bands.

At the turn of the nineteenth century, *Zigeunerkapellen* from Hungary became increasingly active in villages and small towns. Despite the name *Zigeunerkapelle* (the singular form), the groups were usually composed only in part of Gypsy musicians. And the rise of the groups was sparked precisely by the flowering of esteem for Gypsy music in Hungary. The bands rapidly grew from their initial two-instrument lineup to three or four, with fiddlers and dulcimer players joining the fray. Already established musical bands were called—as if allowing for their upward development—Gypsy orchestras, though they would have at most ten to fourteen musicians.

The most typical four-person group comprised two fiddlers—the first of whom was known as the *prímás* (referring to the lead violin part, called *prím*), while the second violinist played what was known as *contra*. Popular *Zigeunerkapellen* also included a double bass (playing mainly an incidental percussion role) along with a dulcimer. By 1800, the Leipzig-based *Allgemeine Musikalische Zeitung* had published an article describing just this makeup for a typical Gypsy band (May 18, 1800; quoted in Sárosi 1987, 238).

The Dulcimer, or *Cimbalom*

Over time, the range of instruments used by the *Zigeunerkapellen* would increase, as demonstrated by the use of the dulcimer. In the seventeenth century, dulcimers were widespread in those European regions occupied by the

Turks, while as early as 1596 an account noted a Gypsy musician playing on an instrument that resembled a psalterium, or psaltery, caught by the Ottoman bey's (governor's) border guards from Pécs, in Hungary (Sárosi 1970, 11).

The dulcimer used at the time was a small, stringed, legless instrument similar to the zither and emitting a relatively quiet sound. It was diatonically tuned and consequently would have been playable in a single key. Only in 1874 in Budapest did József Schunda develop a concert dulcimer with a four-octave chromatic scale. The considerable size of the instrument (approximately 163 centimeters in length) required that it be placed on a pedestal and equipped with pedals used to muffle the sound. This enhanced type of dulcimer, or cimbalom, was shortly adopted by the local *Zigeunerkapellen* and became popular throughout Austria-Hungary. In 1880, Carl Engel assured British readers that "The Hungarian Gipsy musicians are especially renowned as skilful players on the *cimbalom* (dulcimer)" (Engel 1880a, 221). Stanisław Przybyszewski—an acclaimed, young Polish author—wrote about the instrument as well, recalling his first encounter with it upon his 1898 arrival in Cracow, which then fell under the Austro-Hungarian monarchy (Przybyszewski 1959, 305). However, awareness of the virtuosity of Gypsy dulcimer players was not always sharp, even into the twentieth century. Reporting from Hungary in 1923, Christopher Becket Williams felt compelled to explain to the reader not only the appearance but also the way of playing an instrument that, as is characteristic of such accounts, he does not even name. He presents the instrument, on which Gypsies play, as "a cross of a zither with a xylophone." Naïvely, he writes of "instruments which may be described as great pianos without the keys," for which the player holds "a hammer in each hand" (1923, 270).

The Clarinet

With time, other instruments joined the traditional Gypsy orchestras, with the next stage featuring the introduction of the clarinet as the fifth member. Initially, clarinet players appeared in fairly rare cases, and specifically on the condition that a dulcimer player were already present. Around the 1840s, the clarinet appeared more frequently in Gypsy bands, both urban and rural (Sárosi 1987, 238–39).

The early view on the clarinet was that it was too noisy, and hence the clarinetist's role was first and foremost not to stand out within the broader sound of the Gypsy orchestra. The clarinet's timbre was viewed as a means of enhancing the atmosphere, and the clarinet's part was therefore to be played legato (Sárosi 1986, 131). Sometimes the clarinet replaced the second violin (*contra*). As recalled by Becket Williams, in Hungarian *Zigeunerkapellen,* "a clarinet . . . plays always in unison with the first violin even in the quietest passages" (1923, 270).

Gradually, clarinets became an established feature in the growing orchestras of Gypsies, who were now called Új Magyar ("new Hungarians"). This new name was promulgated by the Empress Maria Theresa and her son Joseph II as a way of bringing Gypsies into the broader Hungarian fold. By the turn of the twentieth century, expanded ensembles of Gypsy musicians of a dozen or so instrumentalists included two clarinetists, one playing in the key of A or B while the other, on a clarinet of a lighter timbre, played in D or E flat. In smaller groups, the clarinet would be omitted. The nineteenth century saw the sporadic appearance of trumpets in *Zigeunerkapellen,* but brass instruments never permanently found their place within the Gypsy musical tradition in Hungary.

The Function of the *Prímás*

Zigeunerkapellen were most often led by virtuoso violinists. The prestige and playing ability of the group leader (*prímás*), who often appeared in the dual role of conductor and violin soloist, and sometimes also impresario, decided the popularity of the entire orchestra. The *prímás* gave his surname to the name of the group, and he took responsibility for the repertoire as well as its performance. In addition, he was in charge of communicating with the audience during the course of a performance, reading the mood of the listeners and quickly reacting to their needs. The *prímás,* in fulfilling the function of group leader, was completely liable for failure but would likewise, in the case of success, become the darling of the public, the papers, and aristocratic circles. The *prímás* also enjoyed great respect within Gypsy society, admired not only for his musical abilities but also for his personal traits. These bandleaders came most frequently from musical families and married the daughters of other musicians of the tradition they cultivated. Eighteenth- and nineteenth-century Gypsy *prímás*es from Hungary also helped reinforce certain stereotypical notions of the music they played, entering it into the wider context of discourse on national Hungarian music.

Mihály Barna

In the eighteenth century, the semilegendary Gypsy violinist Mihály Barna rose to fame. Remaining in the service of various patrons, Barna gained recognition in 1737 after allegedly competing against eleven other Gypsy musicians in a test of improvisatory ability at an aristocratic wedding reception (Sárosi 1970, 12). Barna played in a four-member *Zigeunerkapelle,* in which he was the only Gypsy—one member, notably, was enough to warrant the "Gypsy" moniker.

This Gypsy fiddler is famous today thanks largely to Grellman's work, but at the time he played, his virtuosity extended beyond the borders of the Habsburg Empire, reaching Poland, among other places (Narbutt 1830, 121). A kind of living memory of Barna would last until the end of the nineteenth century. For example, Engel reproduced a handful of the news clippings about the musician that had circulated for some one hundred years. He wrote that, "Barna Michaly [*sic*], about the middle of the last century [i.e., the eighteenth], played the violin so admirably that Cardinal Count Emerich Eschky had his portrait painted, inscribed 'The Orpheus of the Gypsies'" (Engel 1880a, 221). Barna's growing legend included false claims of credit for authorship of the famous *Rákóczi March* as well as kinship with the renowned female Gypsy violinist Panna Czinka.

Panna Czinka

Panna Czinka (ca. 1711–1772)—aka Anna Czinka and also spelled Panna Cinkova and variants (Ševčikova 1992, 117–26)—was one of the eighteenth century's most famous Gypsy musicians. As tradition would have it, she came from an extremely musical background and was thus continuing a family tradition. Her uncle had been a well-known *prímás*, and her father played in the musical group sponsored by the landowner János Lányi. Apparently Czinka had already—as a nine-year-old girl—aroused sizable interest in her violin playing. As a consequence, Lányi took her under his patronage, sending her to a professional for lessons. To her last days, Czinka considered herself indebted to Lányi; she would wear the red uniform worn by his servants and indeed ordered that she be buried in this uniform (Waigand 1970, 299).

At age fourteen or fifteen, Czinka married a double bass player who was a smith by trade (Sárosi 1970, 11–12). Together with her husband, brothers-in-law, and later her own children (four sons and one daughter), Czinka created one of the best-known Gypsy bands of the day. In summer, the band toured the country, giving concerts, and in winter the family returned to their home on the grounds of Lányi's estate, on the banks of the River Salza (Hungarian *Sajo*). According to nineteenth-century popular opinion, Czinka played so fantastically that Hungarians themselves had a splendid house built for her, though she preferred to live together with her family in a tent (Engel 1880a, 221).

The numerous references to Czinka's music in late eighteenth and early nineteenth-century works on Gypsies attest to her soaring popularity (Czacki 1835, 54). And by the time of her death, in 1772, her elevated position among Gypsy musicians in Hungary was confirmed by a mourning song written by students in Gemer County (Hungarian Gömör-Kishont). The words *Lessus inobitum*

Czinka-Pannae fidicinae were in Latin. Not only were her origins considered regal ("descendit avorum regia progenis"), possibly from the Pharaoh himself ("Aegypti Dominus Pharao, notissimus orbi, ultimus ipsius sanguinis auctor erat"), but even her external beauty was celebrated ("Corpore crassa fuit, struma sedebat, onus. Talis erat facies, qualem nativa sub axe aestifero arva colens") (Waigand 1970, 299–310). This last point was particularly interesting given that, during her lifetime, she was not considered beautiful, owing to her extremely dark complexion. Yet she was admired for her self-conduct and ability to express herself in Hungarian—a quality not frequently seen among Gypsies—along with her enchanting violin playing. After death, these qualities were transmuted into a portrait of external beauty, and such a portrait would persist for some time (Sárosi 1997, 5–6).

János Bihari

The most famous Hungarian *prímás* was the self-taught Romany János Bihari (1764–1825), who hailed from the environs of Pozsony (present-day Bratislava). Around 1801, Bihari founded his own band (initially comprising four fiddlers and a dulcimer player), which expanded seasonally and performed all over the Habsburg Empire: in present-day Hungary, Slovakia, Croatia, Transylvania, and Austria. The trips often took the *prímás* to many cities: he visited, for example, Eger, Pest, and his hometown of Pozsony. During these visits, he stayed in luxury hotels and met with many aristocratic individuals. In 1824, on the journey home from a concert in Eger, Bihari's carriage overturned, crushing his left hand. Despite intensive rehabilitation efforts, the hand remained paralyzed and the role of bandleader passed on to someone else.

Bihari performed at the most notable of happenings, marking them with distinction. Beginning in October 1814, he and his orchestra spent a year in Vienna, allowing them to play before the numerous politicians and monarchs gathered during the Congress of Vienna. The next year, Bihari and his musicians were invited by Kateřina Pavlovna, the duchess of Oldenburg, to perform at the party to honor her sister, the wife of Prince Joseph, organized on St. Margaret Island, between Buda and Pest, on June 1, 1815.

As these accounts suggest, Bihari enjoyed widespread recognition and was paid generously for his performances. His playing enraptured contemporaries, including Franz Liszt, who compared it to nectar for the ear (Liszt 1859, 471). Bihari was also praised in early monographs dedicated to his oeuvre. These works, however, interestingly avoided giving biographical details. We first have Gàbor Mátray's *Bihari János magyar nepzenesz* (1853), followed several decades later by Ervin Major's *Bihari János* (1928). In the latter work, the author exalts the *prímás* as the greatest "Hungarian" violinist of the first half of the nineteenth century. Bihari himself contributed to this tendency to call his music Hungarian, by performing with his band a repertoire considered to be typically Hungarian, even national, in tone. Yet both the Mátray and Major narratives reflect (particularly Hungarian) intellectual efforts to appropriate certain features of Gypsy culture for the needs of national discourse.

Other *Prímáses*

Other elite nineteenth-century Gypsy violinists included the following names: József Pityó (1790–1888), Marci Dombi (1801–1869), Jancsi Balogh Sági (1803–1876), Károly Boka (1808–1860), Jancsi Kálózdi (1812–1882), Ferenc Sárközi (1820–1890), János Salamon (1824–1899), Ferenc Patikarus (1827–1870), Mihály Farkas (1829–1890), Károly Fátyol (1830–1888), Pál Rácz (1830–1886), and Náci Erdélyi (1845–1893) (Sárosi 1978, 121–34). These musicians' huge popularity directly contributed in the nineteenth century to a deepening conviction as to the extraordinary musicality of Gypsies. *Prímáses* often founded musical dynasties; for example, Pál Rácz passed down his abilities to future generations, while the famous contemporary violinist Roby Lakatos (b. 1965) presents himself as the seventh generation in a direct line from the legendary Bihari (Debrocq 1998, 1).

In 1848–1849, Gypsy virtuosos who had taken part in the People's Spring were to gain renown far beyond their indigenous regions. These musicians were gloriously welcomed, for instance, in Paris—not only this, but their presence was even demanded. The head conductor of all the Gypsy musicians participating in the revolutionary events of 1848–1849, Ferenc Bunkó (1813–1889), gave concerts both in Paris and Berlin; a number of Gypsy orchestras even toured the United States in the 1850s (Fraser 2005, 202). Gypsy musicians became one of Hungary's "exports," promoting Gypsy as well as Hungarian music almost all over the world.

Patrons

The wandering lifestyle of the Gypsy musicians hired to perform at various balls, theaters, and other such venues was undertaken in a search for income. These musicians likewise moved around in the hope of finding wealthy patrons. For their part, those wealthy citizens living under the Austrian monarchy had inherited the practice of hiring Gypsy musicians directly from the Turks. By the end of the eighteenth century, Gypsies had entered into small orchestras maintained by the aristocratic residences, continuing a tradition within the Habsburg Empire of employing musicians for private and public concerts. Particularly, society's most eminent members financed their own *Hauskappellen*, which pointedly emphasized the social ranking of their patrons (Sárosi 1978, 68). For talented young Gypsy musicians, such opportunities often meant the chance to learn music professionally. Remaining under the patronage of rich families, Gypsy musicians could attend prestigious schools, as was the case with Kálózdi, whose patron, Prince Pál Esterházy, enabled him to take up an education at the conservatory in Vienna. A similar chance came to Sárközi. In return for this educational sponsorship, the aristocrats expected the Gypsy musicians to provide them with music to their taste—that is, in accordance with the latest musical trends. Hence, the Gypsy musicians playing at courts strived to incorporate fragments from popular operas and other compositions then enjoying international renown.

Formal knowledge of music among Gypsies, beginning with how to read a score, expanded notably during the nineteenth century, resulting in a sizable group of professional musicians. Musically educated Gypsies, wandering from town to town in search of an opportunity to earn money, brought with them musical innovations from their day's art musical currents. This openness to art music, aided by an ability to read music, helped in turn in their assimilation of new musical trends.

The Repertoire of Hungarian Gypsy Orchestras

The rapidly rising success of the *Zigeunerkapellen* resulted from, among other factors, Gypsy musicians' phenomenal ability to adapt to the varied tastes of their listeners. Having monopolized (as performers) the music market, Gypsies in Hungary easily assimilated popular forms and adapted to public expectations. This skill at adaptation, as exemplified in the quoting of popular tunes, was well known within Hungary by the eighteenth century: for example, in 1790, a performance by a Gypsy group from Nograd during a theatrical event in Pest and Buda showed the Gypsy musicians to be perfectly able to appeal to the theatergoers' tastes (Szabolcsi 1974, 56).

Motivated both by pressure and stimulation, Gypsies met stiff demands, even as their performances did not always achieve the highest standards; these shortcomings could be attributed as a rule to their reliance on intuition rather than knowledge of the principles involved in musical art. Combining fashionable fragments of well-known and well-loved works (including operas) with creative flights, Gypsies transformed heard melodies into something of their own fashion, quite often improvising. The resulting works always contained elements of an earlier melody, one previously known to the Gypsy musicians (Sárosi 1986, 152). Many Gypsies marked these ad hoc compositions with similarly casual titles derived from the surname of the individual who had, perhaps, requested it by humming its main motif. In the early nineteenth century, Gypsies' inability to assimilate the Hungarian singing tradition usually meant that they performed popular Hungarian works of the day in an instrumental form.

The tasks given to Gypsy musicians, particularly those playing at the courts of the wealthiest aristocrats, included the performance of symphonies (Sárosi 1978, 68). The greatest demand, however, came from the gentry and the middle classes, who desired to be entertained to Hungarian rhythms. The aristocracy and gentry also willingly made use of dance music to affirm national identity (Hofer 1994, 46). The composer, conductor, and theoretician Hector Berlioz, on returning to France from a visit to Hungary, remarked in a letter to his sister Nancy on "those great Hungarian balls to which only noble Hungarians were admitted, and where they only performed national dances on national themes played by the *Zingari* [Gypsies]" (Berlioz 1978, no. 1029).

The repertoire played by Gypsy orchestras across the Habsburg Empire was not uniform. An important line of division was drawn between music played by groups in the Hungarian countryside and those performing before wealthy patrons or middle class audiences in more urban areas. In the countryside, for example, Gypsy music did not contain the augmented second interval, among other features widely identified with so-called Gypsy music. Nor did the performance style display the predilection for overt ornamentation, or polyphonic harmonies. Such elements, considered standard for the Gypsy bands playing on aristocratic estates, would become characteristic of Gypsy music in urban areas. Combined with the growing tendency to foster national symbols, this inclination would lead to the association within the European consciousness of Gypsy music with the Hungarian.

Hungarian Dances and Songs

Hungaresca

At Hungarian manor houses and gatherings of a lower social rank alike, dancing enjoyed enormous popularity, and groups traditionally composed of Gypsy musicians provided the accompaniment.

In this context, the flowering of music in a European context can be dated to 1686, when Buda was seized from the Turks. After this cultural shift, musical life flourished in the elaborate residences of the aristocracy, including those of the Esterházy family. Aristocrats, who were often amateur musicians themselves, would take notes on the melodies they heard for later use in domestic performances. The resulting collections of melodies, including those of Zsuzsanna Lányi, László Székely, and Tádé Bodnár, contained varied works that reflected the tastes of their broadly educated, musically cultured creators. As a rule, these pieces conformed to the artistic musical style prevalent at the time, and reflected the recognized canon. Besides works of known provenance, including those of Telemann, J. S. Bach, and Vivaldi, dances such as menuets and ländlers were also performed fairly often among the gentry. Other dances were given titles proclaiming their Hungarian origin. We thus see names such as *ungarischer Janzt, passamezzo ongaro, ungarescha, saltus hungaricus,* and *ungaresca* (Dobszay 1993, 125). The musical layer of most of these dances was characterized by frequent syncopation as well as sequences of tuplets (irregular rhythms) utilizing the short note values, and also the appearance—at the end of a phrase—of typical cadential formulas. The rhythm of Hungarian dances was derivative (most often in an augmented form) of the 2/4 rhythms of the folk dance of swineherds.

Musically educated aristocrats (e.g., József Bengraf, Franz Tost, Joachim Dreschler, and Ágoston Mohaupt) strived to force the typical rhythm of the *hungaresca* into formal and harmonic Viennese norms. A binary dance form (sometimes expanded from a duet into a trio) crystallized in its interaction with art music, and particularly with contemporary harmonic innovations. Also, the instrumental arrangement of two violins, a viola, a double bass, a clarinet, and a dulcimer for performing the dances was established. Dances of unknown origins became increasingly popular, and were usually referred to en masse as *hungarescas*. Given the young Hungarian nobility studying abroad all over Europe, these dances would spread in popularity. For example, the *hajdútánc* form was known in Poland and noted in Jan of Lublin's organ tablature under the name *hajducki* (Brzezińska 1987, 108).

Verbunkos

In the mid-eighteenth century, many Gypsy bands offered their services in Hungary, and their repertoires included Hungarian dances. In combining the stylistic elements of the *hungaresca* with the Viennese and Italian traditions, inflected with Balkan and Slavic influences, popular and art music merged, culminating in the appearance of the *verbunkos*, traditionally performed by young men during military recruitment drives. Indeed, recruitment in the Habsburg Empire took place within a set musical framework from the time a standing army was formed in 1715 up until the 1868 establishment of requirements for military service. The *verbunkos* first appeared in the 1760s and 1770s, even as its geographic origins are difficult to trace, given the wandering lifestyle of the Gypsies who most often performed them (Szabolcsi 1974, 54).

The *verbunkos* either adopted a more varied form, clearly betraying aspirations toward art music (which at the time was meant for listening, not dancing, to), or preserved a simple construction recalling folk origins. The characteristic feature of an instrumental *verbunkos* was rich ornamentation associated with the Gypsy manner of performance. As for the dance, it had a majestic feel and was performed slowly by men formed in a circle or semicircle (Sárosi 1986, 159). The *verbunkos* also helped erode German influences on music in Hungary, which had resulted from the settlement of many German and Austrian musicians (Legány 2006, 851).

As a dance conducive to the presentation of a young man's physical strength, the *verbunkos* was soon considered expressive of the national character in a forceful way (Sárosi 1978, 89). Searching for sources of Hungarian nationality in music, the gentry even picked up on the form from a relatively early stage, from about 1790 to 1810. At balls, where German music dominated, young people increasingly requested the *verbunkos,* manifesting an affinity with the rebirth of Hungary. The emergence of the *verbunkos* as the quintessence of Hungarian national music occurred even as it was performed chiefly by Gypsy musicians. By the beginning of the nineteenth century, the *verbunkos* had risen further to the rank of a symbol (Tari 2012, 81).

According to the periodization proposed by Bence Szabolcsi, the years 1790–1810, during which the *verbunkos* passed as the traditional music of the Hungarian people, were followed by three decades of the form's flowering, from 1810 to 1840 (Szabolcsi 1974, 63). In these years, the *verbunkos* stopped being treated exclusively as dance music. In the 1830s, it was performed as chamber music, popular piano miniatures, and in works for the stage. From 1840 to 1880, the *verbunkos* witnessed the height of its popularity, to be superseded only by the czardas. Among the many non-Romany composers of the *verbunkos* form were Kálmán Simonffy (ca. 1832–1888), Béni Egressy (1814–1851), Károly Thern (1817–1886), Béla Kéler (1820–1882), Elemér Szentirmay (1836–1908), József Dóczy (1863–1913), Lóránt Fráter (1872–1930), and Árpád Balázs (1874–1941). The Romany composers included Mihály Farkas, Pista Dankó (1858–1903), and the famous *prímás* Rácz.

Another Hungarian music researcher, László Dobszay, proposed a different division for the *verbunkos*—not according to chronology but rather based on the various forms the pieces adopted in the first half of the nineteenth century (1993, 125). This division establishes four fundamental ways of functioning within the *verbunkos:*

1. In an original form or one stylized by the various eminent performers of this style
2. As instrumental works serving to strengthen and propagate the national values connected with Hungarian music
3. In the form of short fragments appearing within the framework of a greater whole; for example, in operas
4. In a form fully integrated with the creative idiom of a given composer, an example of which being, according to Dobszay, the artistic output of Liszt

As an alloy of folk and art music, the *verbunkos*, as implied before, has been treated as a musical symbol of Hungarian national history—especially by Hungarian musicologists and ethnomusicologists (Tari 2012, 81). The bestowing of national traits on the *verbunkos* sometimes occurred as a result of complex processes, with the past combining with the present in a completely random way. For example, the melody to the famous *Rákóczi March*, considered the quintessence of national Hungarian music, dates to the seventeenth century. For the next hundred or so years, until the end of the eighteenth century, the melody was accompanied by words about the Rákóczi family and known as *Rákóczi's Song* (and later *Rákóczi's Lament*). The incarnation as the *Rákóczi March* only came later. Transmitted by oral tradition, the melody had many variants, from very simple to exceptionally ornate. During the period of the *verbunkos*'s flowering, the *Rákóczi March* would come to represent the form through its characteristic military motifs and imitations of the notes played on the trumpet (Sárosi 1978, 108). Moreover, the evocation of the Rákóczi family helped boost it to the status of a national symbol. Sárosi contends therefore that the *Rákóczi March* was "not a memory surviving the Kuruc period [1671–1711] but originated from the *verbunkos* period" (1978, 109).

Thereafter, the widespread misperception that the *Rákóczi March* was based in essence on an obscure Gypsy melody came about because of its common performance by Gypsy bands. On the wave of the work's popularity, the piece first appeared in written form in 1820, and a youthful Liszt performed it three years later. The *Rákóczi March* was to be so strongly attached to the tradition of national Hungarian music that it was incorporated by composers wishing to emphasize a Hungarian link in their works (including Liszt, Erkel, and Berlioz).

The publication of the first collections of *verbunkos* pieces came about in the years of their greatest popularity, following Liszt's performance. Between 1823 and 1832, on the instruction of the Veszprem Musical Society, Ignác Ruzitska (1777–1833) published *Magyar nóták Veszprém Vármegyébő* (Hungarian Tunes from Veszprém County), containing—in fifteen issues—a staggering 135 of such compositions arranged for the piano. At the end of the nineteenth century, collections authored by the musician, conductor, and composer Gyula Káldy (1838–1901) were published (Sárosi 1978, 116). The first musicological attempts to determine the origin of the *verbunkos* together with establishing its actual right to represent the Hungarian musical tradition were to appear in the works of Gábor Mátray (ca. 1797–1875), who compiled the first history of Hungarian music (Szabolcsi 1974, 62). His work was to be continued by István Bartalus (1821–1899) and Guztáv Szénfy (1819–1875).

Czardas

Around the same time as the *verbunkos* emerged—toward the end of the eighteenth century—a much faster dance began to be performed in pairs and was known under a series of names, including *friss* Magyar (fast Hungarian), *szabály-tala* Magyar (irregular Hungarian), *rögtönzött* Magyar (improvised Hungarian), and *lakodalmas* (wedding dance). The broad array of types came, in part, from the regional variations associated with these fast dances (Sárosi 1986, 162–63). The dances themselves lacked a single unifying name, but by 1844 they began to be associated with the *csárda* (inn or hostelry) where they were typically performed (Pesovar 1987, 149).

Like the *verbunkos*, the czardas started to take on the significance of a national dance. The czardas was chiefly associated with folk revelry and was, therefore, condemned as a debasement of so-called slow dancing performed at the manor houses, which, in the first half of the nineteenth century, was considered "true" Hungarian dancing (Pesovar 1987, 149). And as early as 1800, in *Allgemeine Musikalische Zeitung*, Hungarian national dances were pronounced as "either slow . . . suitably called recruitment dances, while the faster are referred to as Gypsy or folk."

Around 1835, Márk Rózsavölgyi (1789–1848), a violinist and respected composer of dance (including *verbunkos*) who was of Jewish origin, took steps toward creating a national Hungarian dance that would constitute an alternative to the foreign, chiefly German, dances preferred at gentry balls. Many popular musicians were involved in a similar process of transforming the Hungarian dance tradition, modeling the alternative, among other forms, on the then popular polonaise. Particular attention was devoted to adapting the *verbunkos* to the refined tastes of the listener and viewer, an effort that was also realized in the increased artistry applied to the czardas and its increased prevalence in balls given by the middle and upper classes in the 1840s. The successful promotion of the czardas was interpreted as a victory for the national movement (Pesovar 1987). In time, however, the czardas would be popularized to the extent that it would be viewed, by the 1870s, as almost trivial in character (Szabolcsi 1974, 63).

Hungarian Songs—Magyar *Nóta*

The striving to create a typically Hungarian musical idiom was expressed in an increased interest in folk music. Under the influence of the writings of Herder, among others, the wave of reforms aimed at producing a rebirth of Hungarian nationality. In this context, society was engrossed in the desire to discover the treasures of popular and folk music. The concept of nationality was widely identified with works of a folk character. The aristocracy and the gentry began the trend, later joined in the mid-nineteenth century by the middle classes (composed of former landowners and the clerical intelligentsia), of identifying the source of Hungarian music in the songs they knew. In this discussion, the labels *folk* and *popular* overlapped each other. Beside the name magyar *nóta* (Hungarian song) was *nepies dal* (popular song) and even *nepies mủdal* (popular artistic song) (Sárosi 2001, 864).

Hungarian song meant in point of fact "local song," one composed by Hungarians as opposed to foreigners—with the latter most often referring to Austrians. Songs of a foreign provenance were well known to the middle classes: they desired on the one hand to preserve the standards of art music within their own songs yet on the other hand to locate true Hungarian values in accordance with prevailing national tendencies. As a consequence, inspiration was not sought in the song performed in the Hungarian countryside, which could appear too simplistic for the refined tastes of the Hungarian gentry cultivated in the best of European art, but rather in songs from the late eighteenth century as performed by students.

Upper-class members of Hungarian society took pleasure in the composition of songs, and the public received them rapturously. The composers only rarely, however, performed their works, unaware of how quickly they would become the anonymous property of society at large. Indeed, the names of the authors were soon lost to memory. Songs were popularized through oral tradition or handwritten transcripts.

These popular songs were usually spread by the *Zigeunerkapellen*, which performed instrumental versions. The songs initially underwent a process of simplification and later, under the influence of the art music of the Romantic Age, became permeated with long, sentimental melodies that were well suited to easy harmonization. Sometimes Gypsy bands changed melody lines and adapted the songs for their particular musical ensemble. These adaptations blurred the stylistic features intended by their creators, reinforcing the notion of the forgotten composer and transforming magyar *nóta* into collective property.

The term magyar *nóta*, while identified with this nineteenth-century movement, actually dated back to the sixteenth century, when it was used to define the original folk song cultivated within the Hungarian countryside. By the nineteenth century, the Hungarian gentry, while seeking a true Hungarian quality in music, still had not embraced magyar *nóta*, even as the notion was still developing vigorously. For folk songs in particular, the use of a heptatonic scale was characteristic, along with augmented rhythms derived from the old dances of the swineherds. Church hymns also had a great influence on folk songs. Collections including both popular and folk songs were published throughout nineteenth century. For example, in the 1820s, Mátray published the collections *Pannonia*, *Flora*, and *Hunnia*, in which he considered all the songs—again, without distinction between folk and popular—to be expressions of the Hungarian national spirit. Further collections were published by János Gály (*Eredeti Népdalok* of 1831), István Tóth (*Ariak es Dallok verseikkel* of 1832–1843), János Fogarasi (*Travnyik, Egressy-Szerdahelyi, Furedi,* and *Bognar*), Károly Színi, and István Bartalus (Szabolcsi 1974, 65).

The symbiosis between Gypsy performers and the Hungarian repertoire they willingly performed—which at a specific moment gained the patina of a national symbol—resulted in a network of inseparable links. These would be fortified through word of mouth but also fertilized by musical imagination that resulted in illustrious nineteenth-century works referred to as "Gypsy."

Hungarian National Sentiments in Music

The political vicissitudes of Hungarian history and, in particular, the country's status under Habsburg rule would help shape the country and region's musical culture. Questions of what constituted "Hungarian" versus "Gypsy" music would be central in determining the conception of national music in Hungary.

Hungarian nationalism was spurred, around the turn of the nineteenth century, by intellectuals who argued based on "the conception that Hungary as a linguistically and culturally alien element, surrounded by Slavs, Rumanians and Germans, would disappear through assimilation. . . ." (Kopyś 2001, 30). Relatedly, fears centered on the possibility that external factors could lead to the deterioration of the Hungarian situation within the Habsburg Empire (Kisbán 1994, 56). After the death in 1790 of Joseph II, who had shown inclinations toward Germanization, national tendencies started to evolve "from linguistic questions . . . in combination with concrete political demands" (Kopyś 2001, 131). There then followed a period of reform under the spiritual leadership of Prince István Széchenyi (1790–1861).

The Hungarian aristocracy, the motor behind Hungarian national movements since the Middle Ages, now played the role again, along with other members of the nobility (Hofer 1994, 27). According to Zoltán Szász, the Hungarian "nobility as a whole, without regard to ethnic affiliation, made up the whole *natio hungaricus*" (1996, 392). In their search for original sources for Hungarian values, the nobility and aristocracy turned to folk (or peasant) culture, which at the beginning of the nineteenth century was seen to possess "no symbolic importance, indeed, it was 'invisible' for other social strata (and for the peasants themselves)" (Hofer 1994, 28). A handful of society's upper ranks took part in the quest to "discover" folk culture, which was denoted stubbornly as "Hungarian" rather than "folk" (Kisbán 1994, 54). The Latin term *Hungarus* meant identification with the concept of multiethnicity and multinationality, as opposed to the narrower national associations of the term "Magyar" (Hofer 1994, 36). As Judith Frigyesi concludes, "During most periods of Hungarian history, to be Hungarian meant simply to be an inhabitant of the Hungarian state and had no ethnic implications: a Hungarian (*hungaricus*) was not necessarily of Hungarian ethnicity (*magyar*)" (1998, 54). Moreover, the semantic capacity of the term "Hungarianness" allowed for a varied definition, keeping the dynamic construct connected with the concept of nationality. However, "in the age of growing national consciousness, beginning with the end of the eighteenth century and the spread of modern liberal and national ideals, the conception of *natio hungaricus* became more and more associated with the Magyar population" (Szász 1996, 392).

The process of establishing a folk heritage linked to the construction of the concept of a Hungarian nation was tied to certain choices aimed at advancing concrete national interests. Dances, as we have seen, were enlisted as national symbols, with public performances reflecting unique manifestations of national identity. For the nobility, Hungarian dances contained, on the one hand, a traditional element and, on the other, a bridge to folk culture. In particular, Hungarian dancing differed from its Western and even Southern European counterparts and, thus, allowed for an interesting change for aristocrats, who were so used to performing salon dances of international scope. Hungarian folk dance would thereby become both an alternative to custom and a component in the pantheon of national symbols.

Non-Hungarian (and Hungarian) Composers in Relation to the Category of National Music

In the eighteenth and early nineteenth centuries, non-Hungarian composers—driven by sympathy for Hungarian political independence and an interest in its folk culture—joined efforts to help create a Hungarian national identity and ideology. The route to the creation of the first Hungarian *singspiel* was laid by, among others, the composers Franz Xaver Kleinheinz (1765–1832) and Franz Roser (1779–1830). In 1793, audiences saw the premiere of what was considered the first Hungarian opera, *Pikkó herceg és Jutka Perzsi*, by the Pozsony-born József Chudy (1753–1813).

During this period, Hungarian opera works referencing indigenous traditions—which was almost compulsory—invariably quoted the repertoire of Gypsy bands through excerpts of Hungarian songs or the *verbunkos*. This was the case in the 1839 comic opera *Csel* (*The Intrigue*) by Endre Bartay (1798–1856) and in István Jakab's original libretto. And Ferenc Erkel (1810–1893), Hungary's leading nineteenth-century composer of opera, engaged in this practice. His operas—including his first, the exceptionally well-received *Bátori Mária* of 1840—contain echoes of the *verbunkos*. Later, his 1861 opera, *Bánk bán*, referenced the czardas in a ballet interlude. According to many Hungarian musicologists, Erkel "from the outset of his career . . . was attempting to create his style from a Hungarian musical language" (Legány 2001a, 296).

In the nineteenth century, the development of Hungarian national music was, however, hindered by a lack of greater interest in classical music by the middle classes, which hid their attitudes behind nationalistic slogans (Dobszay 1993, 162). This is why Liszt, who had lived abroad and was therefore seen as a kind of Hungarian ambassador in Europe's salons, was greeted with enthusiasm by proponents of a national musical culture. The links between Gypsy music and Hungarian music were concomitantly discussed fervently, issuing from the specific situation of Gypsy musicians within Hungary (Kisbán 1994, 60).

Franz Liszt's Vision of Hungarian National Music

The Origins of Liszt's Book on Gypsy Music

In 1839, Liszt, who was already recognized as a piano virtuoso, arrived home. As is commonly known, the melodies he would then hear and incorporate in his *Magyar Dallok* (1840) would constitute the beginnings of his famous *Hungarian Rhapsodies*. At the composer's wish, their publication would be accompanied by a foreword explaining their origins. In July 1847, Liszt wrote from Galatz to his friend and partner Marie d'Agoult asking for her help in writing an introduction—or possibly a postscript—based on his notes (Walker 1989, 381). The growing tensions in their relationship meant no reply was forthcoming, and the first fifteen *Hungarian Rhapsodies* were completed in 1853. By 1854, the foreword had grown into a book of more than three hundred pages, in which the composer proclaimed his own concept of Hungarian national music. The book was, however, only published in 1859 (in Paris) and titled *Des Bohémiens et de leur musique en Hongrie*. József Székely (1825–1895) would translate it into Hungarian two years later.

The Ossian Concept of National Music

In the nationalist atmosphere of the early nineteenth century, Liszt aimed to create—following Herder's ideals—a national epos on the level of the Scotsman James Mcpherson's *Songs of Ossian*. Ossianism undoubtedly influenced Liszt's concept as he set out to write his book. In an October 8, 1846, letter to d'Agoult, he described Hungarian melodies as "half Ossian" and "half Gypsy" (Haraszti 1947, 511). The Ossian concept of national music in Liszt's understanding was based, as Detlef Altenburg convincingly presents, on six basic principles (1986, 219):

1. Liszt considered it the right of every nation to create its own poetic ideal reflecting its history.
2. He believed that in Gypsy music lay the potential national epos of the Hungarians, resulting from specific the lack of such an epos in a literary form.
3. He considered Hungarian Gypsies to be the bards of the Hungarian land.
4. He called the music played by Gypsies Hungarian folk music.
5. He characterized Hungarian music as well as music played by Gypsies as being full of pride and suffering, natural and in no way impeded in expression.

6. He characterized the national epos, expressed in music, as being capable of influencing the listener's emotions and soul, thus resulting in a realization of national ideals.

The attempt undertaken by Liszt to create a national epos, supported by a concise concept of national music, derived from his strongly proclaimed patriotic feelings. The composer, born in 1811 in Doborján, Hungary, left his home community at age eleven, yet both privately and publically expressed "the feeling of devotion which I have particularly nurtured toward my native land" (Walker 1989, 386). Sometime after returning from his travels abroad, he would pronounce that, "Only my fatherland has my profoundest gratitude, not only as an artist . . . but as a man" (Haraszti 1947, 504). Nor would his sentiments recede over the years. In the 1870s, he asserted that, "I remain from birth to death Hungarian in heart and mind, and accordingly wish to further the development of Hungarian music" (Legány 1976, 164).

Yet Liszt's interest in creating a Hungarian national musical idiom can be understood to reflect his broader understanding of musical trends and tastes in nineteenth-century Europe. By incorporating folk elements in his own compositions, Liszt could count on a positive response among Parisian *salonnieres* seeking fresh material, especially those from distant European countries. Liszt's friend Frédéric Chopin already understood this situation very well—apart from his multifaceted reasons for dipping into Polish folk music, Chopin recognized that Western listeners were drawn to musical Polishness in a certain form. The myth of authenticity associated with Chopin's mazurkas, polonaises, and other such forms helped construct his image as a Polish national bard and surrounded his work with a romantic aura. Liszt was both a eulogist and a rival of Chopin's, but the former's work with Hungarian source material mirrored that of his Polish counterpart. Likewise, Liszt understood the expectations of him. And the musical forms in his home country were both attractive and ready to incorporate. Some modern musicologists, including James Parakilas and Richard Taruskin, regard these types of nationalistic sentiments as a specific manifestation of (self-)promotion and categorize it as a "touristic" type of nationality in music (Taruskin 2001, 699).

Liszt's Views on Gypsy Music

Liszt's enthusiastic approach to the creation of a national Hungarian epos was closely connected with his assessment of Gypsies as the creators of national Hungarian music. He even considered Gyspies the exclusive conservators of the tradition. He also referred to the popular opinion that Gypsy musicians only performed repertoires composed by Hungarians: in conceiving this inspiring role played by the nobility, however, he always emphasized the Gypsy role. In Liszt's view, the justice in Hungarians claiming Gypsy music as their own lay in former's having allowed latter to cultivate their music.

This controversial thesis identifying Hungarian music with Gypsy music, as proclaimed in Liszt's book, had its roots in a variety of sources. To begin with, the general atmosphere created by music performed by Gypsies in nineteenth-century Hungary influenced the composer significantly. In 1854, Mátray, the early collector and researcher of Hungarian songs, opined that cultured Hungarians did not cultivate a national music, bestowing its care and propagation on the Gypsies alone. Liszt, surrounded while in Hungary chiefly by aristocratic and educated friends, became acquainted with Hungarian music as presented through their prism, as well as that of Mátray (Haraszti 1947, 521). Liszt himself revealed these sources of information on Gypsy music in an 1864 letter directed to Heinrich Ehrlich (Williams 2000, 198). He most often mentioned the names of aristocrats (dukes and barons) who were interested in music in an amateur capacity. During social gatherings, they presented Liszt with musical materials either in notated form or by playing them directly on the piano.

Given this background, it is unlikely that Liszt ever knew Hungarian folk music as it was performed in the countryside and was merely acquainted with the repertoire performed by Gypsies—generally accepted to be folk music (Gárdonyi 1983, 133). Some Hungarian musicologists, such as Sárosi, however, believe that "Liszt knew about Hungarian folk music but—in agreement with the educated Hungarians of his time, musicians among them—he did not consider it worthy of attention" (1978, 142).

The composer's fascination with Gypsy music dated to his childhood, when he would often listen to Gypsy bands. In the spring of 1822, before the entire Liszt family departed for Vienna, Liszt had the opportunity to listen to the great Gypsy violin virtuoso János Bihári. Liszt's later contacts with Gypsy musicians would be equally numerous. After his 1839 return to Hungary, he attended elegant balls, including some outdoors, that were usually accompanied by Gypsy musicians. In an October 22, 1842, letter to d'Agoult, the composer, recalling his moving visit to his childhood home, also mentions a genuine country ball, at which he invited musicians (most likely Gypsies) to play waltzes (Szenic 1969, 134). Liszt regarded Gypsy music with wonder everywhere he encountered it, such as in Sopron, Pozsony, and Pest—and he took in performances of *Zigeunerkapellen* wherever he could. He heard the well-known orchestra of Rácz, and maintained contact for many years with the Gypsy dulcimer virtuoso Pál Pintér (1848–1916) (Legány 1976, 204). In an August 13, 1856, letter to Princess Caroline Sayn-Wittgenstein, he describes his plans thus: "Then I'm running off to the Gypsies, just like I did yesterday" (Liszt 1893–1905, 316). In the same letter, Liszt famously characterizes his split nature as "one half Gypsy, the other a Franciscan [*Zu einer Halfte Zigeuner, zur andern Franziskaner*]."

Liszt's fascination with Gypsy culture also manifested itself in nonmusical decisions—which elicited much consternation from commentators of the day—such as the ordering of a luxury caravan that operated by day as a salon and by night as a bedroom. This vehicle, constructed according to the latest technical achievements, was, at least according to rumor, modeled on the caravan of a certain king of the Gypsies (Szenic 1969, 181). Furthermore, deeply convinced of the exceptional musicality of Hungarian Gypsies, Liszt—following his breakup with d'Agoult—looked after a twelve-year-old Gypsy boy, Jozsy, of extraordinary musical talent who had been presented to him by Count Sándor Teleki. When the boy did not meet Liszt's expectations, the virtuoso handed him off to the boy's brother, who played in an outstanding Gypsy orchestra that performed at the Viennese "Zum Zeisig" club (Szenic 1969, 191–92). Liszt, in his book on Gypsy music, often referred to his experiences with Jozsy, who as a grown man wrote to his former mentor from Debrecen about his work in the Gypsy band of Boka and about the stabilized life of "an ordinary Gypsy" married to a local Gypsy woman. He also wrote of his fond memories of his patron, disclosing that he had christened his son with the composer's name and had a portrait of him hanging at his home (Szenic 1969, 192).

The Reaction to Liszt's Work

The publication of Liszt's *Des Bohémiens et de leur musique en Hongrie* was keenly discussed across the whole of Europe, with news of its contents reaching Hungary and drawing an instantaneous reaction before it was translated into Hungarian in 1861. The same year saw an abridged German edition prepared by Liszt's secretary, the composer Peter Cornelius (1824–1874).

One resounding reaction in Hungary to Liszt's book was the claim that identifying Hungarian music with Gypsy music was an "error." A prime proponent of this view was the twenty-seven-year-old composer Kálmán Simonffy. He had not even read the book, though he had acquainted himself with the fragments published prior to the book's appearance in the periodical *La France musicale*, which the Hungarian press had popularized. In a severely critical letter—written earlier but published in the September 6, 1859, edition of *Pesti Napló*—he addressed Liszt directly and, citing patriotic sentiment, severed contact with the composer. In the same edition of the newspaper, Simonffy included Liszt's private reply to his missive, dated August 27, 1859, in which the composer expressed his surprise at the fervor of Simonffy's opinions, especially given that they were generated without recourse to the actual text. He rejected the accusation of a lack of patriotism and assured Simonffy that in the future he would not react to similar accusations (Walker 1989, 385–86).

Heated discussion on Liszt's book enveloped all of Hungary, where attacks on the composer multiplied. Hungarian public opinion was first and foremost surprised and shocked by the message emanating from Liszt. The luminaries of mid-nineteenth-century Hungarian cultural life weighed in: Gusztáv Szénfy did so on September 14, 1859, in *Pesti Napló,* in an article titled "Liszt on Gypsy Music"; Lajos Ujfalussy published, in *Vasárnapi Ujság,* "One More Word about Liszt and Hungarian Music"; and Gyula Bulyovszky published a piece in *Nefelejts* titled "Talk with a Reader [about Liszt's Book]" (Sárosi 1978, 141–45).

The atmosphere of scandal surrounding Liszt's book was to last in Hungary for several years. The composer was accused of, among other things, lacking knowledge of the Hungarian language, a deficiency he repeatedly and enthusiastically, though for the most part unsuccessfully, sought to remedy. Only by the early 1870s did study result in the concrete achievement of improved pronunciation. His comprehension of written texts also improved, and he certainly possessed a passive knowledge of the tongue, given that his personal servant, Miska Sipka, spoke Hungarian when other Hungarians visited (Legány 1976, 163–64). But he never learned to use the language in day-to-day life, a fact taken up by his adversaries against him.

One of the most ferocious onslaughts against Liszt's views came in 1859 from a professor from Kolozsvár, Sámuel Brassai (1800–1897), who published in 1860 a booklet entitled *Magyar—vagy czigány-zene? Elmefultatás Liszt F. "Czigányokról" irt könyve felett?* (Hungarian or Gypsy Music? Reflections on Franz Liszt's Book *On the Gypsies*), constituting not simply a response to Liszt but also a study on the music of Hungarian Gypsies. In seeking to prove the incompetency of his great compatriot, and basing his claims on historical documents dating from the fifteenth century, Brassai presented a short history of the Hungarian Gypsies' social position, proving their constructive role in the shaping of Hungarian society. In his analysis, Brassai cited musical examples of magyar *nóta,* which in his opinion had mistakenly been associated by Liszt with Gypsy music. Overall, Brassai felt that Liszt had failed to back up his claims with written and musical examples, undermining his purported methodology. Brassai also attacked the overdone, exultative, romantic language of *Des Bohémiens et de leur musique en Hongrie*, calling the nonacademic prose "stupefying." Not only were Brassai's arguments based on a penetrating reading of Liszt's work and its shortcomings, but Brassai made his case using rhetorical techniques such as asides to the reader and direct appeals to Liszt himself. Brassai refers, for instance, to the language "of your country, with which you have not even had the pleasure of mastering a single word" (Brassai 1860, 12–14).

Brassai expressed the opinion held by many Hungarians angered by Liszt's suggestion of Gypsy preeminence in Hungarian national music. Yet in European literature devoted to later nineteenth-century music, Liszt's role in promoting Hungarian music was valued. Most such authors, however—even the most enthusiastic in their evaluation of the composer and his musical and literary works—were aware of the controversy surrounding Liszt's views. For example, Ludwig Nohl, writing superlatively in 1879 on Liszt's literary verve, discreetly suggested that "The weaker portions of these writings are, of course, the historical and theoretical, appertaining as they do to science and research. . . ." (1879, 514).

A short review of Liszt's work was also made by Engel in 1879, with his critique echoing Nohl's: "The style of this book is rather bombastic, and the author states but few instructive facts, although he displays much sentiment respecting the music of the Gypsies" (Engel 1879, 72). This same author also doubted the correctness of Liszt's theory, writing, "F. Liszt . . . expresses the opinion that the national music of the Magyars is, properly speaking, the music of the Gipsies, with whom it originated, and who are at the present day its principal performers and cultivators." He further noted that "If the Hungarian music were the original music of the Gipsies, traces of it would probably be found in that of the Gipsies in other European countries—at least in those where many Gipsies exist, as for instance, in Spain and in Russia" (Engel 1880a, 221).

Other nineteenth- and twentieth-century authors accepted Liszt's arguments, even if indirectly. The overwhelming majority of works on either Gypsy or Hungarian music appearing after 1859 assumed Liszt's thesis as their starting point, as they entered into the assimilative model of discourse about Gypsy music. Engel himself confirmed that "musicians, probably more from relying upon the statement of the celebrated Liszt than from investigations of their own," reproduced his opinions about Gypsy and Hungarian music (Engel 1880a, 221). In a 1907 article on Gypsy music, Albert Thomas Sinclair declared with full force in his first three sentences that "All Hungarian musicians are Gypsies. All Hungarian music is simply Gypsy music. Liszt states this, and it is true" (Sinclair 1907, 16). The author admitted to a fascination with the figure and works of Liszt, writing:

"Liszt (*Des Bohemiens*) has impressed me more than all. . . . Liszt studied, understood and described Gypsy music as no one but a great musician can" (Sinclair 1907, 24). For his part, the Hungarian musicologist Emile Haraszti, who worked from the end of the Second World War until his 1958 death in France, was aware of the controversy in Liszt's thesis, but he nonetheless began his exposition on the relationship between Hungarian and Gypsy music (during the first congress of the International Society for Musical Research in September 1930) by emphasizing the importance of the work (Haraszti 1931, 140).

Yet the equality granted by Liszt to Hungarian and Gypsy music did not appeal to many Hungarian musicologists seeking to reconsider Hungarian national music. Alexandre M. Bertha in 1878 claimed categorically, for example, that Hungarian music had developed independently of Gypsy influences (Bertha 1878, 911). In an article of 1919, Edward Kilenyi negated the identification of Gypsy music with Hungarian music completely, aligning his views with those devised by Dr. Géza Molnár (Kilenyi 1919, 20).

Into the twentieth century, a prominent voice in the discussion of Gypsy and Hungarian music would be the prolific Balínt Sárosi, whom we've encountered in earlier passages. Besides writing numerous articles, Sárosi published in 1971 the influential work *Cigányzene*, which was translated into English by Fred Macnicol. Sárosi sought to cast light on the lingering controversy created by Liszt's claim (Sárosi 1978, 141–50). In doing so, he recalled the historical dynamics governing Hungarian popular and folk music, the history of the *verbunkos*, and also the fate of Gypsy musicians within Hungarian territories. A similar consciousness of the fluidity of the semantics of "Gypsy music" in Hungary has been acknowledged by many other researchers, such as László Lajtha, Ursula Hemetek, Katalin Kovalcsik, and Irén Kertész-Wilkinson. These authors' widely available publications provide reliable correctives to Liszt's so-called error.

Whether Liszt's error has been a target of attack or a source of inspiration or both, the attention devoted to it by scholars shows the way in which his notions on Gypsy music are still alive. In 1994, Alain Antonietto wrote a piece called "Histoire de la musique tsigane instrumentale d'Europe central Etudes tsiganes" (Antonietto 1994, 104–33), in which he rather superficially, and with numerous mistakes pointed out by Sárosi, characterized the history of Gypsy music from Hungary (Sárosi 1997, 4). Two years later, Patrick Williams published a brief book in French devoted to music of the Hungarian Gypsies, based on a short visit to Hungary. Sárosi, reviewing the work, *Les Tsiganes de Hongrie et leur musique*, argued that it was not only modeled on *Des Bohémiens et de leur musique en Hongrie* and that it quoted from the earlier text as if its contents were factual, but also that it contained the very same mistakes as Liszt's work. Williams also seemed to share Liszt's aesthetic views on the correlation between Gypsy music and Hungarian national music, devoting the core of the first part of the text to the controversy surrounding the issue. He claims, as Liszt had once done, that "the Gypsy virtuoso epitomised the political ideal of Hungarianism," a statement that gives him the confidence to conclude that Hungarian Gypsies "occupied a special place in Hungary as interpreters of national music" (Williams 1996, 52). Williams, who also chooses selectively from other materials, including Sárosi's work *Gypsy Music*, writes that, "being paid musicians in the service of authority, Hungarian Gypsies fulfilled a special role as performers of national music. This paradoxical situation was the subject of disputes as to what is 'national' and what 'Gypsy.'" In the book's second part, Williams engages in an ethnomusicological analysis of Romany songs ("Le chant des Rom").

It can be argued that Liszt's publication and the many references to it—either seeking to clarify his thesis or support it—resulted in the consciousness among many music aficionados of Gypsy music as synonymous with Hungarian music. References to Liszt, frequent duplication of his views, as well as attempts to refute his thesis have led to the adoption of a certain image of Hungarian and Gypsy music in Europe, which has—as a consequence—no small influence on the musicians and intellectuals operating today within Hungary as well as abroad.

The Problem of Authorship

Another accusation leveled against *Des Bohémiens et de leur musique en Hongrie*, advanced chiefly by Hungarians, involves doubt as to Liszt's authorship—at least with regard to certain passages. Haraszti, in a 1947 article, argues that, "The question of the authenticity of [Liszt's] literary works offers one of the most curious and most important aspects of the Liszt enigma" (Haraszti 1947, 492). The implication made by the author is that this "enigma" over authorship touches all of Liszt's legacy, with the exception of his correspondence. Liszt's dubious authorship, according to Haraszti, might be traced primarily to his lack of fundamental general education and the close influence of two women with whom the composer had relationships.

In Haraszti's view, Liszt "did not have the qualifications of a learned writer," and he cited the composer's "very neglected" education as the cause (Haraszti 1947, 493–98). The composer apparently regretted the missed opportunity for education, as he later expressed in letters to his son, Daniel (in April 1854), and Caroline Sayn-Wittgenstein (in August 1868). The two women whom Haraszti credits with fostering Liszt's educational development were none other than Marie d'Agoult—the mother of the composer's three children—and Sayn-Wittgenstein, with whom he was attached at various stages of his life. Of these two women, d'Agoult, whom the composer met in 1832 before turning twenty-two, is cited as the figure who "molded, like a sculptress, the soul and mind of her young lover" (Haraszti 1947, 500). D'Agoult's own literary prowess would be manifested by her adoption of a male pseudonym (Daniel Stern) for the publication of her books, in the manner of George Sand. A careful analysis of d'Agoult's literary style together with a reading of her correspondence with Liszt allowed Haraszti to conclude that not only the articles signed by Liszt that appeared from 1836 to 1840 in *Revue et gazette musicale de Paris* but also all documents published prior to 1846 under Liszt's name were—in fact—written by d'Agoult.

Sayn-Wittgenstein's influence on Liszt's writing would concern a later period of his life, including that covering *Des Bohémiens et de leur musique en Hongrie.* In these years, rumors appeared, from Hans von Bülow among others, that the princess should be ascribed authorship not only of certain chapters but of the book in its entirety. As recently as 1936, Bartók wrote, "The rumor that Princess Wittgenstein, with whom Liszt was living at that time, had anything to do with the writing of the book, and the opinions expressed in it about Hungarian music, is not worth any further attention" (Bartók 1992 (1936), 508). All the same, Haraszti suggested that the princess, herself not devoid of literary talents, presumably knew the inside story of the earlier "cooperation" of Liszt with d'Agoult and willingly adopted the composer's previous lover's role, including by editing his writings. She gained substantial editorial experience in this regard by working on his *Life of Chopin,* a new edition of which would appear in 1879. In the case of *Des Bohémiens et de leur musique en Hongrie,* her job presumably involved the task of putting Liszt's spoken ideas onto paper (Haraszti 1947, 508). Hence, according to Haraszti, the book came about based on an idea that "belonged in its entirety to the composer of *Hungarian Rhapsodies*" (Haraszti 1947, 511). Such a view is borne out by Liszt's holding fast to the book's core thesis on Gypsy music and Hungarian music through its subsequent edition and, indeed, throughout his life.

Gypsy Music and Hungarian Folk Music in the Writings of Béla Bartók

Interest in the Concepts of *Volk* and Nation

National ideology interpreted in the spirit of German Romanticism dominated the nineteenth-century understanding of concepts like "nation," "the people," and "nationality" in Hungary and would influence dialogue similarly in the twentieth century. The concept of nationalism was associated with political movements pushing for the country's liberation. Together with the government of Prime Minister Dezső Bánffy (1895–1899), national tendencies increasingly took on the dimension of overt chauvinism, although the very concept of Hungarianness (Magyarság) was never to remain stable (Schneider 2006, 8).

Entering adulthood at the turn of the twentieth century, the young Hungarian composer Béla Bartók (1881–1945) was subjected to these influences, clearly expressing his position in a September 8, 1903, letter to his mother: "For my own part, all my life, in every sphere, always and in every way, I shall have one objective: the good of Hungary and the Hungarian nation" (Bartók 1972, 226; Demeny 1971, 29).

Under the influence of the concept of *Volk*, and sparked by festivities in 1896 marking Hungary's millennium (celebrated grandly in the spirit of national chauvinism), Bartók commenced his work of compiling folk songs in the Carpathian region (Ujfalussy 1971, 43, 60). Beginning in 1905, the composer together with Zoltán Kodály (1882–1967)—who at the time was writing his PhD thesis on Hungarian folk songs—started drawing up transcripts of melodies they heard as well as producing phonographic recordings. Bartók's passion, initially based exclusively on a musical instinct, was to transform itself later into a professional activity. Bartók characterized his research approach by writing: "We Hungarian students of musical folklore ... consider ourselves as academics ... for we take as the subject of our research a concrete product of nature, the music of the people" (Bartók 1992 [1931], 221). Treating their undertakings, therefore, with a sizable sense of responsibility, these two young men—both composers and musicologists—embarked on a systematic and comprehensive description of the musical cultures of Austria-Hungary. Bartók alone collected no fewer than 2,721 texts and melodies (Gerson-Kiwi 1957, 150). The variety of the folk songs with which the scholars came into contact enlightened them unto the need for comparative studies into the musical folklore of the Austro-Hungarian Empire.

The reflections and analyses that resulted from these findings led Bartók to question the generally accepted views on the folk music of Hungarians. Eventually, he would derive from these stirrings a new concept of national music, based on Hungarian folk music.

New Definitions of Hungarian National Music

The sense of nationalist fervor in Hungary at the turn of the twentieth century encouraged searches for the sources of national identity. Attempts to reformulate the theory of Hungarian music also appeared, detached from their nineteenth-century predecessors. All the same, the romantic tradition and its terminology permeated the discourse. For example, in a 1919 article titled "The Theory of Hungarian Music," Edward Kilenyi enthusiastically related the new conception of Hungarian national music, but he used language and concepts betraying a nineteenth-century sensibility: "national melody," "purely Hungarian," "genuinely Hungarian," "Hungarian national music," "candid national character," and so forth. In looking at the limitations of former models, he argued that they simplistically indicated only "good" and "bad" Hungarian music (Kilenyi 1919, 20). As for the theory of identifying Hungarian music with Gypsy music, he defined this as "possible and picturesque," seeing in such an identification the overriding causes of its exceptional popularity.

The question of the traditional nineteenth-century association of Hungarian national music with Gypsy music was to be central in most writing on national music that appeared in Hungary. For instance, in the early twentieth century, such a passage by Géza Molnár was to be found: "All the national characteristics . . . were established long before the Gypsies immigrated into Hungary. That the Gypsy is not possessed of creative talent was thoroughly proved. . . ." (Molnár; cited in Kilenyi 1919, 39). Needless to say, such an attempt to disclaim Gypsy influence on Hungarian traits, and in turn argue against the Gypsy character of Hungarian music, was nothing new and already being wielded in Liszt's day (Engel 1880a, 221).

Other voices doubted the possibility in general of creating an idiom of national Hungarian music. In 1900, Kornél Ábrányi forecast the disappearance of genuine Hungarian music, and simultaneously approached the potential development of Gypsy music with similar skepticism (Ábrányi 1900, 131). Eleven years later, Bartók himself doubted whether a Hungarian music with national features would ever arise, writing that "We did not have, hitherto, a valuable and yet distinctive art music, characteristically Hungarian" (Bartók 1992 [1911], 301).

Béla Bartók's Proposition

In the early twentieth century, the past century's hopes for the creation of a Hungarian national style in music (incorporating the Gypsy interpretations, considered Hungarian, of compositions made by representatives of the upper class) started to slowly disappear, remaining at the level of provincial aspirations (Ujfalussy 1971, 49). A geographic split had emerged whereby German music was preferred in Budapest, whereas in the Hungarian provinces more national traditions blossomed, with music by Gypsies playing a significant role since the early nineteenth century.

Arbiters of opinion such as universities and publications, which were head-quartered in Budapest, evinced fascination with general European trends and copied Viennese and German models. Despite a tendency toward political radicalism, middle class circles preferred a German repertoire, while in smaller, more parochial towns, sentimental music played by *Zigeunerkapellen* reigned supreme.

Early twentieth-century Hungary, therefore, saw an antagonism emerge in musical preference between a high European universalism and a national tradition perceived as dilettantish and not entirely authentic. This dichotomy found its reflection in the creators themselves: educated musicians (including at the Music Academy in Budapest, who favored the Western model) clearly leaned toward German models, while the so-called national tradition was maintained in a repertoire composed by dilettantish writers enamored of popular song. Complaints even arose within musical circles of an absence of clearly defined guidelines conducive to developing young students of musical composition in the spirit of Hungarianness. In 1903, correspondingly, in the popular paper *Esti Újság*, a piece by Aurel Kern criticized the Budapest Music Academy for its Germanic preferences, pointing out that "Brahms is their idol, and the young musicians are taught to worship him" (Schneider 2006, 30).

Consequently, the world of Bartók—a young composer and zealous musical ethnologist—was shaped, on the one hand, by the era's chauvinistic trends and, on the other, by the musicological literature examining the question of so-called *cigányzene*—or Gypsy music within the national context. Aesthetic factors, rooted in a sense of romantic sentimentalism, lay behind Bartók's initial criticism of music performed by Gypsies. Seeking to reconcile his own conflicting inclinations, the composer spoke out against the coidentification of Gypsy and Hungarian music, drawing on his own musicological research in the process. In 1904, he wrote, "Our own Hungarians . . . abhor anything serious, they are much more satisfied with the usual Gypsy slop that makes any cultured foreigner take to his heels. . . ." (Ujfalussy 1971, 60). In that same year, songs he heard sung by a servant girl convinced him that Hungarian folk melodies had a different character from the music played by the *Zigeunerkapellen*, which were hitherto considered representative of Hungarian folk music (Cooper 2001, 18). Three years later, in 1907, Bartók discovered, on a summer expedition to Transylvania, melodies not recalling anything usually considered Hungarian, further reinforcing his sense of an alternative Hungarian national music. The melodies he heard, the most important structural elements of which were based on a pentatonic scale, he marked as belonging to the "old style" (class A) in opposition to the "new style" (class B), with the latter widely associated with Hungarian music.

Additionally, the composer introduced a mixed category, designating it class C (Bartók 1992 [1931], 209).

Bartók's constructively expressed criticism in relation to Hungarian national music did not involve assessing the national value of music performed by actual Romanies but hinged instead on proposing a new interpretation of the term *national music* based on the folk musical repertoire of ordinary Hungarian people, as preserved and still cultivated in the Hungarian countryside. In the collective memory of the culturally isolated Hungarian peasantry, the composer perceived reserves of genuine, authentic folk music that was as if unadulterated even as it was slowly dying.

In proposing his conception, he was aware, however, of its inherent methodological pitfalls: he explained in a 1931 article that, "the concepts of *Volksmusik* and *Volkslied* are unclear. In principle a broad circle of recipients are of the opinion that the country's folk music is homogeneous, when this is not the case, *Volksmusik* is comprised of two parts" (Bartók 1972, 226).

In Bartók's depiction, Hungarian *Volksmusik*'s two distinct types were, one, music played in towns characterized by certain artistic aspirations, and, two, music of the countryside cultivated by ordinary peasants. According to the composer, the semantic capacity of the word *Volksmusik* encompassed the cultural circles of Eastern Europe. This view was to become the starting point for many of his later writings; for example, in 1933, he began an article about Hungarian folk music by recalling, "When folk music of certain Central Eastern European nations is discussed, a sharp distinction must be made between the folk music of the 'educated' or 'partly educated' (mostly urban) classes and that of the peasants" (Bartók 1992 [1933], 71).

As for establishing a hierarchy between the urban and the peasant types, Bartók assertively prioritizes the latter: "Hungarian peasant music . . . is the most important part of Hungarian folk music from the aesthetic as well as the numerical aspect" (Bartók 1992 [1933], 71). Genuine folk music cultivated by an indigenous Hungarian people, for Bartók, offered the prospect not just of an original, authentic Hungarian idiom but also of a break from German-centric cultural hegemony.

Gypsy Music and Hungarian National Music

Bartók's attempts at a new interpretation of national music, although he distanced them from earlier such efforts, were nevertheless deeply rooted in nineteenth-century quests for authenticity and traditions connected with folk music. As we have seen, the composer's findings diverged from those of his predecessors, in that he pointedly criticized characterizations of so-called Gypsy music as typically and fundamentally Hungarian. In his endeavor, Bartók drew attention to the way in which the term "Gypsy music" referred not to music composed by Romany musicians but rather to Hungarian music (class B) performed in towns by *Zigeunerkapellen*. As a consequence, the composer stated that what "people (including Hungarians) call Gypsy music is not Gypsy music but Hungarian" (Bartók 1992 [1931], 206). Notably, he distinguished folk music performed by Gypsy musicians for themselves from the music played for income in the gardens and cafés of the large Austro-Hungarian towns. This radical, even extreme opposition created by Bartók constituted a clear axis for his concept of national music, a proposition that contained traits of novelty and progressiveness.

Bartók's establishment of a polar relation between "Gypsy music" and "Hungarian folk music" was to some degree an artificial construction with heuristic traits aimed at facilitating the discovery of the ideals of national Hungarian music (Frigyesi 2000, 140). And the composer elaborated these ideals in numerous publications, such as the journal *Aurora*. These pieces, in which he advanced a simplified view of the two classes of music, were directed more toward the ordinary reader than toward specialists. To this end, he exaggerated the differences between class A—and the popular *verbunkos* or magyar *nóta* popularized by the *Zigeunerkapellen*—and the more "authentic" class B (Schneider 2006, 11).

As has been implied so far, Bartók looked critically on past attempts to create an idiom of national Hungarian music. In 1911, for example, he wrote in extremely biting terms that Erkel had "tried to solve the task by wedging between musical items of Italian character one or two gipsy-type tunes or *csárdás*. The mixture of such heterogeneous elements does not produce a Hungarian style, merely a conglomerate lacking any style" (Bartók 1992 [1911], 301). Bartók was to maintain this view of Erkel in his later writings. In 1921, he emphasized that Erkel's operas "imitate the style of Italian opera. National features, therefore, are . . . in the form of would-be Hungarian songs, replete with gipsy contortions which are inserted in several scenes" (Bartók 1992 [1921], 474–75). And in 1943, he wrote of the composer as someone who "mingled in his work the then contemporary Italian operatic style with characteristics of Hungarian urban gipsy music. In other words, Erkel's is a hybrid style of composition. His works are still performed in Hungary, but he was and is absolutely unknown abroad" (Bartók 1992 [1943], 361).

Besides Erkel, Liszt was the composer against whose legend Bartók pitted himself within the national context. According to József Ujfalussy, Bartók was unable to avoid this confrontation for at least three reasons (Ujfalussy 1971, 58). First, the musical situation in Hungary, despite the passing of several decades since the great composer's death, had not changed noticeably: the Hungarian musical heritage was based in principle, both in Liszt's and Bartók's day, chiefly on popular songs stylized on folk or the *verbunkos* and czardas dances. Second, Liszt's influence manifested itself in Bartók's own compositions, since the latter understood early on the significant role Liszt played in the development and promotion of Hungarian music. Third, Liszt had raised the question of Gypsy music within his work, something that required explanation and rectification in the light of the ethnomusicological research conducted by Bartók.

Bartók's interest in Liszt reveals itself in his writings as early as 1911, and he would systematically return to combating Liszt's so-called error on Gypsy music, especially as it was expressed in Liszt's book. In 1921, Bartók wrote forcefully on the topic, claiming that Liszt, "in his work *Des Bohemiens*, is perhaps even more extraordinary: he believes that the melodies played by the gypsies and used in his compositions are the creations of the gypsies themselves. According to Liszt, the melodies of the Hungarian peasants have no musical value whatsoever. It is absolutely evident that he was not acquainted with any of them or, at least, with very few, since he never thought to collect them systematically" (Bartók 1992 [1921], 69). Evaluating Liszt that very same year, Bartók admitted that beside certain Hungarian sources of inspiration in his work and his promotion of Hungarian music abroad, Liszt could not justifiably be called a "national composer," for "Liszt as composer has a more international than national character" (Bartók 1992 [1921], 474).

Bartók's longest text devoted to "problems with Liszt" was a February 3, 1936, address to the Hungarian Academy of Sciences marking the fiftieth anniversary of Liszt's death. Ujfalussy evaluated the speech as being highly personal and unusually emotional in tone, particularly in the fragments in which Bartók, quoting Liszt, recalled the echoes of "his own bitter struggle to win recognition as a Hungarian" (Ujfalussy 1971, 325).

Bartók constructed his speech around four questions: Does the present generation understand Liszt's works? Which of his compositions still enjoy popularity? Was Liszt a Hungarian? And what can we make of Liszt's thesis in his book on Gypsy music?

In seeking to answer this last question, Bartók did not retract his former statements but expressed the conviction that Liszt may be only partially to blame for his error. The fault, according to Bartók, could lie in part with the faulty research methods of the nineteenth century. Bartók emphasized further the Romantic era influence on Liszt's work: his search for "frills and decorations, show and glittering ornamentation," and not "perfectly plain, objective simplicity" (Bartók 1992 [1936], 506–7). Bartók also drew attention to the linguistic trap into which Liszt had fallen, as we have seen in his other writings: in nineteenth-century Hungary, the term "Gypsy music" meant Hungarian music performed by the *Zigeunerkapellen* and did not refer to Gypsy music per se. Overall, sympathy permeates this 1936 effort by Bartók, as would have been appropriate for the occasion—a recognition of Liszt's immense personality and musical talent. Bartók interpreted even the publication of Liszt's book as an act of courage by the composer in advancing his own—controversial—views and standing up to his adversaries' attacks. Liszt's attitude was emphasized by Bartók as one worthy of admiration.

Bartók's softening position on Liszt found its reflection in Bartók's later statements, particularly those directed toward non-Hungarian circles. The researcher started to limit himself to a presentation of facts, devoid of emotional color, and to avoid judgemental words in his appraisals. In the course of his Harvard lectures in 1943, for example, Bartók claimed merely that "Liszt . . . discovered what he called and believed to be gipsy music, which was however Hungarian urban music propagated by gipsy bands" (Bartók 1992 [1943], 361).

The Avant-gardism of Bela Bartók's Reflections

In assessing Bartók's bold ideas, one must consider the political factors underlying them. In early twentieth-century Hungary, one of the strongest drivers behind radical liberal movements was the growing awareness of social problems, rooted in the segregation of the middle and upper classes from ordinary people, considered by some to be rabble. As Judith Frigyesi has pointed out, these social stratifications were not new, but the heightened awareness of them among a section of the Hungarian middle class prompted a change in thinking on the subject of Hungarianness (Frigyesi 2000, 45–46). And this change motivated intellectuals to embark on the enormous task of devising a common Hungarian national identity for both the upper classes and common people—with all their range and variations. This shift in focus reflected a broader movement in the radicalization of political life in Hungary—broadly speaking, away from the reforms postulated by Prince István Széchenyi in the early nineteenth century and toward the ideas of bourgeois liberalism, whose noted advocate was Lajos Kossuth (1802–1894).

Europe's fastest-growing city from 1869 to 1910, Budapest blossomed as a center of liberalism (Hooker 2001, 10). The city was simultaneously a site of nationalist pomp, as exemplified in the 1896 celebration commemorating the millennium of the Huns' conquest of Pannonia. To mark the occasion, the Hungarian parliament moved to a new neo-Gothic style building, and the huge Heroes' Square was constructed. In 1905, construction was completed on the monumental St. Stephen's Basilica, named after the first Hungarian saint.

Bartók was heavily influenced by both the liberal and nationalist currents. After 1904, he became a sort of eccentric radical: he stopped going to church, and his friends called him an anarchist. He wore traditional Hungarian dress and insisted that even in his home Hungarian would be spoken and not German, even though the composer's mother, Paula Voit, was of German origin. One of Bartók's biographers, János Demény, pointed to the 1905 revolution in Russia and other political movements in Europe as additional sources for Bartók's thinking on the Hungarian national question (Ujfalussy 1971, 72).

Beginning in 1903, Bartók was strongly influenced by liberal views and by his discovery, in his judgment, of the authentic songs of the Hungarian people. His mixed state manifested itself in creative indecision: on the one hand, he revered the elite, refined music that he had studied, while on the other, he sought to serve the national cause, an effort that led him to Hungarian ethnic traditions and their associated simple and popular music. Even in the previous century, this synthesis of refined art, linked with progress and innovation, with a domestic traditionalism had constituted a great challenge for composers who harbored nationalist aspirations (Schneider 2006, 9). Bartók himself dreamed of achieving this fusion and hoped that the result would be a music bearing true Hungarian traits (that is, a rejection of Gypsy music) while also fulfilling the standards of a new music (Ujfalussy 1971, 57).

Bartók's efforts at following these two different paths would ultimately elicit much criticism. In particular, the modern strains in Bartók's work were seen as lacking beauty as well as being un-Hungarian, more a homage to the avant-garde than to a national tradition. Bartók, who sought musical solutions to breathe life into "the facade of empty nationalism" (Frigyesi 1994, 278), ultimately alienated himself to listeners. Most members of the middle class decisively rejected Bartók's new artistic vision. And conservative circles rejected outright the possibility of a dissonant, modernist version of Hungarian national music—associated with the cult of progress—preferring a romantic orientation.

Given the aesthetic stakes in the argument over Bartók's new creations, the subject of Gypsy music invariably reentered the fray. It was invoked both by Bartók's supporters (who rejected it as the basis of Hungarian national music) and his opponents (who glorified not so much the Gypsy music itself as the Gypsy musicians as symbolic figures connected with Hungarian nationalism).

For example, Haraszti, in the May 1, 1929, edition of the journal *Budapesti Hírlap*, sharply attacked both Bartók and Kodály, accusing them of falsifying the picture of Hungarian music. The author defended the national status of Gypsy music, maintaining that it reflected the sublimation of genuine Hungarian feelings and the Hungarian soul. Haraszti wrote about the ideal of Gypsy music being close to the Hungarian "atavistic way of thinking." In the article's conclusion, the author admitted that "the Gypsy is Hungary's own militant irredentist, whose like[ness] as an artist cannot be found anywhere else in the world. Hungarian sighs are carried to the four corners of the world by the gypsy violin and Hungarian hearts are heard beating in his music" (Ujfalussy 1971, 273–74). The removal of the equals sign between Gypsy and Hungarian music—proposed by Bartók—was in this context evaluated as a conscious blurring of the image of Hungarian music through its replacement by folk music and the diluting of Hungarian music to that of folk music.

Haraszti was particularly fierce in his defense of the place of Gypsy music in the social consciousness of Hungarians, asking rhetorically: "Should we then, at such a time as this, deny [the Gypsy musician] as a Hungarian?" (Ujfalussy 1971, 274). Haraszti was to maintain his position a year later during the congress of the International Society for Musical Research. In presenting to foreign delegates on links between Gypsy and Hungarian music, this Hungarian musicologist spoke up for the value of Gypsy musicians for Hungarian society. Stating that "independent" Gypsy music does not exist, Haraszti admitted that it was difficult to authoritatively differentiate between authentic folk melodies and mere popular melodies adapted by Gypsy musicians. In conclusion, although the author did not mention Bartók by name, he severely criticized his conception (Haraszti 1930, 143–45).

Posterity would be noticeably kinder than Haraszti to Bartók's ethnomusicological legacy; numerous interpreters of his thinking have drawn attention in their works to the spectrum of factors influencing the composer's convictions and their evolution. Szabolcsi showed—in a series of articles published in the 1950s—the composer's ideas' natural continuation, including as they played out in concepts such as patriotism, humanism, and fraternity (Szabolcsi 1964). A subsequent biographer, Breuer, continued the tradition of interpreting Bartók's thought as the organic and consistent evolution of nationalist ideals (Frigyesi 1994, 256). For his part, Ujfalussy posited that Bartók's method was characterized by a dialectic principle with a clearly drawn connection between the critical deconstruction of the past and the construction of a new system of values corresponding to the contemporary world. As Ujfalussy writes, Bartók's route to the formulation of a finalized philosophy was, however, "both difficult and prolonged" (Ujfalussy 1971, 58).

Arguing from a similar frame, Frigyesi proposed a new interpretative concept for the dichotomy behind Bartók's views, suggesting that the composer's writings "document two stages in Bartók's ideological development" (Frigyesi 1994, 256). The first of these stages was characterized by the chauvinism typical in Hungary in the tumultuous fin de siècle; the second remained under the clear influence of the mature composer's faith in the brotherhood of peoples and multiethnic coexistence. Meanwhile, David Malvinni has drawn attention to the courageousness of Bartók's views: his opposition to prevailing musicological dogma and his belief that lofty, inspiring music could only be the work of genius, along with acknowledgment of an alternative source of artistic creativity—the collective Hungarian people (Malvinni 2004, 143).

The concepts advanced by Bartók in his works were continued and expanded on by Kodály. In the foreword to the 1960 English edition of a book on folk music in Hungary, he returned to the problem of the identification of Hungarian music with Gypsy music, writing: "Generally speaking, Hungarian music is still identified with gipsy music and folk song is confused with popular art. Yet in its narrower sense, Hungarian folk music has little or nothing in common with the music offered over the radio as 'Hungarian folk-tunes' or since Sarasate as 'gipsy melodies.' Performed by gipsy orchestras or in other popular arrangements such music has been the basis of all generalizations about 'Hungarian music' for nearly a hundred years. Nor is it in any way the creation of gipsies, as it is still frequently asserted as a result of Franz Liszt's monumental error" (Kodály 1960, 7). One of the arguments quoted by Kodály to support his theses (and those of Bartók) was the "conspicuous absence of gipsy composers" in the genre (Kodály 1960, 9). Alleged Gypsy composers are considered by Kodály to be "never more than second rate imitators of the regular Hungarian style" (Kodály 1960, 9). And Kodály describes the practices of such Gypsy composers as follows: "Gipsy composers follow faithfully in the footsteps of other native and assimilated Hungarians, the most prolific[,] Pista Dankó[,] is even strongly under the influence of indigenous Hungarian peasant music. He wrote more than four hundred songs to contemporary Hungarian texts, whereas other gipsy composers confined themselves to the wordless and instrumentally conceived csárdás" (Kodály 1960, 9).

The views of Bartók and Kodály on the question of Gypsy music in Hungary clearly helped shape the national discourse. The radical nature of their overarching thesis restarted a debate on the role of this music in the creation of national Hungarian music and was cause for a unique "re-evaluation of . . . [the] nation's belief system" (Malvinni 2004, 142). This was particularly so in the context of the counterarguments of Bartók's opponents, who adhered to an assimilative type of discourse in which Gypsy music was used as an element in the constructed image of national music in Hungary.

🌿 🌿 🌿 🌿 🌿

CHAPTER TWO

Spanish National Music

The Gitanos' Musical Traditions in Spain

The Appearance of Gypsies in Spain

The music of the Spanish Gypsies, known as Gitanos, arose as a result of the intermixing of several cultures carrying specific historical experiences: Andalusian culture displaying its Arabic influence, Jewish culture, and the culture of the Andalusian Gypsies themselves. The music of the Andalusian Gypsies started with the arrival of the first Romanies in Spanish territories at the beginning of the fifteenth century and grew and took shape over subsequent centuries (Fraser 2005, 76).

At the time of the Romanies' arrival, their leaders referred to themselves as princes and counts and were initially well treated on the Iberian peninsula; "the Spanish nobility would in fact remain protectors of the Gypsies and give them valuable succor" (Fraser 2005, 97). Their situation, however, would soon worsen. After 1480, with increased numbers of Gypsy settlers on the peninsula, the first anti-Gypsy edicts were issued.

The specific attitude taken toward the so-called Gypsy problem was an outgrowth of Christian Spain's relations with the Muslims, who were finally driven out of Andalusia in 1492. Many Gypsies settled in Andalusia, which under Moorish rule had been a wealthy region with an intensively developed agriculture and textile industry. Cultural life blossomed, and the society was a synthesis of Arab, Jewish, and Christian influences. The Inquisition put an emphatic end to the run of tolerance and coexistence. Even before the official expulsion year of 1492, the Jews were asked to vacate Seville in 1483, along with the city's Moors, as the Muslims of Spain are known from a generalizing Western perspective, reflecting the new fate of Spain's non-Christian citizens (Roth 1995, 283).

The Gypsies were seen, in a sense, to fill the space left by the Moors—and, with their dark complexion and dark hair, they even looked similar—particularly given that the Gypsies willingly took up the traditional Moorish occupations: not simply smithery and trade in horses, with which the Gypsies had earlier been associated, but also masonry, tailoring, baking, and butchery. In the society's search for misfits, Gypsies were often likened to Arabs, and even considered progeny of the Arabs. Some went so far as to suggest that the Moors had never left Spain but rather simply dressed themselves in Gypsy garb and reinvented their customs.

In Spain, the conviction developed that a Gypsy was such by choice: someone who did not adhere to either human or divine laws, regardless of ethnic origin. In turn, both the social and political attitude toward Gypsies resulted from the belief that Gypsies, at least as an ethnically separate people, simply did not exist. Correspondingly, those lacking a permanent abode or steady occupation and who wandered from place to place were considered cutthroats and social outcasts. The view of Gypsies as socially dangerous apostates was expressed famously in the Prematica (pragmatic sanction), issued in 1633 by Philip IV (1605–1665) and declaring unequivocally that "those who call themselves *Gitanos* are not so by origin or by nature but have adopted this form of life for such deleterious purposes as are now experienced" (Fraser 2005, 161). Discussions on the Gypsies were fueled by publications, chiefly by representatives of the Spanish clergy, accusing Gypsies of all possible crimes: betrayal, theft, child abduction, lasciviousness, and heresy, just to begin with.

At the beginning of the seventeenth century, however, several prominent Gypsy families gained royal prerogatives exempting them from the anti-Gypsy laws. From among the representatives of these families (including the Bustamante, Rocamora, Montoya, and Flores families) were enlisted soldiers in the royal army, who saw action in the protracted war in the Netherlands (Leblon 2003, 36). During this period of military involvement, many Gypsy children were born of the relationships between Gypsy soldiers from wealthy families and non-Gypsy women from northern Europe. The offspring were distinguished by blue eyes and blond hair, previously uncommon for Gypsies but after that point characteristic for certain Andalusian Gypsies.

Yet even the families of Gypsy veterans from the Flanders campaign would ultimately be subjected to repression under the increasing Gypsy restrictions. Gypsies would invoke their fair hair and eye color, sometimes effectively, against such restrictions. Families of so-called Flemish origin lived close to one another, often in large clusters. The restrictions meant that Gypsies typically lived in urban areas (Leblon 2003, 44), which were most prominent in Andalusia at the end of the sixteenth century. Besides Madrid, the largest Spanish cities (i.e., numbering more than thirty thousand inhabitants) were situated in the south of the country (Ruiz 2003, 54). By the eighteenth century, the regions of Cadiz and Seville housed around half the Gypsy population, with the rest spread across the country. Gypsy groups settled in Almeria, Malaga, and Granada; in the last of these, they dwelled in caves on the slopes of the Sacromonte.

The abandonment by most Spanish Gypsies of the nomadic way of life, resulting from the restrictions imposed on them, eased the integration of Gypsies with Spaniards, both culturally and socially. The policies enacted from on high caused opposition among Gypsies particularly within those territories densely inhabited by them (e.g., Andalusia). Yet, paradoxically, Gypsy resistance would strengthen the bonds between Gypsies and non-Gypsy society, also in revolt against the overcentralizing authority in Madrid. Both the Andalusian Gypsies and other locals felt the effects of the day's overwhelming poverty. In seventeenth-century Spain, "the lowest in the social hierarchy were the slaves ... and the Gypsies" (Ruiz 2003, 64). The latter had to additionally bear the burden of persecution, intolerance from the authorities, and accusations of theft and beggary. The Madrid authorities, looking for a scapegoat for the empire's collapse, often tagged the Gypsies. The limited assimilation by Gypsies in Andalusia, therefore, constituted an act of opposition against the ruling order. They, for example, sent their children to school with other children and attended Catholic mass. Even the language of the Andalusian Gypsies—with the Romany language banned—adapted, moving closer to Spanish, with the resulting dialect known as *caló*.

As for the anti-Gypsy decrees, a 1717 action restated and intensified the regulation of 1633 (Leblon 2003, 25). In particular, Gypsies could no longer work as smiths, and their settlement was limited to forty-one specially designated cities. In addition, a Gypsy faced the death penalty if he was found in possession of a firearm. Gypsy nomadism diminished as a result of the 1717 decree, but the law's attempt to disperse Gypsies throughout the country failed: most remained in the south. And overall Gypsies did not assimilate into Spanish society to the degree expected by the regime. As a result, in 1749 King Ferdinand VI, who was initially reluctant to take radical steps, consented to the proposal of Bishop Gaspar Vázquez Tablada to pursue a full-scale cleansing of Spain's Gypsies, by way of consigning them to forced labor. Only fourteen years later did the royal edict of Charles III free the imprisoned Gypsies.

In the second half of the eighteenth century, a somewhat different view of the Gypsy question in Spain emerged, as exemplified in a 1783 document signed by King Charles III. This document emphasized, first and foremost, that Gypsies should not be viewed through the lens of criminality; moreover, they were permitted to perform most professions previously barred to them, and they could live in towns as they chose (Leblon 2003, 39).

During the years of severe restrictions, Gypsy music transformed slowly, owing to the Gypsies' attachment to their tradition of music-making. The musical traditions were chiefly cultivated among Gypsies from privileged families (the *flamencos*) and those possessing a permanent home (the so-called *caseros*) and, to a lesser degree, among the nomadic *andarrios* and *canasteros*. Although the anti-Gypsy legislation forbade Gypsies from gathering together, the strongly rooted traditions of collective music-making were to survive. The emergence of the *caló* language and the preservation of characteristic melodies would decide the later shape of Gypsy music in Spain and be reflected particularly in the phenomenon of flamenco.

The Music of the Gitanos

The nontypical situation of the Gypsies in Spain, as explored earlier, resulted in a specific melding of Gypsy and Spanish music. More specifically, this music would incorporate elements of Gypsy, Andalusian, Jewish, and Moorish culture, creating an intricate phenomenon combining song, dance, and instrument playing that, by the end of the nineteenth century, would earn the name *flamenco*.

The initial phase in the formation of flamenco occurred from the mid-eighteenth to the mid-nineteenth century. This period included the composition of prison songs, known as *carceleras*, a musical response to anti-Gypsy persecution and especially the events of 1749. These songs were performed without guitar accompaniment, and even without clapping, and they covered topics such as prison conditions, the lack of money, and the wait for release. The motif of death also recurs in these songs, although historians cannot precisely estimate the number of Gypsies who lost their lives during this period (Volland 1990, 251–66). The subsequent easing of the legislation toward Gypsies brought with it a change in musical practices: for example, a piece from 1781 describes a dance of Gypsy women during a church wedding ceremony performed to the guitar (Fraser 2005, 143).

From the mid-nineteenth to the mid-twentieth century, Gypsy music grew constantly in popularity. In the 1840s, the large Spanish cities of Madrid and Seville saw the appearance of *cafés cantantes*—premises where music was performed live. Certain researchers believe that one of the first *cafés cantantes*, in the environs of Cadiz, bore the name Cafe Flamenco, marking the origin of the name for musical form (Starkie 1935–1936, 20). Other academics follow J. Blas Vega, who claims that the first *café cantante* was more likely El Cafe de los Lombardos, in Seville, opened in 1847 (Fraser 2005, 207); still others "correct" this claim by arguing that the first café was opened in 1842 in Seville on Lombardo Street (González-Caballos Martínez 2008; accessed February 9, 2008). One thing remains certain: from their beginning, all *cafés cantantes* abounded with song and ensured performers regular contact with the public. In the nineteenth century and later, both Spaniards and Spanish Gypsies took every opportunity to gather in such cafés to perform and listen to flamenco (Mulcahy 1990, 234).

The dominant mode of nineteenth-century flamenco played to a male lifestyle that passed at an established tempo, with much emphasis placed on music. Evening meetings in local taverns presented for men an opportunity to sum up—over a glass of wine—the events of the day. Alcohol-laced feasts were conducive to discussions in which "The air, thick with smoke and the musky scent of wine, starts to resonate with their passion. Eventually, one or another of the singers produces a texture of sound that sets teeth on edge, induces chills, and raises goose bumps. This is a signal moment in the art of flamenco" (Washabaugh 1997, 51).

Most flamenco repertoire was accompanied by the guitar. Now and then, a deft guitarist would show off his skills during short interludes between a song's verses. A contemporary visitor to *cafés cantantes*, José Inzega (1828–1891), describes the scene:

> When listening to these *cantaores*, so long-winded and untiring in their singular specialty, with which they show off like finished artists, one fancies that they are advancing, with their swift triplets, their interminable semitonic scales ascending and descending, and all the other oriental embellishments, through the twistings and turnings of a trackless labyrinth, where it is impossible to follow them. And again, they dwell unbearably on the long notes, and close with a dying susurration like the mournful sough of the wind through the branches; they hold our senses in suspense between desolation and ravishment with those everlasting "ays" that move our hearts—that one can feel, but not imitate. (Istel 1926, 503)

Both women and men employed in the *cafés cantantes* usually worked only temporarily, involving a sizable turnover in artists (Molina and Mairena 1963, 50). They could count, though, on a relative degree of financial independence. Still, the outstanding majority of Spanish society viewed the world of flamenco performers as less privileged than the middle classes, and women connected with flamenco held a relatively low social status. But it was the performers themselves who maintained this image of wild women directly connected with nature, personifying Gypsy freedom in opposition to the rigors of the civilized world (Mulcahy 1990, 247). Hence, the fascinating performances of "genuine *cantaores* from Andalusia" (Inzega 1888, xiii) reduced the role of the Gypsies singing there "to the level of prostituted performers . . . to delight wealthy gawkers attracted more by the romance of the Gypsy than by the value of *cante* Gitano" (Washabaugh 1997, 35).

Yet in the nineteenth century, another dimension developed in the public performance of flamenco, dominated by female singing. This form was connected with carnivals and fairs and involved the gearing of flamenco to the reception of an external recipient who, increasingly often, was a foreign tourist. International fascination grew especially in the late nineteenth century. Soon, however, criticism emerged in response to the form's popularization. In the early twentieth century, performances given in nightclubs (*tablaos*) were critiqued as a trivialization of the true art, as in the pamphlet *Escenas y andanzas de la campaña antiflamenca*, in which the Spanish writer Eugenio Muñoz Díaz (1885–1936), who used the pseudonym Eugenio Noel, wrote that "One of the evils of flamenco is the deterioration in dancing that it has provoked. Tonight there is no voluptuosity, refinement, or subtle grace. Our dancer is an indecent type; androgynous and tortured. His female companion disgracefully wields her body like her soul: without art or science, only to earn a few pesetas" (Noel 1913). Interestingly, the 1880s and 1890s were to be sentimentally remembered as the period of genuine flamenco art (Starkie 1935–1936, 12).

Fascination with flamenco was reflected in Spanish literature of the later nineteenth century. Even earlier, around 1847, the early Romantic author Serafín Estébanez Calderón, known as El Solitario (1799–1867) provided perhaps the earliest descriptions of the phenomenon in two novellas, "Asamblea general" and "Un baile en Triana." Academic interest in the form increased in the twentieth century; in 1958, for instance, the Catedra de Flamencologia, an academic institute, was founded with the aim of studying flamenco. Likewise, flamenco festivals increased in the mid-twentieth century.

Nineteenth-Century Sources of Interest in the Music of Spanish Gypsies

Regional divisions in Spain were a source of both cultural and musical difference. The characteristic pride taken in local identity was noted by the early nineteenth-century French observer of daily Spanish life Prosper Mérimée (1803–1870), who, in a letter of October 25, 1830, wrote from Madrid that "small-town patriotism is as strong in Spain as in France" (Mérimée 2001, 21). Others, particularly foreign travelers, in romantic presentations of both Spanish culture and music, concentrated particularly on Andalusia. For example, the English writer Richard Ford was enchanted by the dance he saw in Andalusia (Ford 1846), as was the Frenchman Jean Charles Davillier some decades later (Davillier 1876).

The propagation of the image of music-making Spaniards, particularly of those Spanish Gypsies living in Andalusia, was furthered by Englishman George Borrow (1803–1881), based on his travels around the Iberian Peninsula. In crossing Europe, he had come into contact with Gypsies living in various countries, including Russia, Hungary, and Turkey. His works drew on his own experiences as well as the works of others, including Grellmann and—in the case of the Hungarian Gypsies—Richard Bright's 1818 *Travels from Vienna through Lower Hungary*. In his 1843 work, *The Bible in Spain; or, the Journeys, Adventures, and Imprisonment of an Englishman*, which would bring him much acclaim and success, Borrow describes the customs of the Spanish Gypsies, presenting them as a people enraptured by song and dance (Borrow 1905, 61). His work of two years earlier, *The Zincali: An Account of the Gypsies of Spain*, devotes surprisingly little space to the music of Spanish Gypsies, concentrating instead on poetry.

In Borrow's books and other nineteenth-century texts on Spanish Gypsies alike, two aspects stand out. First, the authors treat the music as a distinctive product of Gypsy culture, although with features akin to those of Andalusian folklore. In many letters, these writers leave a certain space for the reader to interpret the music of Spanish Gypsies as being de facto Spanish music. The second feature typical of these accounts involves the examination of Gypsy music through the lens of three elements: song, dance, and instrumental pieces. In *The Zincali*, Borrow had already presented the singing and lyrical texts of the Gypsies as an intrinsic whole. Similar to other nineteenth-century authors, Borrow implies clearly that Spanish Gypsy music is connected to various musical traditions, with roots similar to those of Spanish music. He writes explicitly that, "The couplets of the Gitanos are composed in the same off-hand manner, and exactly resemble in metre the popular ditties of the Spaniards" (Borrow 1841, part III, chapter 1). He does not, however, go so far as to equate Gypsy music with Spanish music outright, acknowledging that Gypsy music had retained certain distinctive features even through its interaction with Spanish forms. Borrow bears out this view in writing about Gypsy songs: "In spirit, however, as well as language, they are in general widely different, as they mostly relate to the Gypsies and their affairs, and not unfrequently abound with abuse of the Busne or Spaniards. Many of these creations have . . . wafted over Spain amongst the

Gypsy tribes, and are even frequently repeated by the Spaniards themselves; at least, by those who affect to imitate the phraseology of the Gitanos" (Borrow 1841, part III, chapter 1).

Borrow's viewpoint on the convergence of Spanish Gypsy music with Andalusian music was widely shared within nineteenth-century Europe. Even Liszt, in his work on Gypsy music in Hungary, expressed such a view in the chapter devoted to Gypsies "somewhere else" (titled "Die Zigeuner anderwärts" in the 1883 German version). Liszt complained, in typical romantic style, of his lack of luck in acquainting himself with the musical situation of Spanish Gypsies. The melodies he managed to listen to were, he writes, "fragments of songs that were more Andalusian than Gypsy, and a dire accompanying guitar without a trace of originality" (Liszt 1883, 162).

Other authors from the later nineteenth century would display similar ambivalence about the originality of Andalusian Gypsy music, although generally using a fairly careful tone. This owed in part to fears of recommitting Liszt's "error," which gave Gypsies the rights to their country's music. For instance, Engel, aware of Liszt's position, in an 1880 text on the music of the Gypsies generally, devoted several passages to the music of the Spanish Gypsies, writing that, "most tunes attributed to them are in reality Spanish tunes, and of Moorish rather than Gipsian origin" (Engel 1880b, 389). In describing compositions of the nineteenth century associated with the Gypsies, collected in books of traditional songs and bestowed with the nickname *La Gitana* or some other such title, Engel writes of a repertoire "played by the Gipsies, or perhaps composed by them after the models of these Spanish dance-tunes" (Engel 1880b, 390). Yet out of a corresponding desire to assure the reader of the existence of genuine Gypsy music in Spain, he mentions an example of a prelude as being authentically inspired by Gypsy song. He notes different constructions in the piece, as compared with its Spanish counterparts, as well as melodic similarities with other Gypsy melodies. The crowning argument, however, as to the authenticity of the quoted fragment's Gypsy provenance involved—according to the author—the affirmative words of Spanish musicians themselves.

In describing the music of Spanish Gypsies, Engel devoted space especially to dance, examining this matter both in relation to Spanish as well as Oriental influences. According to Engel, Spanish Gypsies had preserved "some of their ancient Hindu characteristics," particularly visible in the "oriental mode of dancing" (Engel 1880b, 389–90). The exotic aspect to the dance appeared, in Engel's view, in women's performances characterized as "wild" and seen as a pretext employed by "wondrous Gypsy girls" to seduce rich men. Almost forty years earlier, Borrow had used almost identical terms to characterize the dances of the Spanish Gypsies. Indeed, Engel did not distance himself from the influence of Borrow, citing his works as sources. In discussing the typical instruments used by the Spanish Gypsies in the later nineteenth century, Engel, like Borrow, emphasized the guitar (modeled on and referred to as the Moorish guitar), the tambourine, and the castanets (Engel 1880b, 390).

The International Debate over Gitanos' Music

The growing popularity of Spanish Gypsy music was reflected in the early twentieth century by a corresponding rise in interest in the subject by both Spanish and foreign researchers. These scholars sought particularly to place flamenco within the context of national Spanish music. When, for example, in December 1907 (during the thirty-fourth session of the Royal Musical Association, founded in Great Britain in 1874) Henry Cart de Lafontaine presented a synopsis of Spanish music, the association's vice chairman, Charles Maclean, mused that the Gypsies' "influence on secular music must have been enormous" (de Lafontaine 1907–1908, 42).

Awareness of the significance of Gypsy influence on Spanish music, however, was not always accompanied by academic competence, often manifesting itself in stereotypical views on the subject. The nineteenth-century works of Borrow, himself considered almost a Gypsy, were the basic information source on the culture of Spanish Gypsies. Yet even the proliferation of thinkers and texts on flamenco did not result in a fuller understanding flamenco's origins and stylistic provenance. The already-mentioned de Lafontaine, in defining *cantos flamencos*, admitted that, "Cantos Flamencos stand for a wide collection of compositions ranging from the 'solea' or 'soledad,' a melancholy song and dance in a minor key, to the 'tona' and 'liviana,' which are not dance measures, nor are they accompanied by the guitar" (de Lafontaine 1907–1908, 32). In failing to offer a precise characterization of flamenco's musical parameters, he left a large field for interpretative possibilities: minor keys he associated with melancholy and revenge, while the songs' subject matter he linked to personal experiences connected with failure and misfortune. Referring to popular etymology and thus propagating stereotypical views on flamenco, he attempted to explain the origin of flamenco forms' names, such as *soledades* (alternatively *soleas* or *soleares*), *tonas*, *livianas*, *seguidillas* (and, more precisely, *seguidillas gitanas*), *peteneras*, *deblas*, and *martinetes*. For example, according to his sources, *soledad* was so called to honor a certain Soledad, most probably a well-regarded singer and dancer, while *peteneras* could be traced to a flamenco songwriter called

Petenera, which was tied to *paternera*, referring to an indigenous inhabitant of the town of Paterno in the province of Cadiz.

Spanish and Gypsy music were also conceived with respect to region. During the sixty-second session of the Royal Musical Association of Great Britain, in December 1935, Gypsy music from Spain was presented within the context of Andalusian folklore and folk music. During this session, the Irishman Walter Starkie (1894–1976), a well-known researcher on Spanish culture, presented an exhaustive paper on the topic. Starkie's talk constitutes a valuable reference as to both the level of interest in and approach to the music of Spanish Gypsies within early twentieth-century European culture. Despite its comprehensive scope, his paper concentrated on the music of Gypsies from Andalusia. A central association made by Starkie was that between the Gypsy musician and the national bard. He emphasized that, "In all those countries the gipsy has played the part of national minstrel, keeping alive among the people the old songs and dances" (Starkie 1935–1936, 2).

Starkie, like former scholars on the subject, focused on the unity of singing, dance, and instrument playing in Gypsy music, defining this unity as a Gypsy ritual. Starkie also focused on structure, paying particular attention to the melody and manner of execution. He characterized the melodies as ornamental, abundant in grace notes, with a tendency for a falling movement in their final cadences. The manner of performance, meanwhile, he defined as flowing and the musical timbre as nasal, even metallic, citing the examples of Gypsy singers Niña de los Peines and Niña de la Puebla.

Starkie classified Gypsy dance as a noble form of entertainment, remarking on the dancers' flowing, graceful movements and on the special attention devoted to the arms and hands. In describing Gypsy dance in Spain, Starkie emphasized the role of rhythm: "Watch the gipsy dancer: his eyes are closed, and his body quivers as if possessed by a demon of rhythm" (Starkie 1935–1936, 10). As for instrumentation, the author focused on the guitar, then enormously popular and highly regarded in the Gypsy context, noting that, "The guitar is the ideal instrument of the wanderer," an allusion to the nomadic lifestyle ascribed to the Gypsies. He characterized the guitar itself as "inexhaustible in the effects it can produce"—yet he noted a sonic ideal: "every attempt is made to give the instrument a metallic tone" (Starkie 1935–1936, 10–11). He defined the technique of guitar playing as serving the dual purpose of providing harmonic accompaniment and melody.

Despite its precise characterization of the music of Andalusian Gypsies, Starkie's terminological imprecision signals a common drawback of early twentieth-century characterizations. The ambivalence in the terms reflects a certain incoherence in the perception of the music of Andalusian Gypsies—on the one hand identified with flamenco, and on the other with Andalusian Gypsies treated as the exclusive source of flamenco. Although Starkie's paper's title, "The Gipsy in Andalusian Folk-Lore and Folk-Music," shows a certain level of precision, the author also talks of "the Spanish Gypsy," "Gypsy singers from the south of Spain," and so on. Further, the author refers to the music of Andalusia when he actually means the music of the Andalusian Gypsies. The confusion is heightened by Starkie's inclusion of vocabulary derived from the Spanish: we hear terms such as "*cante jondo*," referring to Gypsy singing in Spain, and "*baile gitano*," referring to dance, and "*el toque* flamenco," in reference to the characteristic guitar playing. The words *flamenco* and *gitano*, therefore, are used almost synonymously, although this connection is nowhere stated explicitly. Yet, in a seeming contradiction, the author seeks to explain the difference between singing defined as *cante jondo* and *cante flamenco*: "*Cante Jondo* was limited to the purer and less corrupted style of singing. People used the word *Cante Jondo* as a synonym of *Cante Gitano*, whereas *Cante Flamenco* was used for every sort of Andalusian folk-song, even those from the other provinces sung in South Spain. Singers who are not gipsies often introduce gipsy words, such as *parné* (money), *ducas* (sorrows), *Undebé* (God) into their songs, and there are many *coplas* without Romany words that are gipsy in origin" (Starkie 1935–1936, 12).

Hence, this publication, and others by Starkie, did not, even according to his contemporaries, totally explain the question of flamenco. Another researcher into Spanish folklore and particularly the music of the Andalusian Gypsies, Irving Brown (1888–1940), who wrote *Adventures with Gypsy Songs and Singers in Andalusia and Other Lands* (1928), accused Starkie of repeating certain common opinions without offering his own personal spin. Brown meanwhile proposed his own definition of the form: "Flamenco is simply another term for Gypsy, with special connotations" (Brown 1938, 207).

Brown added to the emotionally charged debate by concluding that "Much nonsense has been written on the subject of 'flamenco,' chiefly by Northern Spaniards jealous of the popularity of Andalusia with the tourists" (Brown 1938, 207). Such views followed on those of de Lafontaine, who had warned of a mistaken understanding and definition of flamenco, particularly among tourists: "The ideas entertained by tourists as to what is 'Flamenco' or not are generally found to be most erroneous, and those cafés that, particularly in the capital of Spain, advertise themselves as providing the real unadulterated gipsy element, only present a hotch-potch which to the stranger is bewildering and to the citizen tiresome" (de Lafontaine 1907–1908, 33).

Moorish Influences in the Music of Spanish Gypsies

Early twentieth-century scholarly discussions of the music of Andalusian Gypsies focused on its exotic ethos, a focus that stemmed from a cursory analysis of the music and an awareness of the Gypsies' Eastern origins.

In Spain during this period, ties between Gypsy music and "the Orient" took on a special resonance because of the perceived close historical and cultural links between the Gypsies and the Moors. The Arab influence on Spanish music, and particularly Gypsy music, was emphasized. For instance, de Lafontaine presumed Arab influence in "moulding and fashioning the national music of the country they so long inhabited" (de Lafontaine 1907–1908, 25). He pointed to, among other things, the guitar's popularity in Spain as an inheritance from the Arab love of the lute, the guitar's precursor and prototype. Also, the widespread Spanish custom of clapping to songs was, in de Lafontaine's opinion, similar to Eastern customs. Moving eastward from the Moorish lands, de Lafontaine tied the ornamental richness of Spanish music to Egyptian music; he also emphasized that shouts of *ole!* and expressions of recognition through a drawn-out *a-a-ah* were recognizable in Eastern music. Writing about Spanish dances such as the bolero, seguidilla, *tirana, polo,* and *sevillana,* he noted their exotic connotations, and corresponding links to Romany culture, although without specifying their Eastern provenance. The *polo,* he wrote, was in its primitive form of "purely gipsy origin"; the seguidilla, he wrote, was the "purest musical product of the [Gypsy] race" (de Lafontaine 1907–1908, 31, 33, 37).

In 1907, the same year in which de Lafontaine published his observations, Albert Thomas Sinclair published an article explicitly treating Gypsy music and its connections with the Orient. He focused, however, not on Spanish but on broader European Gypsy music as a conglomerate of varied performance practices. He contended in his thesis that Arab influence could be seen in Gypsy music across the continent, including in Hungary and Spain (Sinclair 1907, 16).

Duende in Spanish Culture

Federico García Lorca (1898–1936), a Spanish poet born in Andalusia and fascinated by the music of the region, presented his own conception of the nature of flamenco. For the musically gifted Lorca, "besides poetry, music may have been the most important artistic activity. . . ." (Stanton 1974, 94).

Following Lorca's successful debut as a poet, he met with the composer

Manuel de Falla, who drew inspiration from Andalusian material for his own compositions. Thereafter, de Falla, Lorca, and other Spanish intellectuals and artists of the day, including the painter Ignacio Zuloaga (1870–1945), organized the Primer Concurso Nacional de *Cante Jondo* (First National Competition for *Cante Jondo*) in 1922 in Granada. Lorca ensured the artistic frame for the event, reading poetry from his collection *Poema del cante jondo* (1921). The singing contest itself, held at the Plaza de los Aljibes on the Alhambra grounds on June 13, attracted many well-known *cantaore* participants: Diego Bermúdez (1850–1923), known as El Tenazas de Morón, Manuel Torres, Tomás Pavón, and Pastora Pavón, known as La Niña de los Peines. The jury, led by José Antonio Chacón Cruz, awarded first prize to two performers—Bermúdez and Manolo Caracol (1909–1973).

The initial meeting with de Falla, who shared with the young poet a fascination for folklore—and Andalusian and Gypsy singing—was to have a profound impression on Lorca, whose own work was permeated with Andalusian influences, prominent among them Gypsy folklore. After publishing *Poema del cante jondo,* he produced *Romancero gitano* (1924–1927). In his works, Lorca referred subtly and allusively to *cante jondo*, modeling himself on the *siguiriya, solea,* and *petenera* forms used in Andalusian music (Stanton 1974, 94). The poet's fascination with the themes of love and death were linked intimately with his intense interest in flamenco. Yet for Lorca, Andalusian song was a means of departure to create an original style, not a source to be imitated; "rarely does he borrow an individual verse or two" from original songs, writes one scholar (Stanton 1974, 95–102).

Adding his voice to national and international debates over the identity of flamenco, Lorca authored two lectures: "Importancia historica y artistica del primitivo canto andaluz llamado cante jondo" (1922) and "Teoria y juego del duende" (1930). The first lecture was divided into three parts: one, a historical outline of *cante jondo*; two, a discussion of its textual layer; and, three, the shortest, a look at the performers.

In briefly presenting the history of "deep singing," Lorca drew on the authority of de Falla, though freely citing other music scholars, including Hugo Riemann. According to the poet, citing de Falla, three historical facts lay behind the creation of *cante jondo* in Andalusia: "the assimilation by the Spanish Church of liturgical singing, the invasion of the Saracens as well as the arrival in Spain of numerous Gypsy groups" (Lorca 1987, 236). Lorca considered the last of these factors the most important, and he emphasized that without the Gypsy input Andalusian singing would not have gained its final—wondrous—form. The poet did not blanketly attribute the *cante jondo* to Spanish Gypsies ("the said song did not belong exclusively to them") but considered that "these people, arrivals in Andalusia, combined our primordial indigenous elements with those equally ancient that they had brought with them and gave the final forms to what we today know as *cante jondo*" (Lorca 1987, 236–39).

In the second part of his first lecture, concentrating on the textual plane, he described not only the subject matter (chiefly suffering, yearning, sorrow, death, and love) but also the deeper melancholy and pathos evoked through vivid word pictures. Lorca cited examples from actual flamenco songs but also exalted the radicalism of the form—one that did not stop at half measures—and the anonymous genius of *cante jondo*'s creators.

The third and final section of the lecture, devoted to performers and their songs, included figures Lorca knew personally and those he knew only by name. Nor did he differentiate between Spanish and Gypsy singers, treating them all, both men and women, as "superb interpreters of the human soul" (Lorca 1987, 258).

The second of the lectures on *cante jondo*, eight years later, was given first during the poet's visit to Havana and later in Buenos Aires. The lecture was devoted to answering the question of the phenomenon's Andalusian origin. In pursuing this end, he developed the concept of *duende* to describe a means of expression unique to Spain.

For Lorca, duende was first and foremost a form of "power and not a behaviour . . . a struggle and not a concept"; he also understood duende in a metaphysical way as "the spirit of the earth," reflecting the land's internal struggles. Aligning himself with other authors, Lorca emphasized duende as "a mysterious power that everyone feels but that no philosopher has explained." Lorca's definition of duende also excluded certain spheres, such as Lutheranism and its predominant doubt and "the Catholic demon, destructive and not very intelligent, who disguises himself as a bitch in order to enter convents" (Lorca 1965, 127). Through this discussion, the poet uncovered false popular interpretations of duende across nineteenth-century Europe. Indeed, as early as 1830 Mérimée had sent a letter from Valencia relating the belief of the Spanish people in witches (who take the form of beautiful maidens); the Frenchman then devoted several lines to the question of duende, claiming that "in Spanish there does not exist a word to correspond to our 'spirit/ghost.' Duende, which may be found in a dictionary, is rather the equivalent to the word 'imp'" (Mérimée 2001, 76). Lorca, opposingly, concentrated on a positive interpretation of duende, which according to him was most fully realized in music.

Instead of striving for an objective definition, the poet concentrated on duende's sources and associated emotions, perceiving its origins "in every cell of the blood" and ascribing its power to the burning of the blood. He emphasized duende's link with strong emotions and compared the intensity of duende with religious ecstasy, "a profound, human, and tender cry of communion with God through the five senses." The poet also drew attention to the uniqueness of duende, which "can never repeat itself" (Lorca 1965, 129, 131, 137).

In his second lecture, Lorca devoted attention to song and dance alike. In flamenco song, he discussed the voice's metallic timbre, which he poetically characterized as "moss covered." Specific examples of duende in flamenco, he wrote, included the work of Pastora Pavón, who sang "without voice, breathless, without subtlety, her throat burning, but . . . with duende." The poet also noted that duende dwelled within the freedom of song interpretation. In his view, the public was "not asking for forms but for the marrow of forms, for music exalted into the purest essence" and transformed under the influence of duende. This would result in the artists suddenly undertaking "a radical change of all forms based on old structures. It gives a sensation of freshness wholly unknown, having the quality of a newly created rose, miracle. . . ." In this way, duende and "its effects are felt by everyone" (Lorca 1965, 131–32).

The uniqueness of the Andalusian duende, associated with flamenco, constituted in Lorca's understanding the heart of Spanish culture. The poet affirmed a distinction between *cante jondo*, understood as the oldest, purest level of Andalusian singing, and flamenco, which was seen to include the musical influences of the whole of Spain. Exploiting the semantic capacity of the latter term, he wrote of the "great artists of Southern Spain, gipsy or flamenco. . . .' The author himself, however, blurred the boundary between *cante jondo* and flamenco when, fascinated with the figure of Pavón, he characterized her as "an Andalusian flamenco singer . . . of Spanish genius," as if forgetting her Gypsy origin.

The Gypsy Character of the Flamenco Phenomenon

As has been suggested so far, flamenco refers to a multitude of musical-dance forms that, from the linguistic, historical, and psychological points of view, constitute the product of Spanish Gypsies from Andalusia. On the one hand, flamenco is a form of artistic expression, while on the other it is a way of life, a philosophy. It is suspended between an identification with Gypsy spontaneity and a commercialism that involves public performances belonging equally to Gypsies and non-Gypsies. Flamenco is not purely a musical phenomenon, it is also sociological: historical and social changes still affect flamenco, giving the form its colorful diversity and force.

From the musicological point of view, flamenco is created from three basic elements (Miles and Chuse 2000, 597) that fall in a strictly defined hierarchical order (Zern 1990, 215):

1. *Cante*—singing is the most important component of flamenco, having evolved over centuries and still absorbing new influences. Flamenco singing represents several dozen forms with a characteristic structure, which are linked by the specific manner of performance together with a deep life philosophy conveyed in a text usually written in the Andalusian dialect of Spanish. To the most popular forms belong traditional songs constantly undergoing minor transformations. The authors both of the music and texts are most often anonymous, although some texts have been credited to famous Spanish poets, including Manuel Machado, Manuel Balmaseda, and Lorca himself. Flamenco is disseminated mainly through the oral tradition, even though the first professional collections of printed flamenco songs started to appear in the 1880s.
2. *Baile*—dance constitutes the spatial realization of the musical ideas. In flamenco, the border between song and dance dissolves, and consequently many forms are characterized as dancing songs as well as song-dances.
3. *Toque*—instrument playing concerns first and foremost the guitar, which became the accompaniment to flamenco in the nineteenth century; earlier flamenco was performed without instruments. Characteristic flamenco instruments also include castanets, percussive hand clapping (*palmas*), finger snapping (*pitos*), and a special stick for beating rhythms. *Toque* blossomed in the early twentieth century during a period when the development of *cante* had slowed.

The Role of *Cante*
Flamenco *cante* can be divided into (1) origin, (2) stylistics, (3) character, and (4) subject matter.

THE QUESTION OF ORIGIN Flamenco songs are characterized by varied provenance: many, as we have seen, display Gypsy or Andalusian origins while others come from elsewhere in Spain and also from Latin America.

The variety within flamenco resulted from the adaptation of traditional

Spanish forms by the Gypsies after they arrived in Spain. Spanish ballads, or romances, which dated to the later fourteenth century, were the first to undergo such adaptation (Katz 1962, 83). Gypsies also quickly took up the popular seguidilla dance form, prevalent throughout Spain, in which boundaries between song and dance were fluid (Miles and Chuse 2000, 592). The Andalusian variant on the seguidilla was named *sevillana* and, over substantial transformations, would lead to the Gypsy *siguiriyia*. Additionally, in the nineteenth century, the *alegria* arose, based on the Spanish dance *jota* (Zern 1990, 216), as well as the bolero, drawing inspiration from its namesake performed in the eighteenth century in the Cadiz province (Leblon 2003, 12). Traditional Spanish Christmas carols entered the Gypsy repertoire under the name *villancico*.

Typically, Gypsy features are considered to include a rough voice, a tearful falsetto with numerous breaks and intervals, and a tense, almost hysterical vocal timbre. This vocal tension, clearly audible in Gypsy flamenco performances, is interpreted by some commentators as reflecting the Gypsies' struggle to endure especially difficult periods during their stay in Andalusia (Manuel 1998, 185).

The Andalusian character of flamenco is detected first and foremost in its Arab influences, such as the tendency to enrich the melody with melismatics and to use from four to seven pitches representing the palette of various modal scales (Manuel 1998, 185). One common mode is the Phrygian, with its characteristic falling tetrachord including, for example, the notes A, G, F, E or A, G sharp, F, E. Particularly the second variant, which contains an augmented second between the G sharp and F, is ascribed to Arab influence (Cunningham and Aiats 2001, 139).

In the late nineteenth and early twentieth century, Latin American–based songs, including the *guajiras* and *colombinas*, became widespread (Zern 1990, 216). And the spectrum of flamenco songs would widen even further, with new forms ranging from Cuban *guarachy* to African *guineo, mandingoy,* or *cumbe* (Leblon 2003, 11–12).

THE STYLISTICS OF FLAMENCO SONGS Researchers maintain that around fifty styles, or *palos*, of flamenco can be identified (Katz 2001, 921). Within the framework of each operate melodic phrases called *falsetas* together with predetermined rhythmic schemes—*compas*. Flamenco is also characterized by its verse construction, with the verses, called *coplas*, usually comprising three to five lines (Miles and Chuse 2000, 598). Three basic *palos* of flamenco are associated with Gypsy music—*tonás, siguiriyas,* and *soleares*—and these are sometimes supplemented by a fourth, the extremely popular fandango, of

Spanish origin (Leblon 2003, 61). The story of Gypsy adaptation of local forms for their own ends is at the same time the story of the formation of the three basic styles of Gypsy flamenco just outlined.

The term *toná* refers to the original songs—usually devoid of accompaniment—that constituted the prototype for flamenco. Most frequently maintained in the Phrygian mode, with its characteristic cadence, they are performed in a heavy manner. The *toná* style was rooted in romances adapted by the Gypsies, derived from the lengthy, monotonous, traditional ballads that also found a use as lullabies called *nanas*. Among the most popular forms of *tonás* are prison and work songs: *martinetes* and *carceleras,* later joined by *deblas,* with their rhythm mimicking the pounding of a blacksmith's hammer or the bellows used for maintaining the fire at a smithy, where Gypsies often worked. The prison songs, as we saw earlier, found their starkest moment in the anti-Gypsy laws and mass internment of 1749. In musical terms, including tonality, the *carceleras* and *martinetes* are identical (Kramer and Plenckers 1998, 112); their only difference is in subject matter: the former tell of the adversity of prison, the latter work at the forge. Other songs belonging to the *toná* style, *seata* are usually performed by a soloist during the religious processions over Holy Week, most frequently on Maundy Thursday or Good Friday. Through the songs, the Gypsy vocalist attempts to grasp the agony of Jesus Christ as he lay dying at Calvary. Often Gypsies have brought their own experiences of suffering to texts, personalizing in this way the torment of Christ and transmuting their own pain into the symbolic realm (Quintana and Floyd 1972, 56).

The second-oldest flamenco style, called *siguiriya,* or crying song, comes, as noted earlier, from the seguidilla, which dates to the eleventh century. When this joyful, almost carefree dance song was absorbed early on by Gypsies and transformed into the *siguiriya,* the latter incarnation shed its previous serenity and became one of the most "sentimental, solemn and deep of all flamenco songs" (Matos 1958, 11), with its characteristic augmented second between F and G sharp. In addition, the metric structure would be interrupted and changed by the addition of syllables, shouts of *olé!* and *anda!* at the beginnings and ends of lines, and clapping; words were broken up and lengthy pauses inserted, particularly on the penultimate syllable of the last line of each verse (Leblon 2003, 51–53). *Siguiriyas* are most often performed to guitar accompaniment, but are sometimes unaccompanied.

Traditional Spanish ballads preceded the third flamenco style, *soleá.* Especially popular among these songs were *alboreas,* appearing in wedding receptions. *Soleares* emerged along with the gradual loosening of the anti-Gypsy laws by

Charles III around 1800. However, the archetypical *soleares* tell of pain and suffering, separation and lost love (Zern 1990, 216).

The last of the main styles, fandango, permeated flamenco naturally, given that the dance form was strongly linked to Andalusia. It is usually characterized by an instrumental introduction, followed by several expressive chords signaling the beginning of the verse, which comprises five eight-syllable lines based on up to six musical phrases (Miles and Chuse 2000, 595). Advanced harmony, melody inflected with typical flamenco yells and even laughter, and fully sensual dance performances have made fandango one of the most expressive forms.

All the forms absorbed by Gypsies through flamenco underwent lesser or greater transformations. Some have died out, while others have been reborn in a changed version both within and beyond the framework of flamenco.

THE CHARACTER OF THE SONGS The songs performed among Gypsies may be classified in basic terms. Serious, almost sad songs accompanied the oldest current within flamenco, called *cante jondo* or *cante grande*. Songs of a lighter nature, often performed in public, became known as *cante chico* (Quintana and Floyd 1972, 53). Another song type that sometimes appears—*cante intermedio*, or *cante flamenco*—is a hybrid bearing the traits of both *cante jondo* and *cante chico* (Miles and Chuse 2000, 597). However, Gypsies and Andalusians alike consider only *cante jondo* to represent genuine flamenco art (Quintana and Floyd 1972, 56).

The different types of songs reflected a dual approach by Gypsies in Spanish territories. Namely, the large discrepancy between the lighter and more serious forms resulted from the Gypsies' willingness, on the one hand, to adapt the more pleasant forms deeply rooted in Andalusian tradition and their adherence, on the other, to themes associated with gravity and even tragedy. The Gypsies enacted their sorrow in the gloomy songs of *cante jondo*, describing their bitter lot in Spain. Writing from Spain in 1954, the English author Victor Sawdon Pritchett (1900–1997) described *cante jondo* as a form of intimate experience: "Frequently, the songs are sung privately, for the singers' own consolation. For, despite its howling, it is an intimate music, perhaps for a singer and a couple of . . . friends only. It can be sung in a mere whisper. . . . One seems to be listening to a sudden, lyrical or passionate statement or exclamation, torn out of the heart of the singer" (Pritchett 1954, 127–35).

Meanwhile, the joyous *cante chico* became a musical product for public consumption, lending itself to entertainment through familiar songs. During musical gatherings (called *juergas* in Andalusia) in taverns, bars, and private houses, the Andalusian gentry, known as the señoritos, listened attentively to *cante chico*.

The simple mechanism of pandering to public tastes guaranteed not only recognition and applause but also financial favor. The *cante chico* started to enjoy popularity at around the same time, in the later nineteenth century, performed in public in *cafés cantantes*. The songs, with their comical feel, dance rhythm, and pleasant lyrics, also served a therapeutic role, transporting listeners from their everyday troubles.

Indeed, the manner of performance for both *cante jondo* and *cante chico* varied according to the particular performers and their individual styles (*estilos*). Most performers preferred a nasal, metallic vocal tone, often suggesting an off-key delivery. The improvisatory quality of flamenco meant singers sometimes held notes for varying lengths or reached high notes by chromatic steps and with free-form rhythms, reflecting the unconventional value systems of flamenco. Any such techniques would be aimed at fitting a given mood, a basic component of flamenco.

As a result of strongly individualized styles, the fame of singers became central to the legend that rose around flamenco. In the nineteenth century, singers performing at *cafés cantantes* were held in esteem. In the early twentieth century, as the Lorca section indicated, Spanish literary figures also contributed to the flamenco lore. Lorca described passionately how "the Andalusian flamenco singer Pastora Pavón, La Niña de los Peines[,] a sombre Hispanic genius with an imagination matching that of Goya or Rafael, *El Gallo*[,] was singing in a small tavern at Cadiz" (Lorca 1965, 130). Such praise helped establish a cult around Pavón. Even many years later, Gypsy children in Spain learning to sing from their parents still dreamed of singing "in *jondo* style like La Niña de los Peines" (Quintana and Floyd 1972, 59). The construction of such legends—aided by writers and academics who didn't always check their facts—helped extend the fame of the *cantaores* beyond Spain's borders. In a romanticized telling, Irving Brown, discussing the Concurso del Cante Jondo of 1922, assured the reader that "The prize-winner was a man of seventy three, El Viejo, who walked to Granada from Puente Genil, carrying the same stick he had used at the age of twenty to tap the rhythms" (Brown 1929, 149–150).

In the later twentieth century, flamenco singing became the preserve of professional or semiprofessional performers, as the *cante* itself underwent a far-reaching process of professionalization (Quintana and Floyd 1972, 59).

THE SUBJECT MATTER OF THE SONGS As earlier examples have shown, flamenco songs are seen to express, first and foremost, the pain of the persecuted Gypsies of Andalusia or even the whole of Spain. Despite this emphasis, scholars also refer to the period of prosperity under Moorish rule, when Jews,

Muslims, and Catholics coexisted (Manuel 1998, 176). Still, even when the focus is on oppression, commentators note that the sorrow in these flamenco songs does not imply resignation; the expressive *jondo* speaks of a man broken but not resigned, depressed but also full of hope, sad but always believing in a better tomorrow (Quintana and Floyd 1972, 60).

Two researchers of flamenco, Bertha Quintana and Lois Floyd, after analyses of *jondo* songs—based on interviews, both public and private performances, phonographic recordings, as well as primary and secondary written sources—distinguished eight dominant motifs in flamenco songs (Quintana and Floyd 1972, 60–66):

1. Love and faithfulness—covering the separation of lovers and related sorrows, along with the question of whether a wife would remain faithful while awaiting her husband's return (e.g., from prison). Songs dealing with sensual love focus on either its unattainability or dreams of future shared fulfillment; alternatively, songs may include recollections of lost fulfillment. Themes also include a son's love for his mother, usually found in prison songs. Much rarer is the reverse: songs in which a mother expresses love for her children. Absent in this context are expressions of love for God or other religious feelings.

2. Jealousy—usually appearing together with the motif of love, often elaborated by descriptions of hunger or even death. The suggestiveness of this motif on the listener's imagination has made it prevalent during public performances.

3. Revenge—an unusually popular theme given the history of Gypsies in Andalusia. But such songs also often involved rejected or betrayed lovers serving as their heroes. The motif of revenge is furthermore connected with warnings or threats. Because these songs contained radical, and intimate, content, they were invariably performed in private venues, where the subtext could be taken in and interpreted by listeners.

4. Pride—covering the rejection of a non-Gypsy lifestyle. Pride issued, among other things, from the sense of long-lasting persecution and isolation in Andalusia.

5. Freedom—along with the sibling theme of liberty, this motif was highly prevalent in *jondo* songs. Freedom and liberty are glorified when desired (e.g., in prison) and lamented when lost.

6. Gypsy persecution—leaving its mark, as we have seen, on the texts of songs filled with regret and frustration. Some such songs, if too drastic in

their sentiments, were not seen as fit for public performance. In prison songs, the motif of Gypsy banditry often appeared as well, extolling the noble opposition to discriminatory authorities.

7. Sorrow—omnipresent in flamenco songs. This motif constitutes the quintessence of *cante jondo*, imparting the meaning and pathos of Gypsy life.

8. Death and destiny—coupled with an obsession with one's inevitable fate. This motif of the human lot heading inevitably toward its end combines with the mystery of the life cycle, which is understood as the most intimate of all experiences.

The Function of Instrument Playing (*Toque*)

FLAMENCO INSTRUMENTS Certain authors maintain the *cante* essentially stopped evolving at the beginning of the twentieth century (Zern 1990, 217). Initially, instruments served only as accompaniment in flamenco song and dance. The most common instruments were idiophones, or those producing sound through vibration—as noted earlier, castanets and tambourines and, of course, the guitar. To beat out a rhythm (for example, on the back of a chair), a special stick was used, sometimes plated with iron at the end to produce a more resonant sound. All such instruments penetrated flamenco as the legacy of early Gypsy settlers in Spain. Until the seventeenth century, two types of wooden tambourines were chiefly used: the larger *pander* and the more common, smaller *panderetta*, which was ringed with bells called *sonajas*, on either or both sides. Gypsies also, particularly when dancing, wore such bells around their ankles. And noninstrumental techniques prevailed and still survive today, such as hitting one's hand on a hard object, clapping (*palmas*), or snapping (*pitos*), sometimes accentuated by the stamping of heels (*zapateos*).

One reason the guitar only emerged later in flamenco involved the high cost of purchasing one. And even today, forms like the *debla* or *martinete* are performed a cappella. The rise of the guitar as an accompanying instrument, as suggested elsewhere, was swift, beginning around 1850 (Zern 1990, 217). Over the next thirty or so years, it gained such popularity that one could hardly imagine a Gypsy *juergas* without one.

THE ROLE OF *TOQUE* The bond created between the singer (and possibly dancer) and the accompanying guitarist takes on a symbiotic character in flamenco. The guitarist is responsible for creating an appropriate mood and often for inspiring the singer or dancer. Mutual respect and recognition govern this relationship, as well as trust, close cooperation, and shared responsibility for the overall effect. At the same time, each performer maintains a broad margin for independent expression.

For the guitarist, this independence manifests itself in improvisation—the essence of a flamenco performance. Hence, every flamenco guitarist must possess the ability to improvise. Together with that of the dancer or singer, this improvisation allows for the magic and charm of performance to emerge collectively from the performers.

In the late nineteenth century, flamenco guitarists began expanding beyond their role as accompanists. This growth could be heard in the development of the solo fragments between *coplas* into something approaching performable pieces in themselves (Quintana and Floyd 1972, 52). In the early part of the next century, Ramón Montoya (1880–1949), fascinated by the classical guitar's sound, helped popularize the instrument in its augmented role. He himself performed in venues such as Paris's Salle Pleyel in 1935, enjoying great success. But the public in Spain was not yet ready to accept the flamenco guitar as a solo instrument for the concert hall (Zern 1990, 218).

Montoya's achievements were succeeded by those of Juan Maya "El Marote" (1936–2002), who heralded the development of the technique of playing with the right hand. Other innovators included Sabicas (Agustín Castellón Campos, 1912–1990) and Mario Escudero (1928–2004). All the while, the former techniques of *rasgueo* (hitting of the string) and *alzapua* (plucking with the thumb) were maintained, leading to virtuoso performances enriched by effects such as tremolo, arpeggio, and *picados* (right-hand technique), which incorporated the middle and index fingers, resulting in increasingly diverse harmonic effects (Manuel 1998, 186). Later in the century, flamenco guitar incorporated jazz sounds and, thereafter, those of pop and rock. This assimilation of varied and often unconventional influences—including enhanced harmonies and rhythmic syncopation—helped popularize flamenco the world over.

Dance (*Baile*)

As early as the seventeenth century, groups of often exclusively women Gypsies performed dance publicly all across Spain. In a troupe, women always outnumbered men. This imbalance was explained partly by the public's view that scantily dressed women performing hip and leg movements verging on the erotic was acceptable, whereas strong Gypsy men displaying their vigor posed a potential threat to established social relations (Weinzweig 1990, 227).

In Gypsy flamenco, particular body movements are vehicles of expression, part of a scheme in which formal choreography is secondary to subtle gestures (Philips 1990, 270). Similarly, flamenco dance marks not only a physical art but also a means of nonverbal communication—and a way to escape reality. The escapism in flamenco is manifested equally in the prominence of its costumes. Extravagant clothes are aimed at drawing attention, shocking or arousing the public's interest at the very least. In wedding-type performances, light-colored, richly embroidered costumes dominate. Such garish ensembles have occasioned comparison to flamingos. The singers of *cante jondo*, for their part, prefer a fairly conservative style of dress, devoid of embroidery and dark in color, in keeping with the nature of the songs (Quintana and Floyd 1972, 58).

Public appreciation and demand for Gypsy dance has often been conditioned by the idea that it is unadulterated by civilization, natural and original. This authenticity has been seen to issue from its having been passed down from generation to generation. And, indeed, Gypsy dancers have absorbed the ethos and movements of flamenco dance by observing other dancers. Such a situation applies especially amid large, close-knit families, with Gypsy children at a young age naturally looking to their elders to understand flamenco dance and music. Those performing in public, correspondingly, have often been linked by family (Philips 1990, 268–69).

Flamenco dance derives its strength from the varied elements it absorbs, and from the interplay of the Gypsy and non-Gypsy worlds. In turn, public performances help to constantly renew the authenticity of this art form (Weinzweig 1990, 227–28), which thrives because of its complexity yet also continually invokes its historical richness and sources.

Flamenco *Nuevo*

The spectacular success of flamenco gave its performers access to an international stage. At the same time, this success opened flamenco performers to international influences. First, there had been the Gypsy encounter with Andalusian culture; this was followed by an encounter with national Spanish culture. As the twentieth century commenced, the forces of globalization themselves would have an increasing effect on the form. Wider audiences imbibed flamenco. In particular, this last phase occurred in the era after strongman Francisco Franco's death in 1975, with flamenco performers migrating to cities outside Andalusia and learning other musical and dance styles. The term *nuevo flamenco* was created to designate the resulting musical idiom, in which tradition combined with Catalonian rumba, along with rock, pop, blues, Latin American music, Arabic, and African forms.

A pioneer in incorporating jazz and Latin American rhythms in flamenco was the non-Gypsy guitarist Paco de Lucia (b. 1947). His collaboration with the Gypsy singer Camarón de la Isla was to produce hits such as "Soy Gitano" and "Caminando." In the mid-1970s, the duo of Lole and Manuel popularized blends of flamenco, poetry, and expanded instrumental forms. *Nuevo dia*, the album they issued following Franco's death, symbolized a new era of idealism and freedom in Spain (Miles and Chuse 2000, 599). Lole [Montoya] and Manuel [Molina Jiménez] also fused flamenco with Arab music. In the 1970s, so-called flamenco *arabe* came into being, cultivated by Lole and her mother, known as La Negra. In the 1980s, flamenco's ascent was marked by the spectacular international success of the Gipsy Kings. The same decade saw flamenco reimagined by groups such as Ketama and Pata Negra, which added salsa and blues to the mix. There also arose rock *gitano*, inseparably linked with the slogan *poder gitano* (Gypsy power), and *nueva canción andaluza* (new Andalusian song). In their lyrics, both of these forms looked into questions of urbanization and unemployment then being addressed by small groups of students and political activists (Manuel 1998, 194). Those inspired by the mass popularity of flamenco, with its array of influences, would particularly include musicians of Romany origin.

Theories on the Origins of Flamenco

Research on the nature and origins of flamenco, and its ties to Spanish Gypsies, dates roughly to the early twentieth century. Early works include Irving Brown's *Deep Song* (1929) and Walter Starkie's *Spanish Raggle-Taggle: Adventures with a Fiddle in North Spain* (1935). As one would expect, identifying an unequivocal origin of flamenco has proved daunting, given the variety of forms it comprises and the centuries over which its variants evolved and crystallized. Also to be expected, proposals as to flamenco's origin have met with sharp criticism—as have proposals regarding the very term *flamenco*. One such claim was made by Francisco Rodríguez Marín, in his *El alma de Andalucía en sus mejores coplas* (1929), when he likened the clothes of flamenco performers to birds' plumage. This claim was ridiculed immediately as being unscholarly.

Theories on flamenco's beginnings have concentrated on several basic concepts. The composer Manuel de Falla attempted to synthesize these in a booklet prepared for the *cante jondo* song competition in 1922, discussed earlier in the section on Lorca. De Falla assured readers of the noble origins of *cante jondo*, while also establishing:

1. Its close links with Byzantine psalms, which penetrated the Mozarabic (referring to Christians who lived under Muslim rule in Spain) liturgy adopted by the Church in Spain.
2. Connections with the Orient, resulting from the Arab invasion of the Iberian Peninsula.

3. The closeness of *cante jondo* and the music of India, notable particularly in similarities in the use of enharmony to perform modulation, the ambitus of melody not surpassing a sixth, a predilection for the persistent repetition—almost to the point of obsession—of a single sound, richness in ornamentation in fragments of a heightened emotional force, as well as interjections enacted by dancers and guitarists. The composer also saw an analog between music of the East and that of Andalusia with regard to vocal performance—involving the filling of the space between two close pitches as well as the role of small intervals in the creation of *cante jondo* (Starkie 1935–1936, 13).

4. Its Andalusian provenance (elaborated earlier).

Variety in Concepts on Flamenco Provenance

Inspired by de Falla's booklet from the 1920s, other Spanish authors published works discussing the history of flamenco and analyzing its forms. José Carlos de Luna, for example, published *De cante chico y cante grande* in 1926, followed seven years later by Pedro (and Carlos) Caba Landa's *Andalucía, su comunismo y su cante jondo*. The latter text attempted to explain the essence of *cante jondo* as well as the phenomenon of Andalusia itself. Two years later, in 1935, Fernando de Triana published *Arte y artistas flamencos*, with information about famous flamenco performers and richly illustrated with photographs.

Two opposing tendencies can be noted in such early twentieth-century works. The first follows the thinking of de Falla, comprehending flamenco within a broad context of various influences. For instance, Starkie, in commenting on folklore and Andalusian music, noted the Moorish, Jewish, and Gypsy influences (Starkie 1935–1936, 12–13). In 1943, writing about the musical heritage of southern Spain, Otto Mayer-Serra considered "Arabian civilization, the artistic contribution of the gipsies, the musical influences brought from the New World to the port of Cadiz, the possible remnants of certain forms of Byzantine chant" (Mayer-Serra 1943, 4).

The second way of interpreting flamenco favored a selected source, belittling the syncretistic dimension. Such discussions have considered only the Jewish, Byzantine, Arabic, or pure Andalusian origin of flamenco. In 1930, Máximo José Kahn (under the pseudonym Medina Azara) suggested that flamenco was of Jewish origin, basing his assumptions on the similarity of certain flamenco forms to Jewish religious songs; Starkie himself, while also fitting within the first school, backed up this claim in his own writing (Starkie 1935–1936, 13). Three decades later, Hipólito Rossy refuted his thesis in the book *Teoria del Cante Jondo*. Yet most scholars today agree that some flamenco forms have Jewish origins, including the *peteneras*, which dates to the pre-Inquisition days. The similar use of *ay!* in Jewish and flamenco music provides a specific point for comparison. In the words of Israel J. Katz, "On the basis of aural perception alone, many collectors who traveled to the various regions of the Sephardic diaspora were led to speculate upon the possible relationship between the Sephardic music and such popular forms as the *saeta*" (Katz 1962, 84).

The theory of the Byzantine origin of flamenco was formulated by a Catalonian, the musicologist and musician Felipe Pedrell (1841–1922), who noticed the similarity of flamenco to the Mozarabic liturgy. As for the broader Arab roots of flamenco, most works on the subject acknowledge this provenance, citing both historical and geographical factors. Blas Infante ardently defended the Arab origin of flamenco in his work *Orígenes de lo flamenco y secreto del cante jondo* (1929–1931), deriving the term *flamenco* from the Arabic *felahmengu* (Blas 1980). Use of similar instruments, such as the percussion and lutes in Spanish cities like Malaga and in Morocco, has figured in recent discussions on the flamenco-Arab connection (Leblon 2003, 69).

Tomás Andrade de Silva, in his *Antologia del cante flamenco* (1958), completely negated the Gypsy origin of flamenco, considering Andalusian folklore to be its only source. Other writers, however—particularly Spanish ones—leave no doubt as to the role of the Gypsies in the shaping of the music of southern Spain; in the 1920s, the German composer Edgar Istel (1880–1948) joined de Falla and Lorca in writing about the Gypsy infusion in the music of Spain (Istel 1926, 501).

Among later twentieth-century Spanish-language publications on flamenco, an invaluable source is Ricardo Molina and Antonio Mairena's *Mundo y formas del cante flamenco* (1963). Toward the turn of the next century, interest in flamenco would be demonstrated through the creation of websites and blogs such as www.flamenco-world.com and www.flamencoolimpico.com.

The Idea of National Music in Spain

At the end of the nineteenth and especially at the beginning of the next century, music performed by Gypsies became a reference point for Spanish composers interested in creating a national musical idiom. At that historical moment, Spain was viewed as existing on the periphery of Europe, associated with distant journeys, adventures, and, foremost, exoticism. As Anthony Clyne wrote in 1926, "Spanish folk-songs and dances were regarded abroad as exotic curiosities" (Clyne 1926, 266). But within Spain, dating back as early as the 1830s, the motivation and pressure were strong to forge a national artistic identity. The

Spanish operatic tradition known as *zarzuela*, for instance, interspersed dialogue and songs and incorporated traditional instruments such as guitar and castanets in an answer to Italian dominance in musical theater (Mindlin 1965, 17–18). The prevalence of piano miniatures in the later nineteenth century reflected both an attempt to echo the great European masters and to create a national music (Castillo 2001, 129).

The Circle of Felipe Pedrell

Felipe Pedrell, whom we met earlier in reference to the Byzantine origins of flamenco, was known as the champion of a national music in Spain. He pursued this end through his research and compositions alike. His achievements in the former realm included editing the eight-volume collection of Spanish music *Hispaniae schola musica sacra* (1894–1898), which included the works of Antonio de Cabezón and Cristóbal de Morales, and the *Antologia de clásicos españoles* (1908). In addition, his four-volume *Cancionero musical popular español* (1918 to 1922) contained theoretical considerations and a wide range of musical examples from across Spain. Pedrell's musical dramas channeled Wagner both in technique and the use of national motifs. And Pedrell's trilogy—*Los Pirineos* (1890–1891), *La Celestina* (1902), and *El Conde Arnau* (1904)—showed the direct influence of the master of Bayreuth.

In 1894, Pedrell, laid out his vision for Spanish opera, with his romantic outlook including concepts such as genius, masterpiece, and the spirit of the nation. Other components, however, were independent of so-called national themes:

A genuinely Spanish opera will not be merely a lyric drama written on a subject drawn from our history or legends. Nor will it suffice to write it in Spanish and scatter some popular themes here and there, whose appearance of authenticity may poorly conceal the foreign origin of the rest. The character of truly national music is not found only in the folk-song, and in the impulse of primitive epochs, but in the genius and masterworks of the great centuries of art. For a lyrical school to be unmistakably that of one nation, its entire heritage must be mobilized: the constant tradition, the general and permanent characters, the harmony of its various artistic manifestations, the use of certain native formulas that a fatal unconscious power made accessible to the genius of the race. (Pedrell 1894; quoted in Otto Mayer-Serra 1943, 8)

Pedrell's compositional efforts at creating a national idiom drew harsh criticism from his contemporaries. Commentary even four years after the composer's death accused him of having indulged in, among other things, pomp. And in 1943, Mayer-Serra concluded that, "In the field of composition Pedrell's efforts proved less happy [than his role as a promoter of Spanish music]" (Mayer-Serra 1943, 2). Such sentiments have been reaffirmed by later biographers (Burnett 1979, 28). But Pedrell's great service was in reviving Spanish aspirations to create a national music and influencing, through his personality, later generations of both musicologists and composers to continue pursuing this dream.

And whereas Spanish music and Spain may have occupied the margins of nineteenth-century European culture, composers elsewhere in Europe were intrigued by Spanish elements. In particular, Russian composers were known to graft Spanish melodies onto their music. The heirs of Pedrell's national idea, including Istel, admitted that "strange to say, the Russian composers were the first to have success in writing Spanish symphonic music so conceived that on a first hearing it was thought that we had copied the Russians" (Istel 1926, 501). Clyne, in 1926, wrote about the frequent situation wherein "Foreign composers derived suggestions from [Spanish songs], but of course without preserving their true characteristics, translating such ideas thus obtained into the common modes of harmony and rhythm, losing all the essence of racial temperament, national tradition embodied in them" (Clyne 1926, 267). Along with the Russians, with one example being Mikhail Glinka, French composers such as Georges Bizet and later Maurice Ravel (1875–1937) sought to appropriate Spanish themes.

Yet several Spanish composers too—namely the internationally known, virtuoso violinist Pablo Sarasate (1844–1908), who was born in Spain and educated in Paris—propagated themes associated with Spanish exoticism and charm. In 1959, Gilbert Chase referred to Sarasate as the figure "who contributed most efficaciously to 'popularising Spanish idiom' abroad" (Chase 1959, 217). Reference to the Gypsies' music within Sarasate's compositions, particularly his *Gypsy Melodies* (op. 20), helped establish stereotypes about so-called Gypsy music and popularized the very term "Gypsy melody" (Kodály 1960, 7). Contemporary biographers are inclined to consider Sarasate's compositions as the manifestation of the typically nineteenth-century marriage of national music and dazzling instrumental technique (Marco 1993, 4).

An undoubted challenge for composers wishing to create a Spanish musical idiom in the spirit of Pedrell was to both identify the specifics of "authentic" Spanish music and to elevate Spanish music to the perceived European standard. This conundrum was not faced by Spanish composers alone. According to Mayer-Serra, the struggle between two rivaling tendencies—the culling and transformation of a nation's own material and the "Europeanization" of music—"presents itself to all nations without a musical tradition of their own, or where musical evolution, vital and original in former centuries, has been interrupted for a considerable period. The latter is the case in Spain" (Mayer-Serra 1943, 1). The creation of a recognizable Spanish musical idiom was therefore to take place through a return to Spain's musical folklore, with compositional techniques already valued in Europe serving as the medium. Both Pedrell and his pupils Isaac Albéniz (1860–1909), Enrique Granados (1867–1916), and de Falla (1876–1946), each in his individual way, would set out upon this route.

As it turned out, the proportions of Spanish versus European influences in these composers' works would be uneven, resulting in mixed evaluations by their contemporaries. Criticized for the bombast in these pieces, Pedrell was also said to lack invention. Wrote Clyne in the 1920s: "So anxious to make his music expressive, he did not see that it was not sufficient to use the material of folk-music with the technique of European music, but that its own technique must be involved" (Clyne 1926, 267). Clyne further classified Pedrell's attempts at creating a Spanish idiom by combining European and Spanish qualities as a failed "mixture of irreconcilable styles." Clyne was hardly more generous in assessing Albéniz's compositions, the Spanishness of which he called "still largely only a colouring skilfully employed" locally. Clyne accused the composer of employing references to Spanishness superficially, designed for effect rather than to create the basis for a genuine national music. Albéniz, he wrote, "composed in a Spanish atmosphere, but not altogether out of the depths of the Spanish spirit. His music has, as it were, Spanish beauty draped around it with often most subtle charm, but it is not at base a new and altogether Spanish music" (Clyne 1926, 268). Istel, for his part, thought highly of Albéniz: "That Albéniz towered high above his followers, for instance Manuel de Falla, seems to me beyond dispute" (Istel 1929, 127). Albéniz's merits, in Istel's view, included recognition of the beauty of Spanish music, including its Arab and Gypsy contributions: "In general Albéniz's relations with folkwise art are quite special in character; he has borrowed from it only rhythmic and harmonic peculiarities and scarcely any melodic ones, or these last only in that, so to say, he employs certain intervals of *fioriture* cherished in Arab and Gipsy music, without directly making use of Spanish, Gipsy or Arab folk-motives" (Istel 1929, 127).

The Spanish violinist Enrique Arbós (1863–1939), who knew Albéniz personally, tried to explain the composer's receptivity to Arab influences on Spanish music. Albéniz, said Arbós, proudly declared that "I am a Moor," an unusual admission by the Catalonian-born composer of *Iberia* that Istel attributed to two facts. One was the suggestion of Albéniz's Jewish origins, as advocated by

Henri Collet (1885–1951), the French literary critic, composer, and enthusiast of Spain, who pointed to the composer's first name as one source of proof. The second fact involved Albéniz's music itself, in which "This Moorish, that is to say Arabic descent, is not contradicted. . . ." (Istel 1929, 118).

Fascination with Arab and Andalusian culture would find expression in the use of Gypsy musical elements, both in the formation of melodies and the employment of scales. This latter endeavor was characteristic of Granados's compositions (Chase 1959, 161). Andalusia would also inspire de Falla, who was widely considered by contemporaries and those who followed as the genuine implementer of Pedrell's concepts. Not only did the music of the Gypsies inhabiting southern Spain permeate de Falla's musical scores, later to be performed across Europe, but this music also became an integral element of discourse within Spanish national music. Anyone discussing de Falla's desire to create a national music would, first, be compelled to acknowledge Gypsy influence and, second, need to take a stand on it. The vast majority of such stances would be positive.

De Falla's Role in the Shaping of a Spanish National Music

De Falla, as we have seen, felt profound gratitude to his teacher Pedrell, who was the first, in Istel's words, to take up "our national treasure and subject it to luminous analysis." Hence, de Falla "never neglected to sign himself in his letters to the master his 'grateful pupil'" (Istel 1926, 498, 502). And de Falla's role was central in continuing his teacher's project. One 1920s source argued that "there is no composer today more intellectually and emotionally fitted to carry on the work of the modern Spanish school, so gloriously begun by Pedrell, Albéniz and Granados, than Manuel de Falla" (no author 1922, 5). Twenty years later, Mayer-Serra wrote, "It remained for Manuel de Falla to realize the ambitious vision of Pedrell in all its implications" (Mayer-Serra 1943, 3).

And de Falla's task was great. Along with managing the incorporation of foreign versus indigenous elements, Spanish composers aspiring to create a national music were tasked with breaking free from romantic nineteenth-century ideas in favor of innovative styles, such as those produced by Bartók in Hungary and Janaček in the Czech lands. For de Falla's part, his initial attempts at creating a national idiom still contained romantic-national traits. The folk material he used, although subjected to stylization, remained not fully absorbed—not so much as a component of the greater whole but as the basis for the composer's musical style. This absorption was to be accomplished only with time. Mayer-Serra described the composer's ultimate shift in paradigm as an audible transformation from romantic harmony into a subtle orchestral fabric, a departure from emotional emphasis to condensed musical schemes illustrating dramatic development, and the replacement of modulation by simple tonal relations referencing the purity of Spanish polyphony. Hence, de Falla's specific "Spanish neo-Classicism" became a fixture of early twentieth-century Spain, referencing both the country's historical musical legacy and regional influences.

The transformation in de Falla's style was also noted by Istel, who concentrated on the composer's change in approach to the question of Spanish folk music. Initially viewing through "French spectacles and hearing with French ears"—as Istel alluded to de Falla's fascination with French Impressionism—de Falla ultimately crafted works in an *españolada* style, perceived as the international contextualization of Spanishness in music. Ultimately, however, Istel focused on de Falla's shift aimed at reaching "the heart of Spanish folk-music" through concentrating on the folklore of Andalusia (Istel 1926, 504).

By 1926, de Falla's compositions utilizing folk music already constituted a model for "sublimation, a genuine new life born, as it were, from the union of diverse elements and not only a mingling, a conglomeration." The composer was thus considered an icon of Spanish music (Clyne 1926, 268). His role in creating a national music was likewise acknowledged in broader European circles. A booklet published in London in 1922, aimed at acquainting the reader with various composers, stated: "On looking at Falla's music more closely, the first thing that inevitably attracts is its national colour. Those who have grown into the habit of accepting the pseudo-Spanish music of composers such as Moszkowski as faithful reproductions of Iberian popular expression, will remain untouched by the deeper and more subtle art of Manuel de Falla" (no author 1922, 5).

The composer, the text continued, had achieved this result through probing the Spanish spirit, not just copying conventions: de Falla did not "resort to actual quotations of folk music save in rare cases where such a process is fully justified. Nevertheless, his remarkable knowledge of his country's popular music had proved invaluable to him, for it has yielded essential elements of Spanish folk-song in all its varied aspects. . . ." The text continued: "This combination of nationality and personality gives his music a complex character." As for Gypsy influence, the text gives the specific example of "Oriental elements, which have been perpetuated by the gypsies . . . in the score of the ballet *El amor brujo*" (no author 1922, 5–7).

In an obituary for de Falla in *La revue musicale*, Collet reaffirmed the Gypsy contribution to his work, defining the composer's death as "the loss of the first Gypsy composer" (Collet 1947, 28).

꒰ ꒱ ꒰ ꒱ ꒰

CHAPTER THREE

Gypsy Music
and Exoticism

The Category of Exoticism
in European Musical Culture

Exoticism in music typically falls into two categories: "distant" exoticism, or music mainly of the East but also including Africa, the Americas, and other locales beyond Europe; and "near" exoticism, or music produced in the European purview but that is, for various, often geopolitical reasons, marginalized. The first of these categories is closely connected with discussions of the Orient in literature, as explored famously by Edward Said and Timothy Mitchell. The second category involves a fascination with previously unknown, "local" musical cultures that dwell at the nexus of folklore and exoticism.

"Distant" Exoticism

Although we cannot demarcate exactly the line between exotic and non-exotic music, we can agree that the arousal of interest in non-European musical cultures originated in the sixteenth-century era of great discoveries. Travelers on colonial expeditions, and later the missionaries and administrators who joined them, devoted much attention in their diaries and monographs to the musical customs they observed. Jacques Cartier (1491–1557), reporting on his visits to the New World in the mid-1530s, wrote about dance and music practices. In 1578, Jean de Léry (1534–1611), describing Brazil in *Histoire d'un voyage faict en la terre du Brésil* (1578), included examples of antiphonic singing and dancers in feather-bedecked costumes.

In the seventeenth century, particularly its second half, world-political dynamics spurred an increased interest in Turkish music. The writer Giovanni Batista Donado, for example, included three Turkish tunes in his pioneering publication on Turkish literature. In 1686, one of the first European operas on a Turkish theme appeared: Johann Wolfgang Franck's *Der glückliche Gross-Vezier Cara Mustaphaen,* composed a mere three years after the siege of Vienna (Ringer 1965, 117). The Marquis de Ferriol, the French ambassador to Turkey in 1707–1708, recorded the details of the famed dervish dance, as mentioned in Franz Joseph Sulzer's 1781–1782 work, *Geschichte des transalpinischen Daciens.* In 1782, Mozart also referenced Turkish subject matter in his opera *The Abduction from the Seraglio.*

Central European awareness of the Turkish style (*alla turca*) focused on the battle music played by Turkish military bands. Elements of this style included a 2/4 meter, duplicated melody in octaves, and grace notes often moving one tone lower or higher, all based on a spread tonal chord with the occasional addition of an augmented fourth as well as simple accompaniment utilizing, in principle, a basic triad (Scott 2003, 158). The Turkish style often favored an excessive use of consonance of a third interval as well as a fixing on minor keys (Bellman 1991, 218). By the mid-eighteenth century, the European reader could become acquainted with a wide range of Turkish instruments, as drawn up by Charles Fonton in 1751. A shortened form of this report appeared in the 1831 essay "Essai sur la musique orientale" in *Revue et gazette musicale.*

The Enlightenment period saw an increased interest in exotic musical cultures, joined by intensified research and more publications on the subject. Mungo Park (1771–1806), for instance, shed light on the music and dance of African peoples in his *Travels in the Interior Districts of Africa Performed in the Years 1795, 1796, and 1797,* while Captain James Cook (1728–1779) described musical practices observed among inhabitants of the Pacific islands in *Voyage to the Pacific Ocean . . . in the Years 1776, 1777, 1778, 1779, and 1780.*

These observations, and the popular opinions and scientific projects associated with them, would leave a mark on European musical productions. Such works typically reflected generalized, idealized views of "exotic" cultures rather than encounters with their complex realities. Quotes of melodies and other direct cultural references were, therefore, rather rare. The prevailing major-minor scales were used instead of the pentatonic scale. Writing of Henry Purcell's opera *The Indian Queen* (1695), an adaptation of a play by Robert Howard and John Dryden on Peru and Mexico, the eminent twentieth-century biographer Jack A. Westrup explains that the work was devoid of "attempts to enhance the music with local colour. For all the music tells us, the action might be taking place in St. James's Park" (Westrup 1995, 142). Likewise, in Jean-Philippe Rameau's opera *Les Indes galantes* (1735), the Persians appear to be no different from Purcell's Peruvians (Scott 2003, 157). Sometimes these efforts yielded comical results. Referencing the exotic, for example, Nicolas Dalayrac (1753–1809) based the middle part of the overture to *Azemia, ou les sauvages* (1786) on Rameau's equally inauthentic *Les sauvages*, from a half-century earlier. Yet indeed, this lack of subject unity was common in drama of the era dealing with nonexotic matters as well. In this context, the theater decorator and costume designer had the principal responsibility of crafting the visual effects of productions.

Eighteenth-century European writers were especially fascinated by the music of China. The author of the most valuable such work, *Mémoire sur la musique des Chinois tant anciens que moderns* (1779), was the missionary Joseph Amiot (1718–1793), while several decades earlier the French Jesuit Jean-Baptiste du Halde (1674–1743) penned *Description géographique, historique, chronologique, politique, et physique de l' empire de la Chine et de la Tartarie chinoise* (1735), which was based on the accounts of Jesuit missionaries beginning in the sixteenth century. Chinese motifs would later be incorporated into operas, including Nicolas Dalayrac's *Koulouf ou Les Chinois* (1806).

In the late 1700s, the author Abbé Georg Vogler (1749–1814)—whose treatises adapted Rameau's theory of harmony—traveled to Africa in a search for original melodies. In 1806, he introduced the well-received *Polymelos* for piano, violin, and cello, containing adaptations of African and Greek folk songs (Ringer, 1965, 121). The intrepid Vogler also composed the exotically tinged *Der Kaufmann von Smyrna* (1771), along with a series of original concert pieces with African melodies, which he performed as an organist in Vienna.

Europe in the later eighteenth century also saw increased knowledge of music from Arab lands, thanks to the travels of Carsten Niebuhr and his work *Beschreibung von Arabien* (Copenhagen, 1772)—translated shortly thereafter as *Travels through Arabia and Other Countries in the East* (1792). Other such works mentioning music also enjoyed popularity, such as *Voyage autour du monde* (1771), by Count Louis-Antoine de Bougainville (1729–1811). Nine years later, another Frenchman, Jean-Benjamin de la Borde (1734–1794), published *Essai sur la musique ancienne et moderne*.

The immense nineteenth-century interest in the Orient encompassed, to a degree, Japan: among the best known work on the country was Francis Taylor Piggot's *Music and Musical Instruments of Japan* (1893). The Napoleonic Wars, in which Napoleon Bonaparte reached Egypt in 1798, spurred an increased interest in Arab music, with the general himself commissioning from Guillaume-André Villoteau (1759–1839) a collection of materials on the region's music (Myers 2001, 369). The Englishman Edward William Lane (1801–1876), for many years associated with Egypt, included observations on the country's music in *An Account of the Manners and Customs of the Modern Egyptians* in 1836. The French-born Algerian resident Francesco Salvador-Daniel conducted a comparison of the European and Arab musical systems from 1853 to 1865, publishing *La musique arabe, ses rapports avec la musique grecque et le chant gregorien*. North Africa, largely inspired by these publications, would be the backdrop for many nineteenth-century operas, including Giacomo Rossini's *L'Italiana in Algeri*.

According to certain authors, the 1844 completion of the "famous *Odesymphonie la desert*," by Félicien David (1810–1876), marked an important moment in the use of exoticism in music (Bie 1920, 346). David would also compose *Perle du Brésil* (1851), although he was actually thinking of Africa; this work, in turn, would directly influence Giacomo Meyerbeer's *L'Africaine* (*The African Woman*), performed in 1865, a year after the composer's death. Five years later, Giuseppe Verdi's (1813–1901) *Aida* marked a revisitation of Egypt, a country that had played a part in much earlier works, such as Rameau's "L'Egiptienne" in *Nouvelles suites de pieces de clavecin* (1736), George Frideric Handel's "biblical epic" *Israel in Egypt* (1739), and Hector Berlioz's religion-themed overture *La Fuite en Égypte* (1850), as well as *Ballet egyptien* (1875), by the French violinist Alexandre Luigini.

The Far East also figured prominently in the nineteenth-century musical repertoire, such as in Arthur Sullivan and W. S. Gilbert's renowned operetta *Mikado* (1885) and Sidney Jones's musicals, such as *Geisha* (1896). Later, Giacomo Puccini's operas *Madame Butterfly* (1904) and *Turandot* (1926, posthumously) were set in Japan and China, respectively. Moving west, Georges Bizet chose Ceylon as the location for his 1863 opera *Les Pêcheurs de perles* (The Pearl Fishers), and Léo Delibes set his opera *Lakme* (1883) in India—with both countries then under British rule. Areas outside the European colonial reach also attracted the attention of composers and libretto writers. Peter Cornelius, for example, wrote *The Barber of Baghdad* (1858), covering a city then ruled by the Turks. The earlier composers Carl Maria von Weber and François A. Boieldieu had also taken up Turkish subject matter, which was particularly successful in comic operas that included instruments used by the Janissaries (Turkish military units), including a huge drum, dulcimers, and the triangle. Such accessories brought color and, even more important given the form, the opportunity for parody. Still other works fit the exotic mold, including Charles Gounod's *Le reine de Saba* (1862) and *Le tribut de Zamora* (1881), Karl Goldmark's *Die Konigin von Saba* (1875), Jules Massenet's *Le Roi de Lahore* (1877) and *Thais* (1894), Camille Saint-Saëns's *Samson and Delilah* (1877), and Anton Rubinstein's *Sulamith* (1883). Composers, as these examples intimate, were tempted by grand, mysterious titles. Both Nikolai Rimsky-Korsakov, in 1888, and Maurice Ravel, ten years later, named pieces *Scheherazade*.

In studying the emergence of ethnomusicology in the European context, the present-day scholar Philip V. Bohlman has designated stages in the development of nineteenth-century reflections on Oriental music. In the first stage, authors, including Villoteau and Lane, did not undertake any attempts to place their accounts within a concrete historical dimension (Bohlman 1987, 150). In the second stage, exemplified, for example, by Raphael Georg Kiesewetter's *Die Musik der Araber nach Originalquellen dargestellt* (1842), authors forced non-European music into a historical context but one unrelated to the tradition of European music itself. Bohlman considers August Wilhelm Ambros's *Geschichte der Musik*, written from 1862 to 1878, to be the most successful example from this period. Later works took a more holistic cultural and historical approach to non-European music. The final stage in the century's ethnomusicological development, in Bohlman's view, was a total departure from a Western research paradigm.

This flowering of interest in the music of exotic lands would evolve into an academic discipline, aided by technological innovations such as Thomas Edison's 1877 invention of the phonograph. This research would be embodied in the ethnological and musicological work of such luminaries as Erich Moritz von Hornbostel (1877–1935), Carl Stumpf (1848–1936), Franz Boas (1858–1942), and George Herzog (1901–1983). A scientific-academic approach became preeminent, along with the trends of the day, for those who collected musical materials. Bartók himself stated that students of folk music could consider themselves scientists, given that they chose "as the subject ... of research a concrete product of nature, the music of people" (Bartók 1992 [1931], 221). The field also included many women researchers, such as Alice Fletcher and Francis Densmore, who wrote on the musical cultures of Native Americans. Alongside the profusion of scholarly texts, many popular writings appeared with the aim of satisfying readers' curiosity and bringing them closer to this remote music.

The surge in interest in exoticism was expressed both in attempts to understand the musical phenomena themselves and in the incorporation of exoticism, broadly speaking, in many musical works. The German musicologist Carl Dahlhaus maintains that exoticism must therefore be viewed through the prism of the functions exotic elements fulfilled in European musical culture. The author defines exoticism as "the legitimate departure from the aesthetic and compositional norms of European music," which—as a consequence—could guarantee diversity in musical life and prevent monotony, even boredom. Exoticism, according to Dahlhaus, served as an unlimited reservoir of ideas, provided by numerous published travel journals, diaries, and other publications. It also was a source of interest where infatuation with other subjects had waned (Dahlhaus 1989, 302).

In particular, exoticism became fashionable in the nineteenth century at a moment when historicism and medieval mystery—as propagated by Walter Scott—had lost their influence. The invocation of strange, unknown lands in operas and other works offered a distinctiveness irrespective of their authenticity or its absence. On this matter, Dahlhaus writes of "exoticism . . . per se without having to specify . . . exotic land involved" (Dahlhaus 1989, 306). According to another scholar, Derek B. Scott, the essence of "exoticist" referencing in, for example, operas was "the simple fact that they were set in exotic, foreign places" (Scott 2003, 155). Scott argues that instead of requiring an exhaustive knowledge of the subject matter, composers needed only to locate in the score certain so-called Orientalist signifiers, or musical elements generally associated with the exotic (Scott 2003, 158). The turn, even the predilection, toward the exotic in music—as defined by Western creators and audiences—was, of course, a distortion and also a reflection of the West itself.

"Near" Exoticism

The focus on distant exoticism also opened up attention to folk music in the European borderlands, particularly southern Spain and Eastern Europe. Such locales, to use Gilbert Chase's designation, were marked "semi-oriental exotics" (Chase 1959, 291), and inhabitants of the traditional heart of Western Europe could view them as charming and unusual. Eastern Europe, enchanted and undiscovered, became a destination, in no small part because traveling there was cheaper and less perilous than traveling to the Middle or Far East.

Bie, an early twentieth-century scholar, observed that the musical cultures of Central and Eastern Europe vied too late for inclusion in the general European canon, resulting in their association with "wisdom, songs and dance as an exotic collection, ethnological jewels" (Bie 1920, 345). Such a view reflected the author's German-centric musicological standpoint, which considered the German-Austrian current to be identical with that of broader Europe. It also carried forth the dominant nineteenth-century attitude toward Eastern Europe as a distant region of atmospheric color and music filled with "the sinful allure of exoticism" (Bie 1920, 346). As Larry Wolff suggestively argues in his book *Inventing Eastern Europe: The Map of Civilization on the Mind of the Enlightenment* (1994), the distinction between the continent's civilized West and underdeveloped East had been established by the eighteenth century, marked both by the emerging concept of civilization and interest in the phenomenon of exoticism (Wolff 1994). Such an approach led to the splitting off of Eastern European citizens from the West. Censuses conducted in Austria-Hungary in the nineteenth century, for example, considered the following inhabitants "Asians": Hungarians,

Armenians, Gypsies, and Jews (as opposed to the "European" Germans, Czechs, Slovenes, Italians, and so on) (Hofer 1994, 43).

In turn, the concepts of exoticism and folklorism became closely associated in Eastern Europe. Dahlhaus, for example, points out how Western European musicians tapped both through "stylistic quotations interpolated into a polyphonic setting governed by the principles of art music" (Dahlhaus 1989, 305). As a consequence, "exoticism and folklorism . . . have analogous aesthetic functions, manifested musically in the notably stereotype [*sic*] devices they use to represent both local and alien milieu" (Dahlhaus 1989, 305). Indeed, distinctions between near and far exotic forms would be erased through widely used techniques such as empty fifths, Lydian fourths, and chromatic melodies. "Orientalist" works in which these techniques are found include *L'Almee* by Georges Bizet, whereas "near" exotic works such as Edvard Grieg's *Twenty-five Norwegian Folk Melodies and Dances* (op. 17) also employ them.

In assessing the relationship between distant and near exoticism, musicologists have pursued a range of approaches. Some, like Scott, have not sought to distinguish between near and far. For example, he classifies exotic lands as North Africa, the Asian subcontinent, the Middle or Far East, along with Spain and the Hungarian territories, with the last associated with the *style hongrois* (Scott 2003, 155–78). For Spain and Hungary, he links exoticism with the musical traditions associated with the Gypsies. He emphasizes, for example, that in the early nineteenth century, Spanish Gypsies were presented in musical works including operas, particularly through the *style hongrois*. Such analyses show how the field of musicology identifies exoticism in Gypsies' music and culture alike.

Gypsy Matters in the Light of Exoticism

From the moment of their appearance in Europe, Gypsies found themselves perceived as belonging to the realm of the exotic, with this view finding traction in academic settings during the Enlightenment. In fact, they were classified as representing both distant exoticism, because of their Eastern origins, and near exoticism, because they had inhabited Eastern European lands for many centuries and their music had become deeply rooted in the region's landscape.

The Provenance of Gypsies

In their migration West, Romanies traveled from the Greek territories that were known as "Little Egypt" and incorrectly assumed to have belonged to Egypt proper. This misapprehension led some to assume that the Gypsies were descended from Pharaohs. Research in the late eighteenth century, however, driven by an overriding interest in exoticism and founded in the Gypsies' language, identified their origins as most likely being in the Punjab region of India, as we saw earlier.

Despite widespread acceptance of the Romany's Indian origins, occasional dissenting voices still could be heard. In an 1865 article published in the British *Transactions of the Ethnological Society*, a certain John Crawfurd cast doubt on Gypsies' ties to India, based on dissimilarities between the Gypsies' language and Hindi and their skin color. The article, needless to say, was subjected to withering criticism from those in the mainstream (Charnock 1866, 89–96).

Along with the debunking of the Egyptian origins of Gypsies, nineteenth-century researchers took apart the late seventeenth-century hypothesis of the German Orientalist Johannes Christopherus Wagenseil arguing that the Gypsies were descended from German Jews (Pobożniak 1972, 4). Wagenseil's treatise, titled *Buch von der Meister-Singer Holdseligen Kunst,* had sought to prove that Gypsies were merely Jews in disguise. According to this theory, the Jews—accused in Europe of causing the plague by infecting wells—had long-ago hidden themselves away awaiting better times; in 1417, they had come out under the leadership of King Zundel and under the changed name "Zigeiner." In a series of articles in 1880, Engel skewered Wagenseil's conjectures as absurd, farcical, and wholly ignorant (Engel 1880a, 219–20).

The Perception of Gypsy Musical Traditions as Exotic

In the nineteenth century, Gypsies were widely represented in Central and Eastern Europe and many, especially those in the Hungarian territories, were thought by their Western European neighbors to have exceptional musical talents. Such views were expressed frequently in journal articles as early as the turn of the nineteenth century.

Around this same time, Gypsy exoticism was often viewed in the context of another "exotic" idiom—that of the Turks. The highly popular *alla turca* style was thought to be the precursor of the *style hongrois*. By midcentury, the Turkish *mehter* (military band) style of performance coexisted with the *hongrois*, with the latter slowly to adopt certain traits of the former (Scott 2003, 158). During the initial phase of the *style hongrois*, as Jonathan Bellman suggests, it was not even seen as clearly distinct, given that both the *hongrois* and Turkish styles fit the broad definition of exoticism (Bellman 1991, 218). The intermingling of these styles was reflected in the names of Western compositions, including Haydn's "Gypsy-style" "Rondo a l'ongarese," from the finale of the *Piano Trio in G Major,* the "Turkish" finale of Mozart's *Violin Concerto in A Major*, and Beethoven's *Rondo alla ingharese aquariun capriccio* (op. 129) for piano.

The Turkish connotations of the music performed by Gypsies manifested themselves in its basic parameters, including rhythm, melody, harmony, and instrumentation. The rhythm evoked spoken language, using the spondee and dactylic meters. The predominant syncopations of Gypsy music appeared in swinging melodies that then returned to a steady beat, supporting Liszt's notion about Gypsy masters who achieved this alternating effect as if laying the grounds for a dance (Liszt, 1960, 307).

The Turkish melodic references manifested themselves in rich ornamentation, including abundant use of the augmented second—an interval associated with all exotic music and commonly exploited in the so-called Gypsy scale (C, D, E flat, F sharp, G, A flat, B). In terms of harmony, exoticism was expressed in the "habit of passing suddenly to a remote key"; the "system of modulation seems to be based on a total negation of all predetermined plan for the purpose in question" (Bellman 1991, 232). The performers themselves allowed whim to govern their playing, with the extent of their expression depending "entirely upon the inspiration of the moment; which also decides the precise form to be given to the cloud of notes" (Liszt, 1960, 303).

Alongside the Turkish connection was, as noted before, the perceived tie between Gypsy and Arab musical forms. Liszt's early attempt to link Gypsy and Arab music was developed and supported, in 1907, by the American Albert Thomas Sinclair, who in the article "Gypsy and Oriental Music" upheld Liszt as the source of such conceptions. Referring to Liszt, he writes that "Gypsy music clearly was from the orient, and that a careful investigation of Hindu and Arab music would conclusively prove this to be the case" (Sinclair 1907, 20). Sinclair went so far as to suggest that, "there are certain peculiar characteristics common to Gypsy music, and also common to Persian and Arab music" (Sinclair 1907, 18). He further speculated on the influence of Gypsies' wanderings on their musical culture: "It must be remembered that for many centuries hundreds of thousands of Gypsies have been wandering to and fro all over southeastern Europe and into and over Asiatic Turkey. During this period they have been the public musicians of the whole territory. Would their music not naturally be Oriental?" (Sinclair 1907, 23).

In seeking ultimately to conjoin Gypsy music with Oriental music, Sinclair drew up an uneven twenty-point list, consisting of both entirely concrete examples (e.g., the lack of modulation and the presence of syncopation) and enigmatic formulations such as the following: "Something which takes the place of our harmony, particularly in modes in which our system cannot be used"; and "Then there is something peculiarly characteristic in the whole general effect of Gypsy music impossible to describe by words" (Sinclair 1907, 22).

Sinclair dealt very loosely in the terms "Gypsy" and "Oriental," not seeking to establish finer distinctions within them. Yet he did attempt to tie Gypsy music in Hungary and Spain with music of the Arabs, writing, "The Hungarian and Spanish Gypsy music have the same peculiar characteristics, whatever they may be, as Arab music, and must have sprung from the same source" (Sinclair 1907, 21–22). Sinclair also freely intertwined statements on melody, rhythm, and manner of performance.

In looking at Gypsy melodies, Sinclair focused on scales and manner of performance—full of unexpected stops, rapid breaks, and large jumps between individual sounds. He noted impurity in the performance of melodies, particularly in those "unusual intervals" thought of as "falsification" by the West and explained in the article as the effect of including quarter tones. Excessive ornamentation also effaced Gypsy and Oriental melodies, in Sinclair's view. He likened the effect to a "vigorous tree covered by a thick foliage and with beautiful vines and flowering and creeping plants which nearly conceal even the trunk itself from view" (Sinclair 1907, 19).

Sinclair also commented on similarities in singing among Gypsies, Persians, and Egyptians, drawing attention to a shared predilection for glissando, the unnatural prolonging of high sounds (lasting up to several minutes and incorporating grace notes), and sudden shifts from soft and muffled to loud and aggressive.

As for instrumentation, Sinclair writes of violin and dulcimer as the instrumental pillars of Gypsy music in Hungary, sometimes supported by additional violins, viola, cello, and double bass; these latter instruments would play "second or third melodies which support the sole performer's melody, in a way peculiar to Gypsy and Oriental music" (Sinclair 1907, 22). The author also mentioned the castanets, Oriental drum, and flute. As for the improvisatory nature of Gypsy music, both instrumental and vocal, Sinclair emphasized a wildness but also other traits: "Hungarian Gypsies seem to attempt to depict all the feelings, emotions, and passions, the soft, the tender side of life, sadness, dejection, despair, jealousy, revenge, terror, mirth, jollity, gayety, delight, love, hate, to terrify. This is exactly what the Orientalists claim to do. . . ." (Sinclair 1907, 22).

Sinclair devoted least attention to the question of rhythm, mentioning principally the sudden pauses, multiple changes in rhythm and meter, and syncopation. He also sought to link Gypsy rhythms with those prevalent in Persian and Arabic music, reinforcing the overall thrust of his work.

Harmony elicited more coverage from Sinclair, who remarked on the difficulty of defining Gypsy harmony but enumerated shared features between Gypsy and Oriental forms, namely the lack of modulation, a basis in various scales, and the preponderance of the augmented second interval. Sinclair, however, showed caution in that he implied the term *augmented second* but never used it, preferring instead the enigmatic *Gypsy intervals* or *bizarre intervals,* even as he gave concrete examples (e.g., C, D sharp; E flat, F sharp).

Discourse around the turn of the twentieth century on ties between Gypsy music and exoticism was rarely expressed as explicitly as it was in Sinclair's work. Rather, it typically emanated from the ambience of the statement itself. Sinclair summed up the day's conundrum: "To describe such characteristics exactly by words is exceedingly difficult" (Sinclair 1907, 18).

Motifs Accompanying the Exotic Discourse on Gypsy Music

The nineteenth-century discourse on Gypsies and their music was enhanced by the set of motifs deeply rooted within the literature (Balacon 2005) and attended by a duality in the exoticist phenomenon: fascination, on the one hand, and concern and fear on the other, with the latter resulting from the view of the Orient as a hostile entity. On these counts, Gypsy men were considered to have the attributes Eastern heroes, associated chiefly with Arab paradigms. Gypsies were also linked with conceptions of romantic love, or "Gypsy love," deriving particularly from the perceived sexuality of "Oriental" dance as performed by beautiful young Gypsy women.

Romantic infatuation with the Middle Ages and Arab culture spurred a renewed interest in adventure, with representatives of the exotic world playing the main roles. George Byron, among others, helped popularize this vision in his 1813 poem *The Giaur.* The trend would mean that European intellectuals and artists eagerly took up Arabic romances, including their translation (Dziekan 1997, 45).

As the previous chapter demonstrated, Spanish Gypsies were seen to have replaced the role of the banished Moors on the Iberian Peninsula. They correspondingly were ascribed traits associated with the Arabs, such as pride, generosity, hospitality, and courage but also vengefulness and a tendency toward sexual forcefulness. These perceptions brought with them traces of the attitudes described in Arab *sirats* (epics), which extolled the honor code of Bedouin warriors (Madeyska 1997, 65–66). The Gypsies, therefore, may have lived in Europe, but they were well suited to literary concepts associated with inhabitants of distant lands.

The Gypsies, as part of nineteenth-century conceptions of exoticism, were not only sexualized but their sexualization was also tinted with the suggestion of perversion. But the sexual trope more generally was tied to the Arab presence and image in Iberia, with lyric poems from as early as the eleventh century seen as "completely overcome by the passion of music" (Ribera 1929, 115). Such Andalusian representations, at the time of their composition, influenced courtly European literature and, more than likely, the songs of the troubadours. The compositions of the Provençal troubadours, however, added a "civilizational ideal" to the love promulgated by the Andalusians, in which "the theme of love, literary art and aristocratic taste united and created an inseparable unity" (Adamski 1986, 84). Drawing from the troubadours, French intellectuals coined the term *courtly love* (or *fin'amor*), understood as the sublimation of desire in unfulfilled seduction (Duhamel-Amado and Brunel-Lobrichon 2000, 31). The value created from unrealized love was both aesthetic and ethical, arising from the disjuncture between feeling and its fulfillment (Adamski 1986, 86).

The collision of courtliness and sublime love with eroticism would leave spaces to be filled. Around the nineteenth century, exoticism helped fill these spaces, often supplemented by elements of debauchery, to the point that in Parisian brothels "a compulsory element" was black, Algerian, Greek, and Chinese women. Gypsy women were likewise viewed as both erotic and exceptionally beautiful. For example, Teodor Narbutt in 1830 noted the fairness of certain Gypsy women and the beauty and shapeliness of many, who in turn attracted the eye (Narbutt 1830, 78–79).

Miguel de Cervantes himself had long before touched on the sensuality of Gypsy women in "La Gitanilla," one of his twelve *Novelas ejemplares* of 1613, which dealt with a young blond-haired, blue-eyed Gypsy woman called Preciosa. Analyzing Cervantes's work, Charles D. Presberg notes that Gypsy women were treated as sexual objects even by members of Spanish society. In this understanding, "women are *useful*, as 'amigas,' to the extent that they provide men with 'friendly relations' based on animal *pleasure*" (Presberg 1998, 58). And Meira Weinzweig notes that, in accordance with the historical reality, Cervantes depicted the dancing and singing Gypsy groups as including attractive women only, allowing male audience members to derive pleasure from the "erotic stimulation of watching young women dance" (Weinzweig, 1990, 227). In the novella, Preciosa's role is highlighted within a performing Gypsy troupe. Her fair attributes signal innocence, a contrast to her public persona and, in particular, her singing filled with sexual references. Her sexually liberated aura also issues from economic independence. According to Alison Weber, Preciosa represents a negation of the model woman of good behavior and upbringing promoted in seventeenth-century Spain (Weber, 1994, 64). Seemingly the complete opposite of the ideal of a tender mother and faithful wife, Preciosa's persona nonetheless displays a seeming contradiction: on the one hand, she is the embodiment of aggressive sexuality, while on the other, she requires that the young man seeking her hand in marriage spend two years living among the Gypsies.

As for marriages between Gypsies and non-Gypsies (*payos*) in Spain, they seem to have occurred frequently, dating to about the sixteenth century (Leblon 2003, 33). In 1544, Sebastian Münster wrote in *Cosmographiae universalis* that Gypsies "widely accept men from neighboring lands desiring women, who live with them in non-legal unions" (Mróz 2001, 124). During dances themselves, young Gypsy women often alluded to their unmarried status, as if suggesting the (erotic) aim of the dance being performed (Narbutt 1830, 121).

In the nineteenth century, the immense popularity of Gypsy dancing from Spain was expanded further by the scandalous lifestyle of an English ballet dancer, Elisa Rosanna Gilbert (1818 or 1821–1861), known publicly as Lola Montez, who posed as Spanish, spoke with a Spanish accent, and generally pretended to be from Andalusia (Szenic 1969, 183). Apparently Liszt carried on an affair with the beautiful Lola at the same time as his relationship with Madame d'Agoult. The exotic and erotic were linked not only in individual performers such as Lola but also in the works themselves, in which dances featuring half-naked women epitomized the Orient as the love object of the West.

The sensuality of Gypsies and their dance was widely written about and therefore well known within European culture. On the one hand, Gypsies (mainly young women), as an element of exotic discourse, were perceived as an object of sexual desire while on the other they were seen as debauched or as grown-up children, treating life as a game. Sometimes, then, the Gypsies' love of dance was explained in relation not merely to the erotic but also to their love of play (Narbutt 1830, 97).

It can be argued that the exotic context within which Gypsies and their music were perceived was strengthened by the European search for the noble savage, which underscored the discrepancy between civilization and its (alleged) absence. In this dichotomy, civilized Europe constructed itself as superior to the barbarianism and wildness of exotic lands. This hegemony played out on economic, religious, and moral fronts, with Western writers—controlling the means of communication—imposing this notion of difference on the non-European subjects they described. Such writers used the language of the ruler, and the nonliterate individuals described were relegated to the position of subordinates.

Gypsies, consequently, with their oral culture, were relegated to the realms of "exotic barbarians" (Mróz 2001, 8).

Enlightenment notions of the noble savage included an emphasis on simple values, and the Orient was identified with innocence, sentimentalism, and naïveté. Such values were included in later, nineteenth-century works on Gypsies, describing them as "lazy with regard to work, lethargic, devoted to ease" (Narbutt 1830, 80). Elements of the noble savage concept also made their way into works on Gypsy music. Liszt wrote that Gypsies are "amazing in their intensity, they are created by miracles of Nature" (Murphy 2001, 20) and characterized them as a people valuing freedom above all else. The composer also noted the Gypsies' complete lack of interest in the ownership of worldly goods. In Gypsy music, Liszt discovered beauty and primordial honesty (traits seen in barbarianism by Herder, among others) and claimed Gypsies were natural musicians, expressing through music their deepest feelings.

Because of Liszt's emphasis on the exotic in both his writing and some of his compositions, later generations of composers, including Karol Szymanowski, would evaluate his legacy in this light. He wrote in 1925: "Fr. Liszt was according to me a typical 'exoticist' who despite the fact that he himself was a Hungarian drew from Hungarian folk music (rather Gypsy!) the rhythms and melodies for his famous rhapsodies with the very same dazzling talent, intelligence and . . . indifference with which undoubtedly he would have drawn from the rich treasury of the music of the East, e.g., if that music had been known to him better" (Szymanowski 1925, 8–13).

Contemporary musicologists take different approaches to the exoticist connotations of Liszt's work. According to Malvinni, Gypsies' music, in Liszt's understanding, showed not a manifestation of the exotic but rather an awareness of the communicative role fundamentally served by music (Malvinni 2004, ix). Bellman likewise contends that interest in exoticism was neither the only nor the most important motive directing Liszt's actions (Bellman 1993, 130).

The influence of Orientalism on music attributed to Gypsies was to appear also in the writings of Bartók: he wrote about the Oriental fascination accompanying the specific manner of performance observed among Gypsy musicians. Up until 1920, he commented frequently in his writings on the exotic tunes heard in Gypsy music, the presence of which the composer interpreted as remnants of Asiatic musical culture (Brown 2000, 129).

꒰ ꒱ ꒰ ꒱ ꒰

CHAPTER FOUR

Gypsy Music and Race

The Concept of Race in Musicological Literature

The word *race* entered European Romance languages in the thirteenth century as a result of the Arab-Muslim presence on the Iberian Peninsula. During the Spanish Reconquista, from the eighth to the fifteenth century, the term did not carry racist overtones in Spanish texts (Roth 1995, 229). The concept began to slowly penetrate other European languages around the sixteenth century, and only entered mainstream use with the advent of the Enlightenment. Music would often be referenced in the construction of race as a concept: influenced by Rousseau, the view became widespread that nature itself was responsible for the creation of different races and music. Rousseau argued that music was derived from language and, in the words that often accompanied music, he saw the ability of music to reflect racial difference (Radano and Bohlman 2000, 14). The German philosopher Johann Herder later adopted a similar view on ties between music and racial difference, joined by collectors of folk songs around the turn of the nineteenth century.

Around the same time, generalizing or appropriating tendencies took hold with regard to race in Europe. And, as claimed by Richard Middleton (Born and Hesmondhalgh 2000, 23)—drawing on the work of Peter Stallybrass and Allon White, *The Politics and Poetics of Transgression* (1986)—the European confrontation with other musical cultures often entailed a good deal of projection. Seventeenth- and eighteenth-century works in which these dynamics played out include *Musurgia universalis* (1650), by Athanasius Kircher, *Relation d'un voyage à la côte des Cafres* (1686–1689), by Guillaume Chenu de Laujardiére, *Moeurs des sauvages américains* (1724), by Joseph-François Lafitau, and *The Oriental Miscellany* (1789), by William Hamilton Bird (Radano and Bohlman 2000, 17).

In the nineteenth century, influenced by Charles Darwin's theories, perceptions of difference were subjected to evaluation. Works fitting this mold prevailed until the mid-twentieth century, with a typical example being the study of a given musical culture from antiquity to the present day. Such works usually began with chapters devoted to the music of primordial peoples and of countries of the Orient (Bücken 1937, 9).

The first half of the twentieth century lent itself to a linked approach to questions of music and race. De Lafontaine, describing the music of Gypsies in Spain, used the terms *weird race* and *bizarre race,* implying that a race's inherent features would be reflected in the music created by its members (de Lafontaine 1907–1908, 32). Sinclair, discussing Gypsies' music in the same year, similarly described them as "outcasts and a despised race" (Sinclair 1907, 28). Such views were common across Europe: in 1925, the Polish composer Szymanowski expressed his conviction as to the "dependence of the creative individual on the features of his race, its permanent substructure" (Szymanowski 1989, 172).

With time, the quest to preserve purity in music became associated with the quest to preserve racial purity. The darkest manifestation of such an effort began in 1933 with Germany's Third Reich, when musicologists established racial standards to be applied, among other places, in repertoires for public concerts. These attempts also involved reimagining and reinterpreting a musical past (Meyer 1975, 651). Activities aimed at preserving the racial purity of German music found ardent advocates among politicians as well as musicologists, with German propaganda minister Joseph Goebbels representing a flagrant example of the former. He contended that music produced outside the country's borders would be impossible to imagine without the inspiration provided by Germany's operas and symphonies (Drewniak 1969, 10).

The roots of the Nazi application of racial theory to music can be found in Richard Wagner's circle from the previous century, and particularly in Wagner's infamous pamphlet on Jews in music. Two main currents on race may therefore be discerned in the musical scene of the Third Reich, as laid out by the Polish musicologist Andrzej Tuchowski. The first was oriented toward "the problem of formulating the relatively Germanic Nordic racial features within music," and the second was concentrated exclusively on research into the Jewish race.

Through rigorous study, musicologists in the German regime set out to create a method for determining "racial" features in music (Tuchowski 1998, 42–48). These features could be identified, first, by simply listening and analyzing; thus, it was suggested that there was music created by Jews and music not created by Jews (Stutschewsky 1935, 12). The process was aimed at undermining the notion that Jews had any creative disposition, although Jews were allowed a "certain ability to show a copied mediocrity in technique and feel" that could bring about effects of a startlingly high artistic level (Stęszewski 1996, 50). A second method was aimed at determining the racial affiliation of a work. Efforts in this arena stemmed from Hans Günther's *Rassenkunde des deutschen Volkes* (1929), which inspired Richard Eichenauer's *Musik und Rasse* (1932). The latter text presented composers from six different races and detailed how a work's racial affiliation could be determined by researching the composer's biography, including possibly a detailed study of his or her genealogy. The third method involved a formal analysis of works. In 1933, Hermann Matzke claimed that in establishing artistic features "which might be considered as typical for particular nations and races, a science of the arts should approach matters in two ways: the first leading to research into external features (and therefore the formal aspects of art), and the second the internal, that is the spiritual contents" (Tuchowski 1998, 47). The Third Reich's efforts at establishing a system of music and race would culminate with the 1941 publication of Theo Stengel's *Lexikon der Juden in der Musik*, which listed more than eight thousand individuals associated with music of either Jewish or half-Jewish extraction. (One-quarter Jews or those associated with Jews by marriage were exempted.)

Similar attempts to link music and race included those of the musicologist Friedrich Blume, who in 1938 sought a scientific grounding for musical feelings and instincts and emphasized the need to formalize research procedures on the connections between race and music (Meyer 1975, 656). Guido Waldmann, a year earlier, in assessing race as a lens for interpreting history, wondered how music fit this scheme and sought a more sober means of finding an answer than those employed in the past.

Such controversies on race and music would intensify as the field of musicology developed. Yet mainstream ethnomusicologists ultimately rejected the utility of race in their research. For example, Curt Sachs in the 1940s and John Blacking almost thirty years later questioned the heuristic importance of "race" and its usefulness in determining musical phenomena, even as music was acknowledged to play a role in establishing group and individual identification (Baily 1994, 47–48). Indeed, in the opinion of contemporary ethnomusicologists, "music is socially meaningful not entirely but largely because it provides means by which people recognise identities and places, and the boundaries which separate them" (Stokes 1994, 5). Later twentieth-century texts focused on reinterpreting and debunking as arbitrary and selective the earlier attempts at linking race and music (Desfor Edles 2002, 99; Clifford 1986, 18–19). From the embers of this discussion emerged a discourse informed by Edward Said's theory on dominant cultures, a discussion that helped shed light on the situation of Gypsy music.

Controversies around Gypsy Music

Revisiting the Views of Liszt

Franz Liszt's *Des Bohémiens et de leur musique en Hongrie* of 1859 appeared just nine years after Wagner's publication on the question of Jewish music, *Das Judenthum in der Musik*. In both the first edition and, even more so, the 1881 expanded edition of Liszt's book, the category of race appeared, applied to both the Gypsies and the Jews. Liszt and Wagner, however—even as they were linked by family as of 1870—would be viewed differently in the discussion of race on music.

For one thing, Liszt was tagged as Wagner's intellectual inferior, unable to sufficiently comprehend Wagner's vision (Newman 1937, 193). Liszt, for his part, thought about race in varied ways, reflecting the currents of the time. And contrary to popular opinion, Liszt was not "the unthinking, finger-driven virtuoso" but rather someone who read widely in French and German. According to Ben Arnold, "Liszt was at least aware of the scientific discoveries of Darwin and Wallace" (Arnold 1998, 37, 45), including Darwin's *Descent of Man* and Wallace's *Contribution to the Theory of Natural Selection*, as reported by Liszt's acquaintance, the German traveler Gerhard Rohlfs (Guenther 1912, 304–307). Liszt also kept up to date on academic developments and subscribed to *Revue Scientifique*. Given all this background, Liszt's own publication on Gypsy music, while not referencing science directly, would itself enter into later nineteenth-century works exploring the concept of race.

Liszt was also aware of perceptions tying Gypsies and Jews as Oriental cultures within Europe. Yet Liszt sought to distinguish the two groups, as reflected in the book's chapter titled "Contrast with Jews." The verdict for the Jews was similar to that presented in Wagner's *Das Judenthum in der Musik*. Liszt depicted the Jews as a cruel, servile race while (Walker 1989, 388) claiming that Jews—"in being able to master the language of a country (including the musical language) they had come to settle—could not produce real music and engage in the creation of any art of worth. Wagner was to express himself in a similar tone in his pamphlet[,] writing that 'The Jew has never had an art of his own,' limiting their abilities to the mere composition of 'the ceremonial music of their Jehova rite'" (Wagner 1964, 55).

Liszt redoubled his initial statements on Jews in the 1881 version of his book, and the Jewish press responded fiercely, accusing him of anti-Semitism. The music critic Miksa Schütz (pseudonym: Sagittarius) of the newspaper *Pester Lloyd* produced a booklet entitled *Franz Liszt über die Juden*, in which he portrayed the composer as a racist. Having read Liszt's book, Wagner described the father of his wife, Cosima, as "Really—. . . a Jew-baiter" (Walker 1989, 389). But uncertainty surrounded Liszt's true attitude toward Jews, given the unclear authorship of *Des Bohémiens*. In the view of those in Liszt's circle, the composer's friend Princess von Sayn-Wittgenstein, who prepared the 1881 edition for print, was responsible for the chapter on the Jews. Ironically, during the Third Reich, the musicologist Herbert Gerigk (1905–1996), who collaborated closely with the Nazi Party, expressed the "widely held" opinion that Wittgenstein was a "Polish Jew" but he did not consider Liszt anti-Semitic (Weissweiler 1999, 104–5).

Most influential on those who followed him, however, would be Liszt's positive approach to the Gypsy race and Gypsy music. In 1880 Engel, despite describing Gypsies as belonging to hordes and separated from civilization, linked them with attributes such as happiness and sensitivity and spoke highly of their culture as one untainted by contact with concert halls. He also observed similarities between Gypsies and Jews, treating both as Oriental races that had managed to preserve the unique character of their music. He wrote further that, "the two races . . . the Jews as well as the Gipsies evince an extraordinary fondness for cultivating the musical art" (Engel 1880a, 220; Engel 1880b, 391).

Bartók's Thinking

Béla Bartók's research on Gypsy music was marked by the buoyant ethnomusicological mood of the early twentieth century, with its focus on culturally linked phenomena (Brown 2000, 122). Bartók's work entailed questions, whether direct or indirect, about whether Orientalism emerged from ethnic roots or a cultural mix, what the concept of the noble savage meant, and how one might differentiate low from high art. Implicitly, he referred to processes of degeneration and renewal, as informed by Darwin's evolutionary theory. Particularly after World War I, Bartók's research constituted a synthesis of his own investigative results and postulates derived from comparative musicology.

Bartók's written works, produced from 1904 to 1945, fall clearly into two periods. His earlier works include discussions of an opposition between Hungarian and Gypsy music, with the presence of a perceived "norm" identified with deformation and degeneration. Meanwhile, his later works evaluate Gypsy and Hungarian music on their own terms, including through a juxtaposition of urban and rural performance practices.

Bartók's early portrayals of Hungarian music as a healthy organism corroded by Gypsy influences drew severe criticism from the German musicologist Heinrich Möller, author of the fourteen-volume *Das Lieder der Völker* (1931), which examined Hungarian music in its twelfth volume. Bartók had eagerly awaited Möller's work, expecting that it would both verify certain notions about Hungarian music and contain examples of tunes arranged in logical order. But Bartók was deeply disappointed by the work, and expressed his views bitingly and comprehensively in a 1931 article in the journal *Ethnographia*. Möller's work, according to Bartók, lacked any governing order and was something of a "conglomeration that bewilders the uninitiated reader" (Bartók 1992 [1931], 208–9). With a scientist's precision, Bartók enumerated Möller's slip-ups, from incorrect dates to incorrect ascriptions of song authorship to comments on the musical material itself. He also lambasted the author for the foolish assumption that ordinary people sang to piano accompaniment rather than a cappella. At the heart of Bartók's contention with the author, however, was the latter's view, expressed in the volume's foreword, that Gypsy music was central to Hungarian music and that present-day folklorists had belittled such contributions of the Gypsies.

Bartók's critique sparked a sharp exchange between the authors, with Möller accusing Bartók of extreme Darwinism, in which norms (racial purity) and distortions and deviations (impurity) were set at opposing poles. Möller, for his part, claimed to have incorporated Bartók's understanding into the broader context of the Darwinian conception. But Möller argued that his Hungarian opponent's language had linked Gypsy music with second-rateness or degeneracy. In supporting this claim, Möller enlisted Bartók's implication that the natural transformations and evolutions of Gypsy melodies had been altered deliberately, suggesting deviation.

As it happened, Bartok's earlier article "On Hungarian Music" (1911) included references to Gypsy music contaminating and destroying music in Hungary. The piece defines Gypsies as an "immigrant nation" whose music is full of "melodic distortions." In a discussion of performance by Gypsy groups, Bartók pejoratively suggests that Gypsies "drum into the ears of the Hungarian gentry" their songs taken from the Hungarian people (Bartók 1992 [1911], 301). In 1914, writing on Romanian music, Bartók accused Gypsies of perversion and deformation: "Gypsies pervert melodies, change their rhythms to 'gypsy' rhythm, introduce among the people melodies heard in other regions and in the county seats of the gentry—in other words, they contaminate the style of genuine folk music" (Bartók 1992 [1914], 198).

In 1921, Bartók wrote using similar language that Gypsy performers deformed melodies through overuse of tempo rubato and unnecessary melodic embellishments, the inclusion of which he called "strange" or "peculiar" and which obscured the melody's identity as either Hungarian, Slovak, or Romanian (Bartók 1992 [1933], 70).

As outlined in chapter 1, Bartók established distinct views on Hungarian music (as often performed by people of Romany descent) and the heterogeneous, inauthentic form known as Gypsy music. Among his objections to the latter was his view that its performers undid the inherent unity of music and text by performing songs instrumentally. Likewise, the composer considered Gypsy music-making to be derivative and lacking a "uniform character." All these traits were seen to be responsible for the degeneration of Hungarian music (Bartók 1992 [1931], 222).

Until 1942 and the publication of "Race Purity in Music," in the U.S. journal *Modern Music*, Bartók did not speak out explicitly on the subject of racial purity. Considering the political situation and the prewar waves of immigration to the United States, waves that included Jewish composers, one would have expected an article so titled to contain unmistakable views. But, as David Cooper writes, Bartók remained "less than willing to clarify his position on the Nazi doctrine of race purity in his essay" (Cooper 2001, 23). The article begins with the assertion that "in today's times, chiefly as a result of political reasons, so much is being said about racial purity and impurity amongst people" (Bartók 1958 [1942], 41). But the lack of deeper scientific knowledge on the subject, he made clear, prevented him from expressing any further views on the matter. Still, he emphasized that the term *racial* should be reserved for the music and not its creators or performers. Such a statement set him firmly apart from views expressed within the Third Reich (Bartók 1958 [1942], 42).

Expounding the idea of "impurity," Bartók emphasized in this essay that the transfer of melodies and rhythms between races, and the corresponding mix of influences, led to the creation of new styles, helping prevent stagnation and promote revival and diversity in musical ideas. He did not, however, offer any concrete examples to illustrate this process, leaving open his interpretation of the interaction between Gypsy and Hungarian music. He warned relatedly that "the tendency to transform melodies makes the internationalisation of the music of a given people all the more difficult" (Bartók 1958 [1942], 45). Yet, in the same paragraph, he cautioned that internationalization represented a threat to a given style's individuality. Cooper notes that such incoherence characterizes Bartók's entire article (Cooper 2001, 24).

Julie Brown proposes that all Bartók's work should be read as "a catalogue of discursive features standard in any 19th century book on natural history," claiming that his writings always gave a prominent place to what we now know of as hybridity (Brown 2000, 122). In particular, Bartók saw hybrid forms at the boundary of popular Hungarian music and Hungarian folk music, an intermixing that earned his approval given that it resulted in the introduction of elements of Hungarian folk music to original compositions. This was the case despite his negative view on the association of Hungarian popular music with Gypsy music.

Over time, Bartók's writings shifted away from positive-negative dichotomies and toward a distinction between Gypsy music performed in urban locales and rural folk music performed by "non-Gypsies." The urban-rural relation fulfilled a common expectation of ethnological research of the time (Sokolewicz 1974, 64). Around 1920, rusticity dominated the composer's writing. As Brown emphasizes, the change of perspective brought with it associations of ruralness with natural beauty and urbanness with commercial vulgarity (Brown 2000, 130). He also focused more on the economics behind the musical practices of Hungarian Gypsies. And by the early 1930s, Bartók would soften his earlier critique of Gypsy musicians, claiming they operated at the mercy of the upper classes' whims—in effect, treated as property—whether hired for parties, balls, or winter sleigh rides (Frigyesi 2000, 60). This change in Bartók's attitude coincided with his discovery of a new musical hybrid in the form of jazz imported from America, a form Bartók condemned and ranked below Gypsy music.

Part II

GYPSY MUSIC IN THE WORKS

OF NINETEENTH- AND EARLY

TWENTIETH-CENTURY COMPOSERS

In the nineteenth and twentieth centuries, composers—as representatives of Europe's intellectual elite—actively shaped the topos of Gypsy music in European culture. They did so chiefly through their music but also through their published works. These works helped shape the dominant discourse on Gypsies and Gypsy culture within the European tradition, while also reproducing conventionalized notions of Gypsy music.

The Gypsy theme played out with particular flair in professional stage works, both in their spoken and visual elements. These works exploited national, racial, and exotic means of portraying Gypsies and Gypsy music. Compositions designed for the stage opened up broad possibilities for the use of Gypsy subject matter, through lead characters and various embellishments of Gypsy motifs. Gypsy heroes were incorporated in serious or tragic operas and ballets but also in lighter works such as operettas, vaudevilles, and musicals.

In nonstage works, both solo and choral songs were used to convey Gypsy themes, allowing composers to combine their own imagined conceptions of Gypsy culture with prevalent tropes in European literature. Songs from the nineteenth century in particular portrayed the Gypsy by appropriating the verses of Romantic poets.

Instrumental works invariably handled Gypsy subject matter differently from works accompanied by texts. Most common in such portrayals were miniatures, while full symphonic works were much rarer. The references to Gypsy culture usually appeared in a work's title, which also set the work within a national, racial, or exotic perspective. The music, in these cases, and its perceived Gypsy gestures often occupied secondary significance.

Stage Works Employing Gypsy Motifs

Stage works employing Gypsy subject matter, dating from about the 1600s to the 1800s, served to reinforce stereotypes—and particularly so in the 1800s. Very seldom were attempts made to go beyond stereotypical portrayals, and even if such efforts were made, Gypsy heroes were still placed within "typical" contexts. In a work's music, the Gypsy idiom was used only to enrich, and references to instrumentation, scales, and, when applicable, dances were implemented loosely and without the pretension of authenticity.

Musical stage works with Gypsy associations were dominated by the five themes of love, freedom, magic, nature, and evil. This "pentalogue" guided the way in which the Gypsy characters were created, and was supported by stereotypical visuals of Gypsies at their campsites. In addition, stereotypes about Gypsies' musical talents provided an ideal avenue for introducing Gypsy heroes into works. For their part, women characters were often presented as vehicles for an exotic song or dance, with examples including Preziosilla from Verdi's *La forza del destino* and Mab from Bizet's *La jolie fille de Perth* (The Fair Maid of Perth).

As early as the seventeenth century, artists used Gypsies to enhance the attractiveness of a work, such as in Jean-Baptiste Lully's *Le carneval mascarade mise en musique* (1675), in which "les Bohemiennes" appear beside Spaniards, Turks, and Egyptians. The commentary—*"une Egyptienne dansante, est accompagnee de quatre Boemiennes jouants de la Guitarre—"* refers clearly to Gypsies, who are typically portrayed in groups playing away on some instruments (Lully 1720, 129). The Gypsies, treated as a collective hero, were immortalized in the English masque *The Metamorphosed Gipsies,* written by Ben Jonson for George Villiers. The renown of this form was reflected in both the proliferation of lute transcripts and the publication of virginal books. Later stage works included Rinaldo di Capua's two-act intermezzo *La Zingara* (1753), *May-day; or, The Little Gipsy* (1775), by Thomas Augustine Arne, and *The Gypsies,* by Samuel Arnold (1778).

An increasing awareness of literature on Gypsy themes in the nineteenth century translated into more stage works. The success of Victor Hugo's 1831 novel *The Hunchback of Notre Dame* resulted in a flood of operas and ballets based on the story of the beautiful Gypsy girl Esmeralda, with more than thirty such works appearing by the century's close (Laster 2003, 600). Literary models also influenced the creation of Carl Maria von Weber's 1821 opera *Preziosa*, including Cervantes's "La Gitanilla," a novella that would also inspire other musical stage works, particularly the Spanish *zarzuelas* (Dziedzic 1984, 67–70).

Nineteenth-century operas on Gypsy themes enjoyed great popularity, with a select example being *The Bohemian Girl*, by the Irish composer Michael William Balfe (1808–1870). The work would be performed in German, French, and Italian, and would meet with success in Berlin and Russia. Balfe's flair for melody even earned him acclaim across the Atlantic, where the opera's songs were published in popular editions with piano accompaniment. The protagonist's song from Act III, "The Fair Land of Poland," was so popular that it became a "single" in the United States (Janta 1982, 86). While "La Gitanilla" had been the starting point for the work, the librettist, Alfred Bunn, drew more directly from the popular ballet *La Gipsy*, staged in Paris in 1839, with music by Francois Benoist, libretto by Jules-Henri Vernoy de Saint-Georges, and choreography by Joseph Maziller. The performance included the Polish *krakowiak* dance, performed excellently by the Austrian ballerina Fanny Elssler (1810–1884). The principal hero of Balfe's opera, derived from Jane Porter's popular novella "Thaddeus of Warsaw" (1836), was the Polish nobleman Tadeusz, whose fate was linked to a certain group of Gypsies and the family of Count Arnheim. Many guides erroneously cite the opening part as being set in Poland, whereas it actually began in Pressburg (Pozsony, present-day Bratislava), in what was then Austria (Kobbe 1999, 13). The libretto is the source of this error.

First appearing in operas and ballets, the Gypsy pentalogue would later show up in the increasingly popular operettas, such as vaudevilles and lyrical pantomimes. Regardless of whether the works were tragic or comic, the appearance of Gypsy heroes automatically drew the viewer's attention to the stereotypes associated with them. No single treatment of the classic Gypsy motifs prevailed, however; rather, they were interconnected in a sort of web.

Gypsy love constituted a highly popular trope in stage works—in the wake of the bell ringer Quasimodo's love for the beautiful Gypsy girl (in *The Hunchback*) as well as in other contexts. The librettos were, however, usually based on literary works rather than real stories. Alexander Pushkin's poem *The Gypsies* (1827) was to become the basis for Sergei Rachmaninoff's opera *Aleko* (1892), which the young composer wrote for his conservatory diploma. In the libretto, Vladimir Nemirovich-Danchenko immortalized Pushkin's heroine Zemfira, who secretly meets a young Gypsy man and mocks her older husband. Zemfira flouts her husband's dignity, derived from his function as leader of the camp, and forgets he is the father of her child. In desperation, the jilted Aleko kills both Zemfira and her young lover before a crowd. Love, evil, and death intertwine in a single course of events.

Similar themes pervade other works on Gypsy subjects, including the opera *Mignon* (1866), by Ambroise Thomas, which propagates the stereotype of the Gypsy as a dancer, singer, and comedian wandering the world with his band. The German townsfolk observing the Gypsy dance displays are clearly aware of their Oriental origins and emphasize them. Furthermore, Michel Carré and Jules Barbier's libretto uses a series of stereotypical associations. The "Mignon" of the title (non-Gypsy herself but kidnapped as a small girl) grows into a beautiful woman and is forced by the Gypsies to earn her keep by dancing and singing. The Gypsies appear only in the first act, but this appearance clears the way for exotic dances and motifs. The story of Mignon, meanwhile, shows how Gypsies were portrayed in operas as cruel and brutal toward women.

Similar associations with evil appeared in various national operas (e.g., Polish, French, Italian, German, Russian) and most often took the form of the Gypsy-kidnapped child. In Verdi's 1853 opera *Il trovatore* (The Troubadour), the Gypsy woman Azucena is suspected not only of abducting children but also of placing them under spells.

This theme of magic entered opera through instances of fortune-telling and palm reading. The fortune-telling Gypsy, first seen in opera in the nineteenth century, appeared in works such as *La Zingara delle Asturie,* by Carlo Saliva (libretto by Felice Romani), of 1817, and *La Zingara,* by Gaetano Donizetti, of 1822 (libretto by Andrea Leone Tottola: based on *La petite bohemienne,* by Louis-Charles Caigniez, which was modeled on the work of August von Kotzebue). In Charles Gounod's five-act opera *Mireille* (1863–1864), with a libretto by Michel Carré (based on the 1859 work *Mireio* by Frédéric Mistral), a young Gypsy woman tells the fortune of the heroine; in a similar vein are introduced the Gypsy women in Giacomo Meyerbeer's *Les Huguenots* (libretto by Eugène Scribe) of 1836. Verdi includes a fortune-telling Gypsy girl, Ulryka, in *Un ballo in maschera* of 1859—as initially inspired by the character Arvedson from Daniel Auber's *Gustave III ou Le bal masqué* (libretto also by Eugène Scribe) of 1833.

A similar current of magic penetrated the Russian tradition in Modest Mussorgsky's opera *The Fair at Sorochintsi* (1874–1880), with a libretto based on the work by Nikolai Gogol. Here, the Gypsy tells the story of a mysterious red doublet, an outfit that had been owned by the devil himself.

The motif of Gypsies' close relations with nature, too, infiltrated many operas, ballets, and operettas in their set design: Gypsy camps were portrayed in mountains, forests, and other inaccessible places. Foucault might have seen these locales as spatial heterotopias, situated outside typical national-cultural sites of power relations (Foucault 2006).

"False" Gypsies, or heroes pretending to be Gypsies, entered many nineteenth-century stage works, even if "real" Gypsies did not appear. A related example is the choir of false Gypsy women in Verdi's opera *La traviata* (1853), with this insertion amounting to exotic coloring. During the ball, which commences the second scene of Act II, the choir performs a song about the Gypsy gift of fortune-telling. The next song, performed by a male choir, tells of matadors, affirming the nineteenth-century association of Gypsy with Spanish culture.

As heroes who were sometimes protagonists, Gypsy characters played a significant role in stage works up through the nineteenth century. As the twentieth century dawned, portrayals of Gypsy themes only continued as demand from audiences remained strong, reinforcing the pentalogue of love, freedom, magic, nature, and evil.

The Characteristics of Nonstage Works with References to Gypsy Culture

In the same way that stage works such as operas, operettas, and ballets employed textual and visual components to convey "Gypsyness," we might speculate that nonstage works such as songs would have relied on extramusical devices such as texts. Likewise, purely instrumental works could allude to Gypsy subject matter through titles or subtitles. We might speculate further that nonstage works—perhaps even more than stage works—would have relied on musical devices either attributed to the Romany or, at least, linked to them through iconography, such as instruments, or literary treatments. As we will see, however, use of such techniques has not always been the rule.

❧ ❧ ❧ ❧ ❧

CHAPTER FIVE

The Gypsy Idiom in Operas

The Pseudonational and Exotic Context: Georges Bizet's *Carmen*

The "Gypsy" Libretto

In Georges Bizet's (1838–1875) opera *Carmen*, Spain is treated as occupying the edge of Europe. The Gypsies who appear in this 1875 work would fit the stereotypical conceptions and reflect the hidden desires of bourgeoisie drawn to Gypsy music. At the same time, *Carmen*, in a far from sophisticated way, refers to nationalist discourse through the introduction of Spanish and Gypsy heroes.

Bizet incorporated exotic themes in works long before *Carmen*. Even at age seventeen, Susan McClary maintains, his composition of the *Symphony in C Major* contained such material, in particular through the use of chromatics, even as it otherwise was based on classical models (McClary 1992, 33). Similarly exotic material predominated in the composer's stage works. For example, the 1862 opera *The Pearl Fishers* (libretto by Michel Carré and Pierre Étienne Cormon) takes place in distant Ceylon during the annual pearl-collecting festival; equally, the opera *Djamileh* (1871) (libretto by Louis Gallet)—based on *Namouna*, by Alfred de Musset—references exotic motifs. According to Bie, writing in 1920, "As a composer of lyrical operas Bizet is a clear exoticist, embellishing them . . . as far as possible with national colourings, not authentic yet sublime" (Bie 1920, 351).

The Gypsy motif itself would appear in the 1866 work *The Fair Maid of Perth* (libretto by Jules-Henri Vernoy de Saint-Georges and Jules Adenis), based on Walter Scott's popular story of the same title. In this narrative, the Gypsy girl Mab is introduced as a counterweight to the Scottish maiden Catherine, whose purity is juxtaposed with the enticing corporeality of the Gypsy. Yet *Carmen*, in the opinion of many scholars, was to be the true source of the upsurge in nineteenth-century interest in the exotic (Lacombe 2000, 690–701; McClary 1992, 33). Spain's geographic location and its Arab past allowed for both fantastic representations and an examination of a foreign folklore imbued with exoticism.

Bizet's opera was based on the novella by Prosper Mérimée, who in 1845 published a letter in *La revue des deux mondes* describing the story of Don José's love for Carmen. It was widely accepted that Mérimée's story was directly inspired by a tale told him by the Countess Maria Manuela Montijo. As for Mérimée, the idea of presenting Carmen as a Gypsy woman arose naturally from his interest in Gypsy life. In a letter of May 15, 1845, he admitted, "As I had recently been studying the lives of Gypsies I made the heroine a Gypsy girl" (Gabryś 1961, 46). Moreover, Carmen was not Mérimée's first Gypsy heroine. He had already portrayed Mila in his *La chronique du temps de Charles IX* (1829), with the character's Gypsy nature visible in her practice of palm reading and tendency for petty theft.

Mérimée's own interest in the Gypsies was augmented by his 1830 visit to Spain. Traveling south in the country, he apparently encountered Gypsies, and in Granada his fascination reached the point where he seems to have become involved romantically with a local Gitana (Northup 1915, 145). Furthermore, Mérimée—known for his love of languages (he had, for example, mastered Russian)—began learning the Spanish of the Gypsies, taught by the Spanish writer Serafín Estébanez Calderón (1799–1867). In addition, Mérimée immersed himself in nineteenth-century literature on Gypsies, with works more than likely including August Friedrich Pott's *Die Zigeuner in Europa und Asien* (1845). However, the greatest influence on Mérimée's conception of Gypsies was *The Zincali*, published in 1841 by the English traveler and writer George Borrow, whom we met earlier. Mérimée became acquainted with this work in summer 1844—a few years after his first visit to Spain and yet before he had written his novella about Carmen. As one early twentieth-century writer suggested, "For over a decade after his first visit to Spain, Mérimée's interest in the Gypsies lay dormant" and was only "reawakened by the successive publication of Borrow's works" (Northup 1915, 145–47).

Among other sources influencing the decision to portray Carmen as a Gypsy, mention should be given to Pushkin's poem *The Gypsies*, which some consider a direct catalyst for the work. This poetic masterpiece encompasses the clash of two cultures—Gypsy and non-Gypsy—through the story of a Gypsy girl and the boy smitten with her. Nor did Bizet's librettists fail to see the convergence of subject matter in Pushkin's poem and Mérimée's novella. Yet the deep parallelism seems to have skipped over Mérimée's work and instead appears in a comparison of Pushkin's poem with Bizet's opera, pointing to a "double source for the libretto" (Lowe 1996, 75). Literary scholars such as William Edward Brown, Elizaveta Martyanova, and Mikhail Alekseev all argue that the poem and the opera are united not only by their subject matter but also by their narrative structures, which foreground both the heroes' inescapable doom and a specific Gypsy ethos (Lowe 1996, 72). Themes such as the exotic, an ethos of freedom, and wildness form the basis of attempts to fuse fragments of Pushkin's poem with the libretto. In effect, *Carmen* not only reflects the European fascination with Gypsies and their culture but also linkages in European literature.

The Libretto as Compared with Its Literary Model

The source behind the adaptation of Mérimée's novella was likely Bizet himself, while sung verses were written by the composer's father-in-law, Ludovic Halévy, and the Gypsies' dialogues were written by Henri Meilhac. In the work, the stereotyped portrayal of Spanish Gypsy life centers on the destructive influence wrought by the beautiful Gypsy Carmen on the simple soldier Don José. Unable to forgive his unfaithful lover her betrayal, and having reached the limits of his psychic endurance, he slays her with a dagger. The inevitable and fatal power of Gypsy love pervades the work, illustrated musically by the "fate" motif that heralds the approaching tragedy while at the same time symbolizing the beauty of love.

Bizet's librettists, in adapting the novella, sought to create a narrative that was clear for audiences. The libretto, however, still preserved elements broadly associated with Gypsy life, such as dancing, singing, and fortune-telling with cards. Stereotypes associated with the Spanish Gypsies were concentrated in their status on the edge of the law along with their customary freedom. In Bizet's *Carmen*, the Gypsies are shown as common criminals, propagating the general European view of them "as a more or less deviant segment of society" (Mirga, Gheorghe 1997, 15). Yet Carmen's criminal tendencies, in the libretto, are toned down as compared to the novella and her utter freedom is emphasized, with this freedom infusing all elements of her existence. She works, loves, and even lives only based on her own volition. When faced with the choice of coercion or death, she easily chooses the latter in the name of preserving her freedom. Don José, by contrast, represents the non-Gypsy world, with its overriding value being to possess (McClary 1992, 9).

This dynamic of freedom versus (capitalist) possessiveness is reflected in the characters' different understandings of love: for Carmen, love results from a choice based on personal desire, whereas Don José considers it linked inseparably to the right to another person. The quintessential illustration of this divergence appears in Act IV, when Carmen throws her engagement ring to the ground, thereby rejecting love as being linked to property and underlining her Gypsy "sense of dignity and attachment to freedom" (Czapliński 2003, 28).

A sense of primordial desire also marks Gypsy love in Bizet's opera. In Act I, Carmen gives Don José a cassia flower (or a rose), traditionally considered within European culture to symbolize love—and here associated not with Don José's platonic feelings but with his physical desire. Carmen, the femme fatale, is thus the object of carnal, sensual attention—attention intensified by society's prohibitions and repression. She is correspondingly a representative of stereo-typical Gypsy passion and an absence of moral restraint. Carmen's sexuality in the opera is largely derived from the literary model, in which the writer obses-sively describes women's bodies as sites of temptation and thereby threats to men (McClary 1992, 11).

Carmen's sexual freedom, particularly apparent when portrayed visibly, al-ludes clearly to the situation in nineteenth-century France, where illegal prosti-tution constituted an indelible component of the urban scene. The author of the once-banned six-volume *History of Prostitution* (first published in 1851–1853), F. S. Pierre Dufour, wrote of this trade as permeating not only Paris but all Western Europe. Yet in France, moral degradation beginning in the era of Napoleon III, was seen to be accompanied by a rise in prostitution. Difficult economic times, as shown in *Carmen*, offered one incentive for young women who sought eas-ier, quicker income (Dufour 1998, 305). According to Bizet's biographers, the composer had become acquainted with a former prostitute, Comtesse Lionel de Chabrillan (born Céleste Vénard), who climbed from her lowly profession to the aristocracy and ultimately resided not far from Bizet's father's country residence. Such knowledge by Bizet may well have informed the creation of the opera and libretto (McClary 1992, 38).

Carmen herself was modeled on women of easy virtue, characterized in nine-teenth-century France as "mainly enormously cunning, unctuous and false" (Dufour 1998, 310–11). Of low status, she resembled a so-called *fille à soldats*—a girl who entertained and danced with men, mainly soldiers, in pubs and taverns. Even prostitutes considered the *fille à soldats* to be a shameful position, given that such a young woman could count on "being had by drunk men and this in the dark" (Dufour 1998, 329). Carmen's social role in the opera, easily apprehended by the Parisian public and critics, was that of a "mixture of Spanish Gipsy and Parisian cocotte" (Vechten 1920, 135). Such a combination had the advantage of portraying moral laxity as well as explaining the transience of men's interest in Carmen.

Even though Carmen's every appearance onstage provides a charge of eroticism, enhanced by her movements and poses, she remains, as a Gypsy, "the
lowest form of human life possible . . . as her charms are those of Satan himself"
(McClary 1992, 8). Indeed, the Gypsy girl is considered a witch and the embodiment of magical powers, as made clear in a short recitative by Don José in Act
I. Carmen's character also stands in opposition to the Catholic ideal of love and
inseparable union between a man and woman. While a target of reproach, this
role was also an outlet for the hidden desires of nineteenth-century Europeans,
who associated promiscuity with so-called primitive peoples. This trope of
sexual freedom and the exotic, in Bizet's opera, would extend from Carmen to
all Gypsy society. In Act III, the customs officers bend before the allure of the
trio of Gypsy women, showing the interplay of censure and desire. In the song's
subtext, a kiss is a stand-in for the act of physical love, showing these women's
moral laxity and Europeans' weakness for it.

In the opera, Gypsy love is also expressed through conventionalized subject
matter, such as fortune-telling and its implications. In Act III, Carmen's friends
predict her future from cards, symbolizing the inevitability of her tragic fate and
emphasizing the Gypsies' ability to foresee the future so universally ascribed
to them.

Between Spanishness and Gypsyness

In time, Bizet's opera would become a musical icon of Spanishness. Its
alleged Gypsy component, meanwhile, was viewed by the public and critics alike
as part of the national discourse, an end achieved through various references.

This national perspective on the opera was apparent even at its premiere in
1875, chiefly as a result of its libretto. Such an analysis would persist into the
twentieth century. Likewise, in the early 1900s, Bizet's opera was perceived in
the context of Spanish music. In 1920, for example, Bie noted the appearance
of the seguidilla in the opera, identifying this form as a Spanish national dance
(Bie 1920, 351–53). For him, *Carmen* represented a work of exotic connotations
and associations, within which national elements were creatively developed.
Julien Tiersot, who wrote an article marking the fiftieth anniversary of *Carmen's*
staging, also viewed the national context as central. He began his piece by asserting, "Carmen, the work of a musician born in Paris, composed on the novel of a
Parisian author . . . has for half a century enjoyed the prestige of disseminating
throughout the world the spirit of Spanish music" (Tiersot 1927, 566).

Most commentators agree that references to Spanish culture in the opera
do not depart from romanticized notions of a distant land with "local color."
As Czapliński writes, "The suggestiveness of Bizet's music . . . meant that this

work started to act as a synonym for Spanishness and Spanish music, while the inertia of the spreading stereotype did the rest" (Czapliński 2003, 29). Jerzy Gabryś clearly emphasizes that the Spain portrayed in *Carmen* "is a conventional country, a stage country . . . while the music is as French as possible" (Gabryś 1961, 54). A similar viewpoint is advanced by Hermann Heyer, who writes that "despite the Spanish decour, Carmen is a French opera through and through" (Heyer 1967). McClary, responding to the tendency to identify original Spanish melodies in *Carmen*'s score, writes that such efforts failed to acknowledge that "Bizet's research into Spanish music may have been less formal, for such music was fashionable in Paris at the time" (McClary 1992, 52).

Whatever the origins of Bizet's Spanish musical material, *Carmen*'s place in the national discourse emanates from the association of Spanishness with Gypsyness through the heroine and her friends and the piece's setting in Seville, in southern Spain. Colorful references to Gypsies occur through melodies alluding to allegedly authentic Spanish (or Gypsy) songs, dances typical of southern Spain, and characteristic instruments, particularly as props. One melody woven into the score, for instance, is a *polo* written and performed by Manuel García, a Spanish tenor born in Seville. Apparently Bizet stumbled upon this piece in Paul Lacome's 1872 collection, *Echos d'Espagne*, which included, with piano accompaniment, seguidillas, boleros, habaneras, *tiranas, jotas,* as well as García's *polo,* which based on the preface is the only dance in the collection with known origins. García apparently composed the piece in Madrid in 1805 as part of the *tonadilla* "El poeta calculista," according to an annotation. Research by Tiersot in the 1920s would show similarities between the *caballo,* another part of García's 1805 *tonadilla,* and the 1872 *polo.* Yet despite certain convergences, Tiersot wrote that "all the same it is not the same piece" (Tiersot 1927, 574–77). The French musicologist instead drew attention to García's *tonadilla* "El criado fingido" of 1804, of which only the serenade survived. He claimed this serenade bore nominal similarities to the *caballo* from García's 1805 *tonadilla* and to the *polo* that served as the source of Bizet's melody. According to Tiersot, variations in this same melody in two separate *tonadillas* by García may indicate their popular origin, perhaps heard by the composer in his native Seville. As for García's background, he was apparently "of obscure birth, and brought up in Seville, it is said that Gypsy blood ran in his veins" (Tiersot 1927, 577). It is therefore possible that the melody in the *Echos d'Espagne* collection functioned within the repertoire of Spanish Gypsies in the early nineteenth century in the same form that it was immortalized in García's compositions.

In Bizet's opera, the four pitches representing the fate motif also point to the romantic connotations of Gypsy music. The five-*sound* motif (D, C sharp, B flat,

C sharp, A) is based on a repetition of the augmented second interval, with one such interval in close proximity to the next and the B flat acting as an axis (C sharp, B flat, C sharp). The use of the augmented second, therefore, refers to Carmen and her fate, and to Gypsy music more broadly. Fate therefore indirectly becomes a Gypsy motif, a counterpoint to non-Gypsy references, such as those to Don José. This motif and its absence come to represent the incompatibility of the two worlds, their moral values, and their attitudes.

Besides the themes expressed in melodies, dances also offer a focal point in the discussion of Gypsy and Spanish entwinement in *Carmen*. This focus is all the more relevant given the nineteenth-century popularity of Gypsy dance in both Spain and across Europe, as exemplified in the soaring fame of Lola Montez. As it turned out, the dance earning most acclaim from *Carmen* was the piece known informally as "Habanera," of Cuban origin, located in Act I and thereby signaling Carmen's personal credo and love's role in it. Amid a sizable gathering, including her future lover Don José, Carmen describes Gypsy love fairly schematically as a "free bird," an immense force not recognizing human laws and capable of breaking down all barriers. Sensing the dance's importance and its potential impression on the audience, Célestine Galli-Marié (1840–1905), who played Carmen at the Paris premiere, forced Bizet to make various changes to the piece before agreeing to perform it (Wright 1978, 53–64).

According to Tiersot, Bizet aimed to evoke Spanish tradition with "Habanera" (Tiersot 1927, 568), which was modeled on the song "El arreglito" by the Spanish composer Sebastian Yradier (1809–1865), contained in the collection *Fleurs d'Espagne* (1864). In addition, the eventual Comtesse Lionel de Chabrillan (the former prostitute and Bizet's friend) had already helped popularize a version of the song by singing it at the Café-Concert du XIXieme Siecle in Paris. Even Yradier (who changed the spelling of his name from Iradier at the publisher's insistence), despite his Spanish origin, may have written the piece as an "exercise in exoticism" rather than an iteration of a Spanish style (McClary 1992, 51–52). For his part, Yradier would write additional habaneras, including the exceptionally popular "La paloma," after visiting Latin America. Habaneras were stylish in late nineteenth-century France, composed by the likes of Emmanuel Chabrier, Maurice Ravel, and Claude Debussy, in his piano cycle *Estampes*. Sarasate was among Spanish composers to take up the form, as in number 2 of his *Spanish Dances* (op. 21) for violin and piano.

The seguidilla, also used in *Carmen*, aroused associations with flamenco but was probably intended to simply evoke the Spanish character identified with the Gypsy (McClary 1992, 87). Not only was the "Seguidilla" written in an "admirable style," wrote Tiersot, "[but] at first hearing gives a vivid impression of Spanish song" (Tiersot 1927, 571). The lack of an intent to insert flamenco may be inferred from the fact that the melody was entirely of Bizet's invention. The piece's explicit name, however, suggests the intentional reference to Gypsy traditions.

Some writers have argued that neither the "Habanera" nor the "Seguidilla" bear any authentic traits of Spanishness or Gypsyness. Rather, they say these pieces are intended simply as functional markers of the opera's exotic dimension. Furthermore, McClary notes an interesting aspect in the presentation of Gypsy music on the operatic stage: Carmen, in performing her Gypsy dances during the opera, not so much expresses herself as reenacts cabaret routines with names familiar to Parisian audiences, such as habanera and seguidilla (McClary 1992, 57). The Act II stage set representing Lillas Pastia's inn with Carmen's performance of "Gypsy Song" offers an apt example of Carmen as a cabaret performer. Here, though, through harp, viola, and pizzicato cello accompaniment, the composer mimics the flamenco guitar accompaniment to the dances.

"Gypsy Song" bears still other stereotypical conceptions of Gypsy music, including the quickened tempo associated with the czardas, a Hungarian form virtually interchangeable with the idea of Gypsy music among nineteenth-century connoisseurs. Flutes (and later oboes, clarinets, and bassoons) drive the melody into obsessively repeated motifs, played with increasing speed, suggesting the whirl of a dance. Despite echoes of the czardas, Bizet maintains the 3/4 meter typically associated with Spanish folk music, as opposed to the 2/4 time of the czardas. But the "Gypsy Song" devolves into an orgy of song, dance, and utterances, joined by flashy costume, suggesting a common stereotype of Gypsy entertainment.

Certain stagings of *Carmen* also include the "Gypsy Dance" from Bizet's earlier opera *The Fair Maid of Perth*. In the final act, set in the Seville square, the "Gypsy Dance" alternates with the "Farandola" and "Pastorale" from the earlier *L'Arlésienne,* a medley aimed at marking the location's authenticity. The instruments in "Gypsy Dance," especially the Basque drum, suggest the fragment's national Spanish character. The increasing tempo toward the end presents an almost universal stereotype of Gypsy dancing, while the 6/8 meter establishes the reference to Spanish dance.

Alongside melody and dance, as recent examples suggest, instruments are employed in *Carmen* in various ways to indicate Spanishness connected with Gypsy color. One common nineteenth-century trick, hinted at before, was the use of pizzicato for violas and cellos to mimic the guitar and evoke Gypsy Spain. When Carmen sings for Don José in Act II, this use of pizzicato is accompanied by the also quintessentially Spanish castanets (Czapliński 2003, 28). On this count, castanets as a mere stage prop pointed to Spanish entertainment, dance, and song. Castanets also accompany Carmen and her friends Frasquita and Mercedes in Act II, indicating their carefree mien and that of Gypsies generally. In Act III, a violin solo in the fortune-telling scene calls up the widely recognized nineteenth-century image of the wandering Gypsy fiddler, even if this image did not apply to the Gypsies of Spain.

Repercussions of a Racial Dimension

Carmen's popularity very quickly translated into increased interest in Gyp-syness as reflected in Spanish music. In 1883, for example, Sarasate based his *La fantasía Carmen* (op. 25) on fragments from the opera combined with Gypsy elements, resulting in its assessment as abundant with "tunes in the flashy gypsy violin style" (McClary 1992, 121). Early film renditions of *Carmen* would also adopt the opera's Gypsy motifs, such as the silent 1908 movie *Love Tragedy in Spain* and, two years later, *Carmen*.

Sound entered these cinematographic efforts in 1931, with the film titled *Gypsy Blood*. (A silent film version of *Carmen* bearing the same name, produced by Ernst Lubitsch and starring Pola Negri, had appeared in 1918.) The question of ethnicity was underlined by two subsequent screen productions: an American version in 1954 and a Spanish one in 1984.

In the United States, Otto Preminger boldly brought *Carmen* to Broadway in the 1940s and later to the silver screen. The film version was named *Carmen Jones* (1954), and it used Bizet's music and motifs to examine the marginalized status and stereotyping suffered by black Americans. Thus was the Gypsy mar-ginalization in Europe transported to the New World. The film's lead role was played by Dorothy Dandridge, who seduced the simple World War II soldier played by Harry Belafonte and would go on to become the first black American to be nominated for an Academy Award. In Preminger's interpretation, Bizet's opera was a "black musical," in which blackness marked not only the heroes' skin color but also signaled felony, criminality, the seediness of night clubs, and threats associated with the urban agglomeration that was Chicago. The resulting message was so powerful that many white viewers protested what they saw as the sugges-tion of "a mighty Negro state" where whites had little say (Waldorff 1959, 4–5).

Amid the multilayered references suggested by Preminger's work was an indirect tie between black slavery in America and the Gypsies' experience of slavery in Europe. The last vestiges of slavery were only eradicated in Europe in 1856, when Moldavia banned the practice, less than a decade before the United States would do the same for blacks with the Thirteenth Amendment to the Constitution (Fraser 2005, 59).

Subsequent screenings of Bizet's opera confirmed the force of its subject mat-ter. Carlos Saura's *Carmen* of 1984 was part of the director's so-called flamenco trilogy, along with *Bodas de sangre* (Blood Wedding) and *El amor brujo* (Wedded by Witchcraft). Although not a film version of Bizet's opera, the story—loosely based on Mérimée's—used Bizet's music as embellished by the well-known twentieth-century flamenco guitarist Paco de Lucia. As Alicja Helman writes, "This is still Bizet, [but] 'read' through flamenco" (Helman 2003, 565–72). The complicated phenomenon of flamenco permeates the film, as played out in the circles of flamenco dancers and the coexistence of Gypsy and non-Gypsy elements. The result is to show the authentic creators of flamenco as true An-dalusians, ennobled through references to Bizet's opera (McClary 1992, 137). In Saura's film, these individuals are both the creators and imitators of their own culture. By rejecting the mythologized conception of Spain, the director debunks Andalusian-Gypsy exoticism and locates Bizet's opera within "an easily identified iconography" (Helman 2003, 565) emerging from nineteenth-century associations and discourses.

From Idyll to Comedy: Stanisław Moniuszko's *Jawnuta* and *The Ideal* and Ludwik Grossman's *Duch wojewody*

The allure of the Gypsy theme is apparent even in works by composers who live in lands with small Gypsy populations. Polish operas of the nineteenth and early twentieth centuries, for instance, contained a host of Gypsy characters associated with both nearby Hungary and faraway Spain. As elsewhere, Gypsy protagonists in these operas were modeled after figures in novels and other writ-ten works. In rarer instances, such librettos sought to recreate realities actually pertinent in Polish territories.

In 1852, Stanisław Moniuszko (1819–1872) premiered *The Gypsies*, an opera based on a popular poem of the same title by Franciszek Dionizy Kniaźnin (1750–1807), in which the rural life takes on a realistic hue. This poem's popu-larity is seen to have derived from the contrast it provided against the period's artistically weak, seemingly unnatural comedies. More particularly, the poem is considered "a colorful and neat depiction of relations between the Polish rural scene and the world of exotic vagrants, stealing not only petty objects from peasant huts but also horses and children" (Krzyżanowski 1964, 529). Although the Gypsy-kidnapping motif is "conventional . . . [Kniaźnin's] application of the said brought with it much that was innovative, at times authentic, such as the slightly paraphrased folk songs, and the scenes of daily life (the chatter of the gossips, who do not want to allow the Gypsy *smaganiec* [referring here to a dance] to have its say) as equally the dialect used as a means of literary expression" (Krzyżanowski 1964, 465–66). The theme of lost-and-found children more generally also helped guide Kniaźnin's work to success (Jendrusik 1958, 43).

Composers prior to Moniuszko had set Kniaźnin's text directly to music, including Michał Kazimierz Ogiński (1728–1800) in 1786, with the Countess Izabela Czartoryska herself appearing as the Gypsy named Jawnuta, and Franciszek Mirecki (1791–1862) in 1822. As for Kniaźnin's work, it portrays a gamut of stereotypical Gypsy themes. One such theme is embodied in the love affair between the village head's son and the young Gypsy girl, who actually turns out to be the Gypsy-kidnapped child of peasants. This discovery, of course, sanctions the relationship and allows the couple to marry. In the plot, the old Gypsy woman Jawnuta plays the central role of having raised the stolen child. Her wisdom and ability to predict the future earn her the respect of Gypsies and peasants alike. So important was her role that the opera later ran under the title of her name.

Moniuszko incorporated no telltale allusions to Gypsy music in the opera. The score does contain typical Polish dances, such as the mazurka, and a Gypsy literary motif that signals the allegro 2/4 "Gypsy Dance," which also uses minor values through sixteenth notes, thirty-second notes, and sometimes eighth notes. Strings predominate in the "Gypsy Dance," which is accompanied by other instruments. A formal musical contrast also exists in the piece, as expressed in the shift in the strings from arco (fragment A) to pizzicato (fragment B), with these two techniques linked to the presence or absence of syncopation and the introduction of other rhythmic values.

This opera's projection of Gyspy themes on just the textual, and not the musical, level is reflected in an earlier opera by the composer, the two-act comedy *The Ideal*—with a libretto by Oskar Milewski—which premiered in Vilna in 1840. The plot centers on the alleged love of a dandy, Karol, for an unknown Gypsy girl (Preciosa or Esmeralda), a development that shatters Karol's father's matrimonial plans for his son. One point of comedy in the situation is the nobleman father's ignorance that the two names connected with the Gypsy girl have already been immortalized by Cervantes (Preciosa) and Hugo (Esmeralda). Intent on outwitting Karol, the father and the boy's tutor hatch a plot in which fake Gypsies (dressed-up servants) arrive at the manor to be greeted by Karol. Feeling his dreams have been realized, Karol finds among the group a purported beautiful Gypsy girl, who instantly enchants him. In reality, this girl is Emina, who had earlier pledged herself to Karol.

The arrival onstage of the false Gypsies, said to be from Andalusia, allows for the performance of additional songs and dances. In Act II, typical romantic motifs are enacted in a Gypsy camp, complete with carts picturesquely situated in a forest with a smoldering bonfire, with the dark night heightening the scene's mystery. Although conveying a romantic notion of Gypsyness while also mocking the idea of Gypsy love, *The Ideal* was attacked by the Vilna press for its nonsensical, "ridiculously . . . poor libretto" (Kydryński 1984, 378). Indeed, the work would not endure in its original form and would be rereleased, in the 1960s, with a new libretto.

After Moniuszko's time, another opera that touched on the Gypsy motif, although marginally, was Ludwik Grossman's (1835–1915) *Duch wojewody czyli u wód* (The Spirit of the Voivode; or, At the Waters) of 1873, with a libretto by Władysław Ludwik Anczyc (1823–1883). As with Grossman's other works, such as *The Fisherman from Palermo*, this work experienced "widespread audience popularity though failing to attract recognition on the part of critics and experts" (Fuks 1989, 89). Set in the later nineteenth century, at the baths of Galicia, the location near the Hungarian border suggests a Hungarian emphasis. Reinforcing this orientation is that the resort's owner, Lajos Fekete, is a Hungarian who enlists evening Gypsy entertainment in an effort to please his guests. A meeting between Poles and Hungarians at the start of Act II is accentuated by the performance of a czardas accompanied by the lyrics "Hey, Gypsy! What is this? Is your violin asleep?"

The Gypsies' czardas, in the opera, represents the Hungarian nation, even as Polish writing would evince ambivalence about this association well into the twentieth century. In 1953, the prominent Polish musicologist Józef M. Chomiński wrote that "the czardas is rather of Gypsy origin than being inherently Hungarian" (Chomiński 1954, 141). The popularity of the czardas from *Duch wojewody* deserves credit for perpetuating such opinions. And the czardas would exceed the fame of the opera itself, which, despite its skillfully written libretto and electrifying musical style, would not survive the test of time.

The Image of the Gypsy in Poland: Paderewski's *Manru*

The Literary Prototype

In 1901, Ignacy Jan Paderewski (1860–1941) finished his only three-act opera, *Manru*. The work was, in fact, the first Polish musical drama, and the composer had labored on it for more than two years (Paderewski 1984, 348). On a personal level, the opera offered an outlet for Paderewski following the death of his only son, Alfred, at age twenty-one. He considered the performance deadline linked with the work's commissioning from the Dresden Theater a blessing for this reason (Paderewski 1984, 376–77). The May 29, 1901, premiere in Dresden, conducted by Ernest Schuch, was a great success (Opieński 1960, 61). Performances followed across Europe, in Lvov, Cracow, and Warsaw, as well as Cologne, Bonn, Prague, and Zurich.

Paderewski's opera was based on one of Józef Ignacy Kraszewski's (1812–1887) brief "folk novels," *Chata za wsią* (The Cottage beyond the Village)—the others being *Ulana* (1843), *Ostap Bondarczuk* (1847), and *Jermoła* (1857). *Chata za wsią* was published in four installments over 1853–1854 in the quarterly *Biblioteka Warszawska,* and each installment earned acclaim from readers, encouraging the author to keep writing. The book would subsequently appear in numerous editions, including three during the writer's lifetime, the first being in Saint Petersburg in 1854–1855. The book would be translated into Czech, French, Russian, German, and Slovenian, and stage adaptations would include that by Gabriela Zapolska in Lvov in 1884.

Other musical works basing themselves on *Chata za wsią* included the five-act opera by Zygmunt Noskowski, with a libretto by Zofia Mellerowa and Jan Galasiewicz, titled *Chata za wsią* (1884) and later renamed *Dziewczę z chaty za wsią* (The Maiden from the Cottage beyond the Village) (1886). An opera by Władysław Żeleński (1837–1921) would also use the novel's title.

In *Chata za wsią,* Kraszewski sought "to become acquainted with [Gypsy] culture, to imitate the differences through linguistic stylistics, describe the customs, difficulties and conditions of life" (Burkot, 2006, 15). At the same time, the author opposed "extremely mimetic aesthetics," and he did not allow himself "excessive fantasizing" (Olszewska 2004, 201). Kraszewski would draw his basic information on Gypsies within Polish territories from his own research but, even more so, from the ethnographic publications of the day, including the studies of Kazimierz Władysław Wójcicki (Bednorz 1997, 17). Among the writer's visual sketches housed at the Jagiellonian Library in Cracow, dating from about 1834 to 1837, can be found a quite reverential portrait of a Gypsy "with somewhat slanty eyes, broad lips and a bloated face." The small mouth and eyes give the drawing a universal, rather than narrowly ethnic, appeal (Górecka 2004, 228–29). Kraszewski was also known for his linguistic talents, having mastered French, German, Latin, Italian, English, Russian, and Belorussian, among other languages, and he was likewise interested in the language spoken by the Gypsies (Bachórz, 2004, 13). Consequently, he infused *Chata za wsią* with a limited selection of Gypsy phrases, basing these on publications available to him (Klich 1931).

Even though *Chata za wsią* may possibly constitute the first "serious attempt on Polish soil to break the false stereotype of the Gypsy" (Bednorz 1997, 18), the writer seems to have perpetuated these very stereotypes through a kind of amplified sensitivity to Gypsy representations. Just as does Hugo's novel about the beautiful Esmeralda and the bell ringer Quasimodo, Kraszewski's work brims with an almost sickening sentimentality and melodrama, while the rather trivial plot deals in contrasts associated with lyricism and threat.

The novel's emotional layer is reflected in a nineteenth-century tendency wherein artists did not strive "to recreate the absolute truth about life" but instead touched on the canon of prejudices and stereotypes connected with Gypsies (Olszewska 2004, 201). Kraszewski sought to achieve a sort of balance in portraying Gypsies, probing both their distinguishing characteristics and the widespread dislike of them and their corresponding social ostracism. In Kraszewski's view, Gyspies should not be portrayed as ethnically monolithic but rather in the light of individual heroes and antiheroes alike. The Polish characters are treated with a similar attention to variability. In this discussion, the author finally presents dichotomies associated with the Gypsy and non-Gypsy worlds—sin (evil) versus conscience, social dictates versus their transgression—as being subordinated to the laws of nature.

Yet, in the novel, the characters fall into a schematic that includes "stereotypes at various levels of textual architectonics" (Olszewska 2004, 200). Such treatments include references to Gypsies' exotic origins and heavy emphasis on Gypsy women's beauty. The libretto to *Manru* incorporates similar elements, reflecting common European modes of looking at Gypsies.

The lens of the exotic even influenced early performers of Paderewski's work. A telling note appears in the composer's diary reporting on the dress rehearsal of a performance at the New York Metropolitan Opera. He wrote that the American baritone David Bispham (1857–1921), set to play the role of the villager Urok, arrived dressed like "a boy in rags, and as if that wasn't enough, wearing a Turkish fez!" (Paderewski 1984, 384). Paderewski, for his part, had interpreted the character as something far different from the caricature Bispham presented. In his diaries, he described the Gypsy Urok as a village wizard and a Polish peasant. This portrayal set Urok both within (Polish) national parameters and, as a wizard, tied him to supernatural powers and forces.

Elements of Gypsyness

Alfred Nossig (1864–1943), Paderewski's librettist for *Manru*, was a polymath, having studied law, economics, and philosophy, among other subjects, in Lvov and Zurich. He was also a self-taught sculptor, and, as the son of the secretary of Lvov's Jewish community, he was aware of struggles faced by the

Jewish community and eventually became an enthusiast for the idea of a Jewish state. As a contributor to *Manru*, Nossig helped propose the interweaving of Gypsy and Polish highland themes, as had already appeared in the opera *Syreni gród* (Mermaids' Town) (Kozubek 2001, 15–16). The commissioning of the work by the Dresden Theater also spurred the inclusion of a German libretto, among other elements. Modifications to the original literary model included name changes—Motruna to Ulana, Tumry to Manru, Janek to Urok, and so on—and the move from the Podolia region to the mountains allowed for highland dances at the end of Act I (Raba 2010, 145–52). The conflicting worldviews meanwhile are represented by Ulana—the beautiful highland girl seeking happiness beside her beloved husband, Manru—and the Gypsy, who tires of sedate family life and his day job at the forge. All this allows for a presentation of both highland folklore and the Gypsy way of life.

The heroine Ulana, whose name is taken from Kraszewski's novel of the same title, is a simple country girl enamored of Manru. After she moves in with her lover, a child is born, but Manru eventually overcomes internal resistance and abandons Ulana, who herself has been damned by her family for taking up with a Gypsy. Although initially in love with the mother of his child, Manru is ultimately lured away by the Gypsy way of life, with its songs and dance and imperative of absolute freedom. Manru, in turn, falls for the beautiful Gypsy girl Asa. Spurned and alone, Ulana commits suicide. Yet her faithful friend, the village idiot, who is versed in spells and herbal medicine, honors a pledge he had once made to Ulana that she would always remain with her husband and pushes Manru into a mountain chasm.

Despite the numerous changes to the libretto as compared to the literary original—including the accentuation of secondary characters and the ousting and introduction of others—Paderewski's musical drama reflects the spirit of Gypsy and Polish roles presented in Kraszewski's book. One difference is that in *Chata za wsią*, Kraszewski's hero, completely rejected by village society, never works, while in the opera Manru is a smith—a common trade for Gypsies. Yet sustained from the novel are themes of Gypsies' exotic beauty and their links with nature, manifested by mountains, forests, and the remote locations for Gypsy camps. Romantic conceptions of Gypsies as semibarbarians are therefore propagated. The motif of unhappy, and ultimately tragic, love tinged with violence also advances stereotypes. Such themes explain why Paderewski's *Manru* drew comparisons to Bizet's *Carmen*. But Paderewski's work emerged in a vastly different political context from Bizet's, with the Poles still lacking an independent state at its 1901 premiere. The concepts of isolation and liberty from the shackles of civilization, in the opera ascribed to Gypsies, take on a changed significance when viewed in the light of the Polish struggle for sovereignty.

As opposed to some other Polish composers who addressed Gypsy themes, Paderewski used musical, as well as textual, devices often associated with nineteenth-century Gypsy music. These included dances and instruments—such as tambourine (Spanish) and violin (Central European)—but also the use of the augmented second interval to signal the appearance or mention of Gypsy characters. Vocal scores assigned to Gypsy characters also contained irregular rhythms. Paderewski's knowledge of such gestures may have been culled either from his own experience or from texts on Gypsy music, such as Liszt's *Des Bohémiens et de leur musique en Hongrie*, which he was known to possess in Lina Ramann's German 1883 translation (*Die Zigeuner und Ihre Musik in Ungarn*). Doubts about his knowledge of this text arise, however, on seeing that the pages from the copy in Paderewski's private library, stored at a division of Cracow's Jagiellonian University, were never even cut. (While assembling materials for this book in 2008, I myself could see that no one before me had made use of this text.)

Paderewski's opera promoted the commonly held idea of Gypsies as a musical people. This notion adhered in late nineteenth-century Poland particularly in the appearance of violinists in published collections of fairy tales (Zieliński 1896, 117–18). Accordingly, in Act II of *Manru*, the figure of the old violin-playing Gypsy Jagu is introduced, and he performs solo onstage, generating profound emotion. Overall in the drama, Jagu embodies "Gypsy musicality and its artistic soul" (Kozubek 2001, 38).

The musical associations with Gypsies are further underlined in the stage directions: at the beginning of Act III when the Gypsies appear onstage (performing a choral number), the text reads, "From mountain paths groups of Gypsies descend approaching from various sides, and in each of these can be seen musicians, chiefly fiddlers and bassists, colorful costumes" (Paderewski 1901, 89).

The trope of erotic dancing by Gypsy women also appears in Paderewski's drama. Here, the structure of the drama is notable, with group scenes (and dances) predominating in Acts I and III and more individual scenes prevailing in the middle act. Within this structure, Polish highlander dances appear in the first act whereas Gypsy dances occur in Act III, the second scene of which includes Asa's seductive dance, joined by men—with the tambourine she holds (a detail included in the score) attesting to her Gypsy origins. Ties between Asa's dance and the Hungarian czardas appear, among other details, in the use of the minor key and 2/4 meter.

Minor keys are used generally (C and F minor in particular) in scenes with Gypsy heroes, in keeping with the plaintive, melancholy associations with Gypsy music. As we have seen, Paderewski also applied the augmented second, between the third and augmented fourth degree (in C minor: E flat and F sharp) and the sixth and augmented seventh (A flat and B); such techniques appear, for example, in "Asa's Dance" in Act III. Even an oboe solo (G minor) in the opera's opening scene employs the augmented second, from E flat to F sharp, appropriating a motif introduced by the strings and important throughout Act I. The composer's use of the augmented second and variants brought the opera's melodic lines closer to the so-called Gypsy scale, thereby propagating the stereotypical vision of musical exoticism.

Other musical fragments tied to Gypsy characters are marked with the Gypsy quality of improvisation. To create the impression of spontaneity, the composer wrote orchestra parts that repeat sound cells in quick succession, often based on the principle of montage. "Asa's Dance" employs, on the one hand, augmented seconds and, on the other, a four-note motif with a characteristic rhythm composed of a dotted eighth and sixteenth notes. The juxtaposition of these motifs, repeated within a given section without any melodic or rhythmic changes, establishes their preeminence.

Gypsy-associated improvisation, in the nineteenth and early twentieth centuries, was also tied to ornamentation. Consequently, in the Act II arioso by Manru, Paderewski introduced, in both the vocal and orchestral lines, numerous grace notes, other ornaments, and an unusually minute division of values, performed directly before the lengthier value divisions, thus enhancing the melodic line and suggesting its spontaneous character.

One could claim that rhythmic irregularity constitutes the essence of the Gypsy musical picture in *Manru*. The unconventional division of values is manifested in triplets, quintuplets, and sextuplets and, even more frequently, in eighths and sixteenths. Paderewski also juxtaposed regular and irregular value divisions within the space of a single bar, creating the impression of rhythmic spontaneity. In the Gypsy fragments, he also used syncopation. The sense of improvisation is further established through rubato, with the tempo speeding up and slowing down in seemingly unstable ways. Likewise, the tempo is often intensified over very brief periods, giving the feeling of variability often associated with Gypsy exoticism.

Commentary on Paderewski's opera showed awareness of its Gypsy components. As early as 1907, Zdzisław Jachimecki, in his *Muzyka w Polsce* (Music in Poland), questioned the authenticity of the main Gypsy character's singing

(Jachimecki 1907). Much later, Lidia Kozubek would affirm Paderewski's knowledge of Gypsy music (although without citing the composer's sources), writing that "what he derived from authentic models is beyond any doubt whatsoever" (Kozubek 2001, 71). Offering clarification (and perhaps contradiction), she announces that "in the third act the Gypsy music is also typical yet inauthentic" (Kozubek 2001, 79). In particular, Kozubek cites three musical components—rhythmic, melodic, and tonal—in discussing the opera's Gypsy treatments. Her language, however, remains enigmatic in formulations such as "figures of Gypsy rhythm," "rhythmic motifs of a Gypsy character," "scored Gypsy rhythms," "Gypsy motifs," and "a descending Gypsy scale." Each of these components may well have been pivotal in guiding both Paderewski's compositional techniques and Kozubek's approach as a theorist. Whatever the details of this interaction, *Manru* constitutes another example within late nineteenth-century European culture of a nexus between the discourse on Gypsies and Gypsy music and musical attempts to popularize a certain image of Gypsyness.

The National Element: Manuel de Falla's *La Vida Breve*

The Work's Origin

In 1904, the Academy of Fine Arts in Madrid announced a competition for best dramatic work by a Spanish composer. The next year, Manuel de Falla won the competition with an opera, with a libretto by Carlos Fernández-Shaw, titled *La vida breve* (Life Is Short). But the opera would not be staged for another several years, and this staging was only spurred by de Falla's other compositional successes, largely achieved abroad. Only after its 1913 premiere in Nice would appreciation for the work take hold in Spain. Later, the opera was performed in Paris, with a French adaptation of the libretto by Paul Milliet.

From the start, critics from Spain and abroad recognized the opera's Spanish character. Edgar Istel, for example, pointed to the predominance of "local color" in the libretto, and its particular aim of showing the beauty of Andalusia (Istel 1929, 505). In both the music and the libretto, Istel noted the accentuation of Gypsy culture.

As for its plot, the two-act opera told a rather simple tale of love and betrayal, opening up the libretto to charges of containing weak and conventional subject matter (Weber 2000, 154). The story line has much in common with Bizet's *Carmen*: set in Spain, the action centers on the Gypsy connotations of the central hero, a woman. Whereas in Bizet's opera Carmen is the driver of misfortune, de Falla's Salud ends up the victim of her own longings. Yet, symptomatically, in both works the women ultimately die rather than the men.

The protagonists of Bizet's and de Falla's operas are different in other ways. While the fiery Gypsy Carmen embodies a full-bodied Spanishness (Pahlen 1953, 104), Salud is seen as an ordinary Spanish girl living in Albaicín, the Gypsy part of Granada. As it happened, "ordinary Spanish (or Andalusian) girl" was often morphed by commentators into "simple Gypsy girl" (Mayer-Serra 1943, 3; Istel 1929, 505).

The plot details reinforce associations of Salud with Gypsy culture (Hess 2001, 530). In the unfolding action, Salud is in love with the young Spaniard Paco, who despite vowing to love her marries another woman from his social class—"a maiden of his own race" (Istel 1929, 505). The betrayed Salud, supported by an uncle, Salvadore, and grandmother, appears at her lover's wedding. The assembled guests take the arrival of the group to signal the start of the festivities, given the association of Gypsies with song and dance. But Salud exposes the unfaithful Paco, her relatives call him a Judas, and she dies at his feet.

This love-induced death is a motif deeply rooted in Gypsy flamenco, as is the related theme of the death of a young person in the name of love, a theme indirectly linked within flamenco to the torment and death of Christ. The content also "evokes the mythic sacrifice of a young god, whose blood brings hope for renewal" (Stanton 1974, 96). The stage works of de Falla, as well as Lorca's poetry, would incorporate this powerful motif in reference to flamenco. Likewise, the intertwining of love and death seems to have provided de Falla an entry point for addressing the art and folklore of the Spanish Gypsies.

La Vida Breve as a National Opera

From its premiere up until today, *La vida breve* has been considered in the context of national opera (Weber 2000, 154, 178). Musicologists have therefore interpreted the inclusion of Gypsy material as part of an attempt to create a Spanish national opera. In 1917, to this effect, the influential French critic Georges Jean-Aubry cited the melodic material in *La vida breve* as being of Andalusian origin. He warned, however, that neither the rhythms nor the scales nor the cadences and forms were borrowed from folk music but rather simply were inspired by the music of Andalusia (Jean-Aubry 1917, 153). In 1922, an unknown author affirmed this view, writing that "Manuel de Falla does not resort to actual quotations of folk music save in rare cases where such a process is fully justified" (no author 1922, 6–7). Clyne, writing four years later, however, called de Falla's work a "folk-song opera" (Clyne 1926, 268). Manuel García Matos, writing in the 1950s, disproved previous views by demonstrating close links between flamenco songs and the melodies in de Falla's opera (Matos 1953, 33–52). The scholar Carol A. Hess seems to see de Falla's goal as having gone beyond the simple reproduction of folk songs. The composer, she writes, "set himself the challenge of elevating traditional Gypsy music to the highest level of art while preserving its primordial essence" (Hess 2001, 533). De Falla, she continues, tried "to . . . unite art music with the spirit of traditional Gypsy music" (Hess 2001, 530).

The influence of Gypsy traditions on de Falla's work, with the composer himself described as Andalusian "to his core" (Corredor 1955, 225), appears in the three flamenco-associated elements of song (*cante*), dance (*baile*), and instrument playing (*toque*). In the broader historical scene, the influence of *cante jondo* on early twentieth-century Spanish operas drew attention from commentators (Manuel 1930, 24). Clyne saw this influence in *La vida breve* as "the foundation of a new architectonic style. . . ." (Clyne 1926, 268). According to one present-day commentator, the opera was the young composer's first attempt at "explorations of Gypsy *cante jondo*" (Hess 2001, 530). "In the vocal lines of the heroes of *La vida breve*," writes another, "the prosody of Andalusian speech is apparent" (Weber 2000, 154).

In particular, *cante jondo* elements may be found in the opera's frequent use of melismatics and irregular value divisions (e.g., quintuplets, sextuplets) and, most important, in performance suggestions that allow artists considerable freedom (e.g., ad libitum). In Act I, the melodies sung by workers at the smithy evoke the typical *debla* flamenco form. Choral singing addressing toil and the cruelty of fate (the latter in a tenor solo) introduces a melodic motif that is subsequently taken up by Salud. Act II is rich in musical links to *cante jondo* as well: in the first scene, assembled guests exclaim *olé!* when the singer at the reception of Paco and his betrothed, Carmela, expresses his wish to perform a typical flamenco form called *soleara*. Some scholars see the succeeding musical material as deriving from the original *soleá gitana* (Weber 2000, 162–63).

De Falla also used the minor third interval abundantly throughout the opera. In the 1920s, Istel drew attention to this interval in the opera's most prominent motif, which appears, in somewhat varied forms and with modified texts, in Acts I and II (Istel, 1929, 505). This minor third, interestingly, is the enharmonic equal to the augmented second so closely associated with Gypsy music.

Gypsy dances appear most notably in Act II, in which the action focuses on the wedding reception. At the act's outset, dance rhythms resound, accompanied by typical flamenco instruments (castanets and guitar), while in the second scene young guitarists appear onstage. The lively dance is performed in a typical flamenco 3/8 meter with typical rhythmic formulas: one eighth note, three sixteenth-note triplets, and an eighth note. Some scholars also contend that these meters and rhythms were accompanied by an authentic folk melody (Pahlen 1953, 108).

The use of the guitar in particular highlighted the flamenco innovativeness of de Falla's work, deviating from typical opera instrumentation and, thus, sound quality. The guitar sound is especially strongly felt in the dances, and the technique is based on the rather simple *rasgueado*, characteristic of the earlier phase of flamenco *toque* development (Christoforidis 1999, 262–63).

De Falla's opera has been seen by critics to achieve a certain realism in portraying Gypsy themes, even as its characters lack psychological depth (Weber 2000, 178). Some commentators have ventured further that *La vida breve*, owing to its harmonies and elaborate instrumentation, also contains influences of French impressionism (Pahlen 1953, 104). Istel, for example, wrote of de Falla's earlier works employing Spanish folk music, as quoted earlier, through "French spectacles and heard with French ears" (Istel, 1929, 504). And Mayer-Serra viewed the composer's inclinations regarding regional music as having the stylistic trappings of French lyrical opera (Mayer-Serra 1943, 3). Early twentieth-century critics also pointed to the exotic connotations of de Falla's opera, with Clyne saying it was "full of passionate Oriental melancholy" (Clyne 1926, 268) while Roland Manuel, in 1930, linked the concepts of the Orient, Islam, and Andalusia with *cante jondo* and *toque jondo* (Manuel 1930, 37). Present-day scholars have also grappled with questions surrounding the local color in *La vida breve* (Weber 2000, 178).

These hybrid elements of de Falla's opera, falling under the banner of Spanishness, along with its brevity and staging difficulties, limited the work's popularity. All the same, *La vida breve* represents a valid contribution in the Spanish search for a national musical idiom. By the 1920s, de Falla's influence was already considered to issue from "a combination of nationality and personality," which resulted in music of "a complex character" (no author 1922, 5). Needless to say, the Gypsy elements in de Falla's operas, ballets, and purely instrumental works figured largely in his attempts to construct a Spanish national idiom.

CHAPTER SIX

Gypsy Themes in Operettas and Vaudevilles

The Role of Johann Strauss

Interest in Gypsyness

Johann Strauss II (1825–1899), the master of the waltz and the Viennese operetta, also helped contribute to stereotypes of the Gypsy and Gypsy music within European culture.

In Act II of his most popular operetta, *Die Fledermaus* (The Bat), of 1874, the composer introduced a czardas, performed by Rosalinda, pretending to be a Hungarian princess, with the performance serving to substantiate her Hungarian roots. Yet the czardas possesses all the traits associated with Gypsy music, including a two-part construction, consisting of a slow (*lassan*) part and a fast (*friska*) part. The solo clarinet part is marked by ad libitum, allowing for a controlled freedom of performance connected with Gypsy improvisation. Pizzicato in the strings, meanwhile, suggests Gypsy (flamenco) guitar. The piece is also played in the Gypsy-associated minor key, with insertions of the augmented second interval.

The melding of Gypsy and Hungarian music was widespread among nineteenth-century European composers. Indeed, in 1877, for the performance of *Die Fledermaus* at the Theatre de la Renaissance in Paris, the piece would be renamed *La Tzigane* (The Gypsy) (Traubner 2003, 118).

In the 1885 operetta *The Gypsy Baron* (*Der Zigeunerbaron*), Strauss's crowning work along with *Die Fledermaus*, the title also suggests the contents, which include Hungarian-Gypsy as well as Austrian cultural allusions. The 1883 novella "Saffi," by the Hungarian author Mór Jókai (1825–1904), formed the basis for the libretto; Strauss learned of this work in Pest in February 1883 through his third wife, Adela Deutsch, a few months before its publication. As for the plot, it contains the familiar-feeling elements of a non-Gypsy girl who grows up in a Gypsy camp, adopts the Gypsy culture's values, and falls in love with one of its apparent members. Strauss, who for the past few years had wanted to compose an operetta covering Hungarian material, was intrigued.

The novella's author, Jókai, was among the most valued Hungarian romantic writers and was perceived as a great patriot—a participant in the struggles of 1848–1849 and a friend of the Hungarian poet and revolutionary Sándor Petőfi. Although Jókai did not personally contribute to Strauss's libretto, he recommend a true-born Hungarian, the writer and journalist Ignaz Schnitzer (1839–1921), even if the latter was permanently domiciled in Vienna, significantly easing the collaborative process. The close work between Schnitzer and Strauss lasted two years, from 1883 to 1885, moving from the creation of a vision to agreement on the minutest details. Their efforts were aided actively by the then director of the Theater an der Wien, Franz Jauner (1831–1900). The lengthy period of work was Strauss's intention, aimed at creating an opera *buffa* (comic opera). In comparison with his earlier operettas, which gave much space to dialogue and dance—including, for example, *Indigo* (1871), *Der Kerneval in Rom* (1873), *Die Fledermaus* (1873), *Cagliostro in Wien* (1875), *Der lustige Krieg* (1880), and *Eine Nacht in Venedig* (1883)—musical material predominated in *The Gypsy Baron*. The traditionally elaborate end to Act I was accompanied here by an equally momentous end to Act II, along with a dramatic twist. The courage and risk in such a strategy lay in the typical need, in a three-part work, to make all the themes and narrative threads coalesce by the close of Act II in anticipation of a happy ending in Act III. Early critics, recognizing the work as a comic opera, noticed this innovation at both the formal and libretto levels (Kydryński 1985, 232). Even the severe Eduard Hanslick praised Strauss on the pages of the *Neue Freie Presse* for attempting to create grander, increasingly complicated forms (Crittenden 2000, 207).

The Gypsy Baron's premiere on October 24, 1885, at the Theater an der Wien was a huge success, and the work has been performed continuously ever since, in European theaters and those throughout the world (Traubner 2003, 129).

The National Perspective in *The Gypsy Baron*

The Gypsy Baron is inscribed with the specific political situation of the late nineteenth-century Habsburg monarchy. The work's political connotations, often emphasized elsewhere (Klotz 2004, 39), would have been impossible for audiences to ignore, given the 1867 compromise between Austria and Hungary, which—through the so-called Ausgleich—decentralized the monarchy in favor of a dualistic model granting equal political and economic rights to Austria and Hungary. The political fusion had been encouraged equally at the artistic level, and Strauss's operetta was seen through the lens of "enthusiastic Hungarian participation in imperial politics" (Crittenden 2000, 175).

For Hungary, which was more agrarian as compared with the more industrialized Austria, the 1867 accord was an economic boon, with Budapest—formed with the 1873 merging of Buda, Pest, and Óbuda—reaping much of the benefit. In Viennese circles, increased interest in Hungarian culture and folklore followed these economic developments, with Strauss's work representing an artistic attempt to portray the ideal harmony enjoyed by the two halves of the empire, Austrian and Hungarian. From this shared nationalist perspective, Joseph Wechsberg defines *The Gypsy Baron* as "the musical miniature of the dual Austro-Hungarian monarchy" (Wechsberg 1999, 169). This image of cooperation was furthered symbolically by the cooperation between the Austrian composer and the Hungarian librettist, who formed their own personal union.

For all the rhetoric about union, Strauss's operetta was deeply rooted in the Viennese tradition and designed for a Viennese audience, whose expectations, tastes, and imagination all figured in its creation. Also, whatever the advances in Budapest, Vienna remained the empire's cultural and social reference point— and its ideal (Bobrownicka 1995, 14). In the contemporary Viennese perspective, Hungarians were valued for their independent and rebellious character and the nation was endowed with a special respect. In this context, Strauss's operetta portrayed Hungarian Gypsies in an unusually positive light—as courageous hussars who helped form the nation and not as social pariahs (Klotz 2004, 39). The premiere of *The Gypsy Baron* was therefore contrived as a "patriotic spectacle" (Kydryński 1985, 229). Yet even as the work portrayed Hungary and its subjects flatteringly, the subject matter was employed chiefly as a pretext for propagating Austrian ideas. Decades after its premiere, a writer in the journal *Das Vaterland* observed characteristically, on December 27, 1910, "On account of the text, but even more on account of the music, it is a national, patriotic, a true Austrian and Viennese work of classical character" (Crittenden 2000, 170).

Hungarian Connotations

On the day after *The Gypsy Baron*'s premiere, a review in *Fremdenblatt* classified the work as a Hungarian national opera. Given that Hungarian cultural material was considered ideal for the Vienna stage, a question posed nearly a hundred years later by the Polish music popularizer Lucjan Kydryński seems apt. He asked "how it happened that nobody earlier had hit on the idea of basing an operetta on a Hungarian motif," particularly given the attractiveness of Hungarian culture in the eyes of the Viennese. "Hungarian music, violins, dulcimers, wistful romances full of the temperament of the czardas . . . that all spoke to the Viennese imagination. . . ." (Kydryński 1985, 222). Use of romantic Hungarian cultural material also served important political ends in Vienna, given that "Hungary was admittedly always the most troublesome, rebellious and quarrelsome yet the most loved child of the Austro-Hungarian monarchy. . . . [T]he Viennese always stood on the side of 'goulash and paprika,' admired the splendid colourful uniforms of the Hungarian hussars seen on the streets of Vienna, admired the fantasy and jollity of the Hungarian gentry, who would arrive . . . in order to have a most decent time of it" (Kydryński 1985, 222).

Kydryński's question may be elaborated in the very multiethnicity that was Austria-Hungary. Within the territory of the Crown of St. Stephen (Hungary) lived, besides the Hungarians, Romanians, Germans, Slovaks, Serbs, Croats, Ruthenians, and others, including Jews and Romanies (Gergely and Szász 1978, 111). More generally, in the late nineteenth century "the matter of nationality was to be of a leading significance for the history of the region of Central-Eastern Europe," while "ethnic policy in Hungary (with its nationalism and sometimes chauvinism) to a significant degree was conditioned by the need to maintain the social relations in force in an unchanged form" (Kopyś 2001, 129). This sociopolitical context helped shape Strauss's work, which "presents a seductive argument for Austrian hegemony under the Habsburg crown"; its chief ideological aim would be expressed in the presentation of "Hungarian cultural symbols within the framework of protective Austrian hegemony" (Crittenden 2000, 170–73). In this model, Gypsies illustrate the color in—and also help create—Hungarian culture.

The discussion of Hungarian nationality is expressed in a common dramatic convention involving confusion over whether the two heroes, Saffi and Sándor Barinkay, are of Hungarian or Gypsy identity. Although Saffi presents herself as a Gypsy girl, this is far from the truth; indeed, she is later revealed to be the daughter of a Turkish pasha. Likewise, the Hungarian Barinkay is proclaimed a Gypsy baron, even though he is not a Gypsy. Even later commentators on the opera have remained confused over the identities of these characters. Crittenden, for example, describes Barinkay as a Gypsy in her analysis of the operetta's cultural-ethnic themes (Crittenden 2000, 181–82). This same author, in noting the composer's meticulous musical techniques to evoke conventionalized

Gypsyness—such as pizzicato in the strings, oboe against the backdrop of arco strings, and the extensive use of the clarinet—classifies these modes as specific to Gypsy exoticism while simultaneously hinting at "the Hungarian combination of pizzicato strings and clarinet. . . ." (Crittenden 2000, 191). This ambivalence results, as implied thus far, from Gypsies' portrayal in the operetta as integral to Hungarian culture.

Supposed Gypsy "color" would offer a pretext for presenting other ethnic figures within the Habsburg imperial mosaic, including a Jewish character playing Arsena's father. Even as this Jewish ethnicity is not spelled out in the libretto, Alexander Girardi (1850–1918), the first performer to play the role, began the tradition of portraying him this way. The Jew, like the Gypsies, was treated oversimplistically, with his expressiveness and too-explicit ethnic features reflecting the conventions of the day.

Such conventionalized portrayals of Gypsies—including their association with Hungarians—imbue the characterizations and, to a lesser extent, the music of *The Gypsy Baron*. Such treatments appear more specifically in the handling of the thematic Gypsy "pentalogue" of love, freedom, magic, nature, and evil.

The "Gypsyness" of *The Gypsy Baron*

The work's Gypsy connotations were underlined in its very first staging, including through a Gypsy village, "which was intensely realistic, with real horses, straw, even actual gypsy clothes" (Traubner 2003, 129). To create this painstakingly authentic tableau, the Vienna theater director traveled to the environs of Raab (Győr), in Hungary, where he actually purchased from Gypsies clothes for the production (Wechsberg 1999, 170). A real Gypsy cart also appeared onstage (Kydryński 1985, 229). These realist elements propagated Gypsy stereotypes, centering on "their nomadic lifestyle, their reputed intimacy with nature and the spiritual world, their physical appearance (dark complexion, wild manner, bright dress), and their musical talent" (Crittenden 2000, 176).

The colorful crowd of Gypsies presented in *The Gypsy Baron* continues a tradition within operettas cultivated by Jacques Offenbach of introducing a group hero representing a distant, mysterious world; in Offenbach, such a role was filled by non-Gypsy vagabonds, bandits, and smugglers (Klotz 2004, 45). In Strauss's work, two female figures stand out against this collective characterization. One is Czipra, a wise, old Gypsy woman respected by Gypsies and non-Gypsies alike. In real Gypsy groups, such a figure enjoyed authority second only to the group leader (Ficowski 1953,15). Czipra, inhabiting this role, can read cards and tell fortunes. Mysterious powers influence her prophetic visions, which have an impact on the narrative's heroes, including by leading to the discovery of trea-sure hidden in a castle's ruins. Czipra's authority also clears the way for genuine acceptance of Barinkay's leadership by the Gypsy community.

The second female figure, at the opposite pole, is the young Gypsy-raised Saffi. Without knowing her true identity, Saffi expresses ambivalence about Gypsies in the Act I song "So Wretched and So True," which, according to Crittenden, projects a necessary sentiment given the later change in the girl's fate (Crittenden 2000, 187). The song contains a host of stereotypes and superstitions connected with Gypsies: warnings of Gypsy love, which knows no rules or boundaries; accusations of Gypsy unfaithfulness; and warnings that children and horses should be guarded if in the vicinity of Gypsies. She sings, for example, "As soon as a Gypsy appears, when a Gypsy woman fans out the cards, boy lock up your horses, mother keep your child in sight, *tszing rah tszing rah*, this song the Gypsy knows, *tszing rah tszing rah*" (Strauss 1935, 5–6).

The motif of Gypsy love in Strauss's work is closely connected with the stereo-type of "looser moral or sexual codes" among Gypsies (Crittenden 2000, 182). Such portrayals of difference, according to Crittenden, allowed for a voyeuristic pleasure in observation as well as a perceived sense of moral superiority for audience members (Crittenden 2000, 187). This illusion was further facilitated by the juxtaposition of two romantic rendezvous: that of the non-Gypsy pair of Arsena and Ottokar and the "Gypsy" one of Saffi and Barinkay. The relative chastity of the former is represented in a stolen romantic evening, while the latter—despite their short acquaintance—succumb to their desires and, granted permission from the girl's Gypsy mother, spend a passionate night together. The strong connection of these latter heroes with the Gypsy camp sanctions their erotic behaviour. In the late nineteenth century, this particular union was perceived as so bold that the censor demanded that the "relation of the couple Barinkay-Saffi be not ... described in the text as 'a wild marriage' but by means of the term 'a forbidden unlawful marriage'" (Jaspert 1939, 193).

Another stereotype promulgated in the work, although indirectly, is that between Gypsies and raw nature. The tales spun by Barinkay, the Gypsy baron of the title, in the Act I song "Als flotter Geist," about his remote adventures as a trainer of wild animals, an acrobat, and a magician bring to mind the typical associations of Gypsies as dabblers in wandering performance troupes. As for the animal-training component, bear training among Gypsies in Lithuania had been mentioned as early as 1575 (Ficowski 1953, 76) and saw wide comment throughout the nineteenth century (Daniłowicz 1824, 42). The operetta alludes to other traditional Gypsy professions too, such as blacksmithing, as in the

Act II song "Ja, das Eisen wird gefüge," with these words referring to the iron (Czacki 1835, 59–86).

Innuendo provides further hints unto Gypsy themes, such as the references to Barinkay as a Gypsy baron, even though his true relationship to Gypsies is as the son of a landowner who had supported Gypsies by allowing them to camp on his land. Barinkay is therefore something more like a baron *of the* Gypsies. Even so, the young man's hegemony with respect to a group of Gypsies, combined with his aristocratic title, references a long-standing Gypsy tradition of assuming aristocratic titles. In Poland, a mere fifty years after the premier of *The Gypsy Baron,* there appeared a self-proclaimed leader of the Gypsies, Matejasz Kwiek, who gave himself the title of baron (Ficowski 1953, 66).

Interactions between Gypsies and non-Gypsies offer yet another arena for promoting stereotypes. In this sense, even as the operetta sought principally to emphasize the unity of Austrian and Hungarian interests (and, within these, those of the Gypsies), it also highlighted antagonisms between Gypsies and non-Gypsies. Toward the end of Act I, Barinkay, thrown out of the house by Arsena and her family, is derided as a Gypsy baron. In revenge, the young man acts to publicly humiliate Arsena by declaring his preference for the Gypsy girl Saffi over her. From the standpoint of Hungarian society, this act is an affront—and, in the drama, it leads to a violent exchange of views. Yet even had Barinkay preferred Arsena, the daughter of a rich swineherd, their marriage could not have gone forward given artistic conventions forbidding a "Gypsy baron" from wedding a non-Gypsy (Crittenden 2000, 187). Yet despite the initially unfavorable portrayal of the Gypsies in the drama, they eventually gain the audience's sympathy and are presented as a noble people who have found their place within the multiethnic monarchy.

Gypsy associations in the music were contrived quite consciously by Strauss, who was mindful of Viennese music connoisseurs' expectations of a contrast between Gypsy exoticism and Austrian culture. The quintessentially Viennese Strauss thus used Gypsy musical tropes against typical Viennese waltzes, with supposedly Gypsy melodies, in minor keys, exposed against a salon background. Operetta critics would subsequently agree regarding the dual nature of the music. Jaspert described *The Gypsy Baron* as "a happy synthesis of waltz with czardas, of Vienna with Budapest," although not delineating precisely the Hungarian component that was also Gypsy (Jaspert 1939, 191). Much more recently, Richard Traubner considered the operetta "a musical monument to the Austro-Hungarian Empire" (Traubner 2003, 111).

Strauss's musical characterizations of Gypsies corresponded basically to nineteenth-century conventions: Saffi's song from Act I bears similarities to "Habanera" from Bizet's *Carmen*, both in its subject matter and its placement within the opera. Another refrain appears, and is repeated in the Act I finale, based on the mysterious and meaningless words *tszing rah*, which are introduced because of their foreign-sounding, disturbing associations. Thus, they are not merely senseless or meaningless but instead play an important role in making the Gypsy hero exotic. Also noteworthy is the Act II Gypsy choir, whose singing and accompaniment—through content, minor key in the orchestral opener, instrumentation—reference the Gypsy choir from Giuseppe Verdi's opera *Il trovatore*, thereby showing a linkage in the nineteenth-century operatic tradition.

Strauss's achievement of musical exoticism in the Gypsy context came about more broadly through means associated with the "East." Besides instrumentation, he often introduced a free accentuation, chromaticism, an augmentation of the fourth and the diminishment of the second scale degrees, as well as rich ornamentation. Such techniques were embedded in the Western European norm, and the pseudo-Gypsy music that resulted was then enjoying notable popularity in Vienna, where residents had many opportunities to listen to the famous *Zigeunerkapellen*. These groups often performed their own repertoires at the same events as ensembles conducted by Strauss. In 1873, at a ball held by the Russian ambassador, the Gypsy orchestra of Jancsi Balogh Sági alternated with Strauss's (Crittenden 2000, 149).

A knowledge of the *Zigeunerkapellen* did not, however, prevent Strauss from copying baser conventions tied to Gypsy music. In attempting to evoke the Gypsy character in music, he used the conventionalized technique of delegating lengthy solos to clarinets (associated with "Gypsy clarinets") or oboes. Likewise, the work's "Overture" features a melody by the clarinet and then by the oboe. Listeners coming to experience exoticism expected just such instrumentation. According to Kydryński, these instruments sparked thoughts of Hungary and were enlisted to paint a picture of the "endless Hungarian plain" (Kydryński 1985, 230).

As mentioned earlier, Strauss also used pizzicato fragments in the strings to produce the effects of a guitar, which had by then become linked predominantly to Spanish Gypsies. This effect was paired with the operetta's Gypsy heroes, such as in Saffi's song from Act I, and also helped bring out the romantic aura of Gypsies as wanderers (Crittenden 2000, 177).

Minor modes also predominate in the parts reserved for Gypsy heroes. Saffi's song from Act I begins in D minor and only later changes to D major, and the melody line includes, for example, augmentation of the fourth and diminishment of the second interval. In this way, Strauss connects himself to the so-called Gypsy scale, expanding connotations of the augmented second with the exotic. Chromatics, as we have seen, also appear more readily in parts associated with Gypsies.

The Gypsies are also connected with rhythms maintained in an even meter, suggesting a connection with the *verbunkos* or the czardas—with the latter form signaling both Gypsy and Hungarian national traditions. In Act II, Strauss, on Jókai's suggestion, used a *verbunkos* (in "Homonay's Song") allegedly citing the authentic melody from a march from the Hungarian revolution of 1848–1849— at least according to the July 19, 1885, issue of *Fremdenblatt* (Crittenden 2000, 199, 292). To mark the work's seventy-fifth staging, Strauss, who was constantly perfecting the score, introduced to the Act II finale the melody of the *Rákóczi March* (Kydryński 1985, 233).

Rubato, moreover, is tied with Gypsy performance in the operetta, particularly with a slowing down of the tempo, while the 3/4 meter suggests a waltz and is thus connected with Austrians.

By reproducing stereotypes within the framework of *The Gypsy Baron*, Strauss undoubtedly strengthened the topos of the Gypsy and Gypsy music in European culture. The popularity of the operetta, which uniquely combined Gypsy, Hungarian, and Austrian elements, also emerged from an attempt to ensure its commercial—and financial—success. And this latter component would make it the target of severe judgments by later generations. Ernst Křenek, for example, wrote of the tricks used to tap nationalist sentiment and ensure critical acclaim:

> *The Gypsy Baron* represents an ill-advised step into a worse future; it is the beginning of the cultural scandal of later Viennese operetta which dominated the beginning of the 20th century. . . . Sentimentality reared its ugly head along with a distasteful folkloristic arrogance; this led to the habit of seeing the non-German speaking people of the Austrian monarchy as curious, laughable exotics . . . of operetta, a habit whose consequences we are still suffering today. As the same [*sic*], everything is wrapped up in a phenomenal wealth of beautiful music which will always give these works a certain life even when they themselves are no longer interesting as memories of a great period—brilliant, sad and very strange. (Křenek 1966, 21–22)

Despite such dim assessments, others would remind us that it was Johann Strauss, in his fusion of Hungarian and Gypsy culture within the terrain of Viennese operetta, who introduced "onto the stage the Gypsy Hungarian milieu, which then was to bear fruit in many wonderful achievements during the so-called silver and later periods of Viennese operetta. . . ." (Kydryński 1985, 232)

The Heirs of Johann Strauss: Franz Lehár and Imre Kálmán

The Gypsy theme was to play an exceedingly important role during the so-called golden era of Viennese operetta, which lasted from the 1860s (namely, *Die Fledermaus*) until Franz Lehár's *The Merry Widow* of 1905. The tradition would be carried on in subsequent years in works by Lehár and Imre Kálmán (Traubner 2003, 103–274). Yet references to Gypsies remained confined within both operetta convention and the traditional motifs associated with Gypsies, as explored with respect to *The Gyspy Baron.*

The Gypsy Stereotype in the Work of Franz Lehár

In 1910, Lehár (1870–1948) premiered the operetta *Zigeunerliebe* (Gypsy Love), with a libretto by Alfred Maria Willner and Robert Bodanzky, who located the work in Transylvania. Given this location, Lehár and the librettists were able to explore both Romanian and Hungarian folklore as it related to the Gypsies inhabiting these territories. Lehár, for his part, had high aspirations for the work, seeking to elevate it to the status of an opera rather than a mere operetta. Contemporaries boosted Lehár's self-regard in this pursuit, with the Viennese press calling him the "Puccini of operetta" and others claiming that *Zigeunerliebe* "soars into opera" (Traubner 2003, 251–52). The general conception, as well, was that the operetta's subject matter was close to the composer's heart and that he poured all of himself into creating the score.

Two principal portrayals of Gypsy heroes are enfolded in *Gypsy Love*: that of the musician whose fate is sealed within the convention's framework and that of the wanderer closely linked to nature.

In the Act II finale, the (non-Gypsy) countess Ilona defines the social role of Gypsies in a non-Gypsy world when she calls them providers of musical pleasure. Thus, as a collective hero the Gypsies are presented as a singing people whose wedding receptions are "colorful, dancing, exceptional" (Kydryński 1984, 303). The male hero, in this framework, is the Gypsy violinist Joszi, who bewitches women with his virtuoso skills. On a broader, instrumental level, violins and dulcimers, along with other instruments, create a link to the Gypsies of Transylvania in particular. The dulcimer, for its part, is mentioned textually in Ilona's Act III aria.

In Act II, scene 6, Joszi explicates the ethos of the eternal Gypsy wanderer as someone lacking a homeland, a permanent abode, and attachment to the land (Lehár 1910, 17–18). And whereas Stan Czech writes of Lehár's operetta "He is a Gypsy who knows no homeland" (Czech 1942, 134), he also draws attention to the Gypsies' portrayal as a people deprived of their own country and functioning practically within the bounds of the Austro-Hungarian monarchy.

Negative stereotypes of Gypsies, however, prevail in the operetta, characterizing its beginning and persisting throughout, thereby keeping within the day's theatrical convention. Gypsy love, to begin with, is cast in a pejorative light. Joszi, invited to play at the engagement of Jonel and Zorika, seduces the latter, thereby enacting the tenets of Gypsy love (Lehár 1910, 3). Zorika's nanny helps propagate this unflattering portrayal of the Gypsy lover, saying that more than one young woman has been damned by such allure. And Joszi himself is soon revealed to have seduced other women in similar ways. Meanwhile, the love that ensues between Joszi and Zorika is described as "hot as flames but like those very flames extinguishing" (Lehár 1910, 4). Zorika's subsequent unhappy fate confirms both the short duration of Gypsy love and the generally unfaithful nature of Gypsies. The beautiful Zorika is saved in the end, however: her experience has only been a dream—and is therefore a warning against giving in to feelings for a Gypsy and a testament to Gypsy amorality.

Another stereotypically negative view of Gypsies is presented with regard to their relationship to the legal system. In this construction, Gypsies operate only according to their own internal moral code and defy any law imposed from the outside. For instance, the countess Ilona, although secretly desiring Joszi, criticizes the prospect of a Gypsy wedding in a church, even as she admits that such an event would have spice. But the Gypsy himself, unbounded by convention, feels no need for a formal wedding.

In Act I, Hungarians are portrayed as being tolerant of Gypsies, a view that ensures they will consider to perform their music, but also as believers in the concept, in the words of Jonel, of "Gypsy rabble." Zorika's father's disowning of his daughter at the close of Act II constitutes a particularly forceful rebuke of Gypsy culture. Yet Gypsies, despite these negative treatments, ensure color and a romantic aura in the operetta, as exemplified in their dancing processions. At the musical level, Lehár's evocation of Gypsies does not diverge much from Strauss's. Slow waltzes go hand in hand with the czardas, and the wistful sounds of the Gypsy violin mix with the melodious arias supported by a wide range of instruments.

In 1922, twelve years after the premiere of *Gypsy Love*, Lehár returned to the Gypsy motif in the operetta *Frasquita*, which related to the expressive Gypsy tradition in Spain. Set in contemporary Barcelona and Paris, the operetta conveys standard conceptions of Gypsies while also alluding to Bizet's *Carmen*. Whereas in *Gypsy Love* the Gypsies are presented as a people without a homeland (but existing within the variegated fabric of the Austro-Hungarian monarchy), *Fras-*

quita's Spanish Gypsies reflect Lehár's desire to produce an attractive work set in a distant, exotic land. The composer's active involvement with Spain dates to his 1911 operetta *Eva*, which earned him enormous popularity in southern Europe, namely Italy and Spain. Encouraged by this success, the composer reached for a similar audience by covering Spanish subject matter in *Die ideale Gattin* (The Ideal Wife) of 1913, with a libretto by Julius Brammer and Alfred Grünwald (Traubner 2003, 256).

This attempt to seek a sympathetic audience was in line with other contemporary European works covering Spanish Gypsy material, such as de Falla's *La vida breve* and *El amor brujo*. And such works, as we saw earlier, attracted audiences not only in southern Europe but also at Paris theaters. The French comic opera (and particularly *Carmen*) therefore constituted a highly useful reference in Lehár's work.

Yet whereas other works referenced *Carmen* directly (for example, Émile Lassailly's *Carminetta* of 1917), *Frasquita* borrowed prodigiously from Bizet's work in formal, structural, and visual ways, from the arrangement of episodes to the use of props. In the operetta, the appearance of Gypsies at a tavern prompts musical displays both by the Gypsy girl Frasquita and other girls. (Carmen also performed her song and dance for Don José in a tavern.) In a similar way to Bizet's opera, the temperamental Frasquita causes an argument with a non-Gypsy, and the Gypsy girl is blamed for the incident. The social role played by Frasquita, as compared with Carmen, takes on a new dimension when the heroine becomes a dancer in a Paris nightclub.

Visual allusions to *Carmen* in *Frasquita* include the young non-Gypsy aristocrat Armand's lost cigarette case, a reference to Carmen's place of work at a cigar factory. And during the argument between Frasquita and Luisa at the tavern, the dagger's gleam is similar to that in Carmen's hand during her struggle with a factory coworker. The rose (or cassia) symbolizing sensual love in Bizet's opera is used similarly in Lehár's operetta, but with an added element of humor. Frasquita, in presenting a rose to Armand, who feels an urgent attraction to her, demands a whole bouquet in return.

Lehár's work likewise employs the entire gamut of prejudices against Gypsies, such as representations of their thievery, hedonism (e.g., their love of song and dance), and the low morals of Gypsy women, who seduce men in night spots. Such portrayals place Gypsy culture within the broader exotic discourse of nineteenth-century Europe connected with Spain.

This category of exoticism influenced certain musical decisions by the composer, particularly in the melodies sung by the Gypsy heroine, Frasquita. A two-part structure characterized the introductory song, which has a love theme and incorporates, in its second part, the czardas *friska*, expressed through 2/4 meter and characteristic syncopation. Working within the Viennese operetta convention, the composer juxtaposed, even within a single aria (e.g., "Frasquita's Song"), chromaticized melodies and, within the waltz form, quasi-melismatics. The predominant dance rhythms, especially as performed by Frasquita, display Spanish provenance and offer the possibility for artistic interpretation.

The popularity of exotic references in music, often reflected in a work's title, thus found expression in operettas that treated the Gypsy element as affiliated with Spanish culture. In works such as *Frasquita*, the Gypsy theme offered a pretext for colorful, although stereotyped, representations that were, in turn, embedded in the era's academic discourse.

The Gypsies and Their Music as Depicted by Imre Kálmán

The Gypsy motifs in the operettas of the Hungarian-born Imre Kálmán (1882–1953) may not have been central or frequently employed, but they were nonetheless integral to his compositional idiom. Kálmán's first operetta to employ a German libretto (by Julius Wilhelm and Fritz Grünbaum), *Der Zigeunerprimas*, premiered at the Johann Strauss Theater in Vienna on October 11, 1912, to enthusiastic public and critical reviews. In 1913, the work would be performed in Berlin, and the next year it would appear on Broadway in New York (Traubner 2003, 265).

In *Der Zigeunerprimas*, Kálmán had some success in overcoming Gypsy stereotypes through the downplaying of the portrayal of the wandering Gypsy musician. Gypsies are portrayed as educated, intelligent people who experience their own real-world problems rather than as exotic supplements to non-Gypsy society. Correspondingly, the work's conflict plays out among the Gypsies themselves, a departure from the usual convention that pitted Gypsy against non-Gypsy. The operetta's contents are, however, fairly banal, involving the more or less unconvincing romantic tribulations of two couples, with the story centering on the question of the essence of Gypsy music and its performance tradition. The principal heroes are the famous Gypsy fiddlers Pál Rácz and his son Laczi, whom the composer was able to channel through his own experiences growing up in Hungary and hearing Gypsy bands. Kálmán even possessed a photograph with a dedication from Rácz (Frey 2005, 7). *Der Zigeunerprimas*, then, constituted a homage to both this particular Gypsy musician and to all other Gypsy *prímáses*.

As chapter 1 showed, the widespread respect surrounding Gypsy virtuosos in Hungary enabled them to advance socially by marrying into wealthy homes. Thus, in the libretto to Kálmán's operetta, Pál's daughter Sari falls in love with the king, a love that is reciprocated. Sari's centrality is evident in the fact that the operetta is sometimes known in English by her name. Yet Sari's story leads one to the rather conventional portrayal of Gypsy love within the operetta. For example, Pál's son Laczi becomes involved with the beautiful Juliska, whom Pál himself desires as his fourth wife. The son wins this romantic battle, but the real conflict between them is played out on the musical plane. Old Rácz represents the romanticized type of Gypsy violinist who plays simply from the spirit and rose to a high social position as a result of his virtuosity. The young violinist Laczi, meanwhile, has completed his studies at a conservatory and is an immense talent, even if he is also a professional musician. Yet his playing is seen by his father as "contaminated." During the first song in Act I, Pál expresses regret over the transformation of Gypsy music into goods and cites the surname "Rácz" as synonymous with reliable Gypsy music. Yet the son will triumph on the musical plane as well, with Pál ultimately coming to terms with the far-reaching commercialization of Gypsy music.

Despite breaking from schematic presentations of Gypsy characters, the operetta remains true to the principles developed by earlier generations of Viennese operetta composers. Based on their model, Kálmán contrasts Gypsy music with salon music by introducing waltzes, evoking "higher" social circles. Yet the distinct portrayal of Gypsy music sets this operetta apart from its Viennese peers, avoiding their marginalizations and conventionalizations and allowing *Der Zigeunerprimas* to stand out.

Kálmán would never again handle Gypsy content as openly and innovatively as he did in *Der Zigeunerprimas*. In his later operettas, the Gypsy element would be treated as being integral to Hungarian culture. In the popular 1915 *Die Csárdás-fürstin* (Princess of the Czardas), the Gypsy-associated dance form holds no small role. With the action playing out in early twentieth-century Budapest and Vienna, cities in which Romanies were numerous, Gypsies themselves do not appear, even as they are summoned in stereotypical fashion in the musical trio that closes Act III. One of the heroes, Feri, chants the beginning of the melody with the words "Nimm, Zigeuner, deine Geige" ("Gypsy, take your fiddle"; sometimes translated as "Zigeuner, drive our sorrows away"), while Sylvia, the princess of the title, takes up the theme, singing, "Spiel Zigeuner, mir was Feines, Etwas für's Gemüt!" ("Gypsy, play me something nice"; sometimes translated as "Play, oh play, a soothing song to mend a broken dream"). The handling of Gypsy music as a component of Hungarian culture also appears in the 1924 operetta *Gräfin Mariza* (Countess Mariza), set in early twentieth-century Hungary. Arriving at her country estate one day, the countess Mariza is greeted by her peasants and by Gypsy music. She responds with a song with characteristic references to Gypsy music. In Act II, the figure of the Gypsy as a perfect musician is recalled when Tassilo, a count who has fallen on hard times, recollects the fate of the Gypsy musician in Hungary ("Play Gypsies, Dance Gypsies!"). The appearance of the fortune-teller, the Gypsy woman Mina, equally reflects the stereotypical understanding of Gypsies.

Indeed, the figures of the fortune-telling Gypsy woman and the Gypsy band glorifying Hungarian culture became two of the most recognizable features of Viennese operetta and, thus, would influence operettas composed in other settings. The notion of Central Europe as an area dominated by Gypsy music would be reflected stereotypically in works such as Georg Jarno's (1868–1920) operetta of 1907, *Die Försterchristl* (The Girl and the Kaiser). In this work, the Gypsy Minka is a fortune-teller whose singing, accompanied by a Gypsy band brought onstage, praises the beauty of the Hungarian land in the Act I piece "Steht ein Mädel auf der Puszta" (A Girl on the Puszta). Despite the Central European milieu, Spanish associations also enter the operetta through castanets and tambourines in Act II.

The infusion of Hungarian material with Gypsy themes was so prevalent that operetta composers far outside the region would take up the practice. Victor Herbert (1859–1924), for instance, a composer of Irish descent connected with New York's Broadway, spread the romantic Hungarian-Gypsy vision in the United States. In his 1898 operetta *The Fortune Teller*, the main heroine, a Gypsy, tells fortunes, yet her likeness recalls that of Imra, an heiress who had come to the United States from Budapest. Appropriated from Viennese operetta was this fortune-telling association, along with a tendency for deceit ascribed to Gypsies. Musically, the composer used melodies familiar to him of both Irish and Hungarian origin, even loosely employing an Irish melody for "Slumber on, My Little Gypsy Sweetheart" (Traubner 2003, 369).

The Gypsy Vaudeville of Konstanty Krumłowski

The Vaudeville Genre

The vaudeville tradition in Europe, a mainly urban entertainment form, was characterized by frivolous presentations brought to earth by an implied awareness of cultural conditions. The 1899 stage work *Piękny Rigo* (Beautiful Rigo), by the Polish writer Konstanty Krumłowski (1872–1938), fell within this tradition and covered a Gypsy theme.

As for vaudeville's context, early on, spectators congregated in town squares and later in café gardens or small street theaters. They were entertained by peripatetic folk, such as traveling musicians, acrobats, or poets. As a collective, these performers were labeled *Spielleute*, even as they came from different walks of life and were quite distinct from one another (Salmen 1983, 21).

By the early eighteenth century, vaudeville had become formalized, even as it remained closely bound to the rhythms of the city. This formalization meant performances held during fairs would be moved from the marketplace to a nearby theater. And as the formalization of vaudeville took hold, opera *buffa* incorporated some of its elements. In time, light dances, songs, jokes, and even acrobatic stunts gradually penetrated operetta.

Krumłowski was the main Polish purveyor of vaudeville at the turn of the twentieth century. Fascinated by the slogans of the modernist Young Poland movement, he spent stints living with artistic bohemians, acting, and later working as a journalist. His productions mainly addressed the habits and customs associated with his home city of Cracow, as the titles attest: *Przewodnik tatrzański* (1911) (A Tatra Guide), *Śluby dębnickie* (1915) (Dębniki Weddings), *Białe fartuszki* (1919) (White Aprons), *Jaskółka z wieży mariackiej* (1937) (The Swallow from St. Mary's Tower).

The Origin of *Beautiful Rigó*

The factors behind the inclusion of Gypsies in Krumłowski's work included their presence within the multiethnic city. Even more important, however, were the writer's personal experiences. In particular, Krumłowski had likely spent about three years in Vienna in the late 1800s (Babral 1991, 103), when the city was the capital of operetta and garden theaters and much gossip fixed on an 1896 scandal involving the Gypsy *prímás* Jancsi Rigó—a scandal that would be the model for *Beautiful Rigó*. Born in Hungary, Rigó and his band gave concerts in the capitals of Europe. During one of these performances, at the Parisian Alhambra, the violinist struck up an acquaintance with Clara Ward-Chimay (1873–1916), the daughter of a wealthy American—whom the press often referred to as a millionaire for sensational effect. Although married for several years to a Belgian, Count Chimay, and having two children, Clara left her husband, finalizing the divorce in 1897, and took up with the Gypsy musician (Dobos 1981, 171–82). She subsequently traveled with him around Europe, including a visit to Hungary. The romance would intrigue readers and audiences owing to Clara's American origins, her rise to an international marriage, and her ultimate rejection of social status for love. Such details were provided, for example, in the January 28, 1897, edition of the *New York Times*.

News of the affair (and Clara's troubled life) would fill newspapers from 1896 to 1898 as well as after the countess's untimely death in 1916, before which she was married twice following her separation from Rigó (*New York Times*, December 19, 1916). Interest in the couple was encouraged by Clara herself, who posed with her Gypsy husband for postcards and lithographs, including an 1897 lithograph titled *Idylle princiere*, by Henri de Toulouse-Lautrec. Even as this story titillated at social gatherings, such liaisons between Gypsy virtuosos and well-born women, as we have seen, were less rare than the buzz might have implied. The Hungarian musician Elek Vörös, for example, was known to have promised to wed a certain rich Parisian, who went along with the plot—including by planning to divorce her husband—until visiting Vörös's village and learning that he intended to remain officially "single" and had left behind a wife and children in Győr (Sárosi 2004). In time, the once-marquee story of Rigó and Clara would fade from interest. In Hungary, curiously, the main trace of the scandal is a certain gateau named in honor of Rigó Jancsi (Gundel 1992, 130).

Other vaudeville creators besides Krumłowski would exploit the story, including Carl Michael Ziehrer (1843–1922), a famous operetta composer based in Vienna, who in 1898 premiered *Der schöne Rigo* (The Beautiful Rigo), with a libretto by Leopold Krenn and Carl Lindau. But aside from the title and a focus on Gypsy themes, the two works (Ziehrer's was set in Hungary a few decades earlier, with the Gypsies and Hungarians as the main characters) share little in common (Ziehrer, 1898).

Main Characters

In Krumłowski's work, the narrative more or less follows the true story as presented in the press, with one notable exception being that the fictional couple meets in America, not Europe. The retaining of the actual names, including Rigó, Klara (in the Polish spelling), and Count Guido Chimay, also contributes to the work's air of authenticity.

The realism in Krumłowski's work applied not only to the scandal's details but also to widespread associations linked to the Gypsies inhabiting Austria-Hungary. The writer, a citizen of the monarchy, extended the practice of setting the Gypsy image within the wider Hungarian national context, all within the framework of Viennese operetta. His characterizations were stereotypical in the context of Hungarian culture, with understood variations according to class and society, and had prevailed since the mid-nineteenth century. Such a cast "remained in place for a long time, and became established as the stable structure of national alternatives. . . ." (Hofer 1994, 45–46).

In *Beautiful Rigó*, both Gypsies and non-Gypsies are subjected to conventional treatments. Hackneyed themes appear especially when the plot moves to the United States in Act II. Tritely devised characters include the wealthy lady seeking entertainment and diversions outside the home; the affluent, much older husband smitten by her; their sober-minded servant; the black lackey Bob; and the falsely religious, shady Pastor Smith—the American equivalent of Tartuffe. The portrait of stereotypical U.S. glamour, riches, and outsize economic opportunity is set against the mores of the European upper classes, a scenario in which America becomes more a site of exotic interest than the Gypsies.

The comedy in the work's characters is transparent. For instance, the impresario Schmutzbrand (*schmutz* means "dirt" in German) is a far from scrupulous talent scout searching for an easy living. It is he who involves Gypsies in the American tour, believing their artistic talents will garner him profits. Schmutzbrand also recalls a Jewish merchant, a well-known Galician figure. This identification gains clarity when he becomes a traveling button salesman after the failure of his American tour, even as his Jewish ethnicity is never noted explicitly. His Jewishness is also hinted at by the Viennese practice of including certain Jewish operetta characters (e.g., the swineherd Zupan from Strauss's *The Gypsy Baron*). And Schmutzbrand stammers severely as does the Jewish lawyer, Dr. Blind, in Strauss's *Die Fledermaus*.

Gypsies are shown in the vaudeville production through a series of stereotypes, in which they are providers of entertainment in an eternal conflict with the non-Gypsy world. This conflict is expressed in Act I through a Gypsy dispute with the Hungarian landowner Kálmán Arwaj over the rights to the land they live on. Reinforcing negative notions about Gypsies are the imperial bureaucrats entrusted to deal with the matter, who describe the Gypsy group as a band and even rabble (Krumłowski 1931, 42, 44–45, 77, 84). They make just one exception in this assessment—for Rigó—but even him they view as a drinking partner. "Do you know what, that Rigó's alright!" they exclaim. "But only if needed for company" (Krumłowski 1931, 18).

The names given to the Gypsy characters are widely used among Hungarian Gypsies: for example, Rigó's wife is called Csirka, and an old Gypsy is named Segeny. Interestingly, the figure of the original Jancsi Rigó inspired Krumłowski to create the two fictional heroes—the commune head Rigó, endowed with musical abilities, good looks, and a strong will, and the young, talented violinist, Janczi.

To give the Gypsy scenes verisimilitude, Krumłowski inserted Romany terms such as *egaszi!*, *ciurrahan!*, and *czibało*, as well as whole sayings such as *O Beng a tełem o iłu!, Merał me!, Czajori foro, Haj!, Tarno cioro!,* and *Romi ciaworo!* These insertions are especially prominent in the Gypsy group scenes—for example, in Act I. Vouching for his intentions, Krumłowski himself asserted that "the verses in italics are genuine words taken from Gypsy songs" (Krumłowski 1931, 82). The use of Romany also emphasizes the Gypsies' emotional nature (some of the terms are curses), while adding fresh linguistic material and offering a new light in which to interpret Gypsies. Primarily, however, these words allude to the exotic, undecipherable element of Gypsy culture.

The conventional depiction of Gypsy characters extends to their perceived views on love of freedom. By Act I, the Gypsies are already portrayed as being opposed to law and all uniformed bureaucrats and preferring to enjoy themselves. Young Gypsies are also seen as seeking freedom and extensive travel. Janczi, the son of the elderly Segeny, yearns to travel the world as a violinist for recognition and money, though his father dissuades him from such an idea, recommending instead that he stay put and find honest work. Aside from music-making and wandering, Gypsies in the production are linked to their long-associated trade as blacksmiths (Krumłowski 1931, 14).

Yet another scene tied to Gypsy stereotypes, although isolated from the broader plot, involves a treasure to which the Gypsies are presumably entitled but that ends up having been set aside by the miserly old Segeny (Act I, scene 4). While displaying pride in their Indian origins, the Gypsies in Krumłowski's vaudeville production are, on the whole, seen through the distorting mirror of exaggeration and comedy.

References to Gypsy Culture: Love and Music

The central motif of Krumłowski's vaudeville production is that of Gypsy love, with its banal treatment influenced by Viennese operetta. The plot centers on two broken marriages—one Gypsy, one non-Gypsy—and the notion of a spousal swap, a grotesque version of the authentic romances involving Gypsy musicians described in the press. Other traits of Gypsy love as illustrated in the show include its impulsiveness, storminess, and fleetingness. The emotions associated with love, in this conception, can bring neither stability nor long-term happiness.

Gypsies, as a people enraptured by song and dance, are assigned in the vaudeville production instruments typically used in the *Zigeunerkapellen,* first and foremost the dulcimer. The tambourine also appears, arousing Spanish associations, as well as the violin. Gypsies playing string instruments ascend professionally not only because of their skillful musicianship but also because of their personal charm. These players are often exceptionally handsome young men (Rigó is referred to as "a dark Adonis") who enjoy success with women. Even as the term *prímás* does not appear in the production, it is easy to imagine that Rigó, a superb violinist, fulfills this role—not only playing first violin but also leading the entire band. Thus, when Rigó escapes with Clara Chimay, his orchestra automatically ceases to exist, dashing Schmutzbrand's hopes of continuing to profit from the lucrative American tour. (The tour of the United States itself refers to a common nineteenth-century practice among European artists, including Gypsy musicians.)

Dance also makes its obligatory appearance in reference to the Gypsies. The vaudeville characters and theatergoing audiences alike were drawn to the sensual Gypsy women dancing the czardas. Krumłowski's vaudeville work, in keeping with the Viennese operetta tradition, likewise ties the non-Gyspy world to dance—through association with the elegant waltz.

The vaudeville production contained relatively few musical fragments, but they nonetheless fulfilled an important role in establishing the link between Gypsy culture and music. Krumłowski envisaged the creation of sixteen musical fragments, for both vocals and dance; as many as eight of these were composed by Józef Marek, and the remainder were never composed at all. The overall simplicity, if not banality, of *Beautiful Rigó*'s music issued from the contingencies of the genre, which was often staged at outdoor cafés and performed by amateurs or semiprofessionals. As for the musical fragments, they were composed for voice with uncomplicated piano accompaniment, and they had memorable, singable melodies. Both the instrumental and the vocal parts could pretty much be muddled through, with the singer's line doubling that of the piano. In this way, the pianist could coax the proper notes from the singer. Despite their musical simplicity, the songs contained echoes of the Gypsy idiom as conceived within European culture. For example, Rigó's czardas is played at an andante tempo, in 2/4 meter, and in the key of F major. This song contains elements typically considered Gypsy, including the augmented second interval and imitation of the violin through the upper piano registers. These techniques are repeated in the later sections of the czardas, anchoring the dance within the conventions of so-called Gypsy music. The piece also has the quintessential two-part czardas structure: the slower *lassan* and the quicker *friska*—with the latter part entailing a change in meter to 4/4 and a change in key to D major. The *lassan* possesses an internal build, from A to B, with the B section including tremolo in the piano part, evidently suggesting the "quivering" of the dulcimers.

Reference to stereotypes of Gypsy music is also made in "Rigó's Aria with

Chorus." Like the previous song, this piece has a two-part structure. And the fast section contains a change in mode and key typical for the czardas (from D minor to F major), while the accompaniment contains frequent syncopated rhythms and shifting accents. At the close of Act II, the fast part of the "Aria" is reprised, allowing for a collective dancing of the czardas and reemphasizing the importance of the form in the Gypsy context. The lyrics offer this message explicitly, recounting Gypsies' wandering existence and the role of their musical abilities.

In this early vaudeville production, Krumłowski offered the Cracow public a mélange of Viennese operetta and rich Gypsy folklore, even as he would never return to this topic again. For Cracovians, whether or not the work propagated conventionalized portraits, its entertaining character helped promote a better understanding of Gypsy culture, in light of Ryszard Kantor's idea that "entertainment may antagonize ethnic groups, though it may equally unite them; the process of mutually becoming acquainted with alien groups is possible" (Kantor 2003, 17). Hence, the role of Krumłowski's almost forgotten vaudeville work deserves to be reconsidered. Not only does Krumłowski seem to be the main representative of Polish vaudeville (Babral 1991, 100), but the vaudeville he created was also rooted in a local mentality and simultaneously tied strongly to the Viennese vaudeville and operetta traditions.

CHAPTER SEVEN

Gypsy Motifs in Ballet

Gypsy Motifs in European Ballets

As it did in other artistic forms, the exotic discourse on Gypsy culture predominated in European ballet, especially in its visual elements. In Russian ballets particularly, Gypsies would appear at markets and fairs as onlookers, reflecting their age-old national presence.

The Gypsy type emerged in European ballet in the eighteenth century. One instance was Christoph Willibald Gluck's three-act ballet-pantomime *Don Juan ou Le festin de Pierre* (Don Juan; or, The Stone Guest's Banquet) of 1761, with a libretto by Gaspar Angiolini and Ranieri de Calzabigi, in which Gypsy women in Act II perform a showy dance for assembled guests, accompanied by tambourine. In this and other instances, it was Gypsies' exotic appearance and dress, along with their perceived musicality, that encouraged artists to include them in stage works. Such a perspective held up in ballets of the nineteenth century—a period of fascination with mysticism and exoticism. In turn, librettos often incorporated the Gypsy "pentalogue" of love, freedom, magic, nature, and evil.

The most popular ballets combining these motifs include *La Gipsy* of 1839, by Jules-Henri Vernoy de Saint-Georges, which employed the music of three composers: Francois Benoist for Act I, Ambroise Thomas for Act II, and Marc-Aurelelé Marliani for Act III. This work's libretto has no lack of Gyspsy stereotypes, including the kidnapped child, fortune-telling and dance, and allusions to Gypsies' impetuous and impulsive nature. (In the final scene, Sarah, who is found among the Gypsies, lays bare her Gypsy nature when she murders her husband's killer.) Similar in story line is the ballet *La Gitana* (1838), conceived by choreographer Filippo Taglioni (1778–1871) and first performed in St. Petersburg (Beaumont 1951, 129).

Other themes pertaining in ballets included the Gypsy as magician or sorcerer and the Gypsy woman as a creature of phenomenal Oriental beauty and mystery who arrives on a scene as if from nowhere. In the twentieth century, such a portrayal would appear, for instance, in Igor Stravinsky's ballet *The Fairy's Kiss* (1928), for which he himself created the libretto based on Hans Christian Andersen's "The Ice-Maiden." The Gypsy woman epitomizes mystery, riches (her clothing sparkles with valuable jewels), and erotic allure, with her Eastern beauty clearly setting her apart from the country folk. At the wedding celebration, she is distinct from the revelers; her origins are unknown and she disappears unnoticed, perhaps pointing to Gypsies' nomadic lifestyle.

The popularity of Hugo's *The Hunchback of Notre Dame* resulted in many ballet creators including a heroine named Esmeralda. And in later nineteenth-century France, and particularly Paris, the Gypsy woman's traits as a fortune-teller worthy of regal love would be combined with the world of the bohemian artist. Looseness in the term "Bohemian/bohemian" also played a part here, with one connotation referring to an ethnic group and the other to artistic circles. Félicien Champsaur published a modest but interesting pamphlet on this subject in 1887, "Les Bohemiens," envisaging his ballet, in which the figure Djina appears—"reine d'une tribe errante" (Champsaur 1887). The Gypsies depicted in the ballet are stereotypically presented women living on the margins of society.

The connection of Gypsy heroes with devilish powers—a concept present in European culture since the fifteenth century—also influenced their inclusion within many a ballet. In 1845, Adolphe Adam, who previously composed the music to the popular ballet *Giselle,* composed the incidental music to the ballet-pantomime *Le diable à quatre* (The Devil to Pay), which tells of the life swap between a rich countess and the poor wife of a weaver, all brought about by a spell often attributed to a Gypsy. The two women's entertaining adventures are also ended through Gypsy magic.

The ascription of shady dealings to the Gypsies, with their associations with devils and impure forces, found its reflection in ballets across Europe. Magic and Gypsy love intertwined in the 1902 choreographic fantasy *Święto ognia czyli noc świętojańska* (The Festival of Fire; or, St. John's Night), with music by Zygmunt Noskowski (1846–1909). The main heroine of this three-act work, with choreography by Marian Prażmowski, is the Gypsy queen Tyra, who is infatuated with the Hungarian prince Stefan, on whose infidelity the plot turns. Rejecting Tyra, he takes the young country girl Halina as his wife, but the spurned Tyra swears she will win Stefan back. The entrance of Gypsy elements into the ballet both ensures a component of the extraordinary (as in the Gypsy dance from

Act I) and suggests national motifs, with the czardas showing Stefan and Tyra's Hungarian origins.

Even though she is referred to as the Gypsy queen, Tyra is modeled on a romantic, lone heroine, unaccompanied by any fellow Gypsies. The romantic element of this portrayal is accentuated by the images of Satan and fire illuminating the murky night. And Tyra, in making a pact with Satan, embodies the evil associated with magic, sealing her agreement by performing a symbol-filled dance replete with snakes. Tyra thus willingly enlists dark forces to win back her beloved, but when her gambit fails, she throws herself into the river's current. The Gypsy's only ally turns out to be Night—the personification of solace.

The romanticized vision of Gypsies as the children of nature and natural forces thus influenced the locations associated with Gypsies. These locations can be perceived generally as a heterotopia, a forbidden expanse operating outside the typical bounds of European culture (Foucault 2006). Hence, Gypsy camps were most often depicted in forests and desolate districts. In *La Gipsy*, mentioned before, Gypsies set up camp near Edinburgh, with the remote location in Scotland allowing for an intensification of the sense of mystery and seclusion. References to the popular motif of the Gypsy camp enhanced the work's attractiveness and were used elsewhere, for example, by Marius Petipa in the four-act comic ballet *Don Quixote* (1869), based on Cervantes's novel.

In some ballets, Gypsies would be employed in national contexts as an Other with the goal of distinguishing "us" versus "them." For instance, the Gypsies in the opera-ballet *Boruta* (Devil Boruta), which premiered in Warsaw in 1930 and had a libretto by Or-Ot (Artur Oppman) and music by Witold Maliszewski (1873–1939), are treated as background figures against which Polishness can be clearly etched. In the libretto, the devil Boruta and the alluring she-devil Ponęta beguile the Polish gentry with their tricks, creating a pretext for the presentation of various Polish dances (in Act II the *kujawiak, oberek, krakowiak*, while in Act IV the mazurka and the polonaise). The devils, by contrast, perform dances from other nations, including the tango, the foxtrot, and the boston. In Act II, Gypsies appear as musicians in a satanic band led by Rokita, with this representing the Gypsies' membership in an alternative tradition to that of Polish tradition. Such associations with non-Polishness and impure forces, in turn, subject Gypsies to vilification according to the European cultural tradition as an alien ethnic group posing "a threat to the Christian model" (di Nola 2004, 311).

Gypsy elements are also set up as a contrast against Polishness in the 1921 ballet *Pan Twardowski* (Sir Twardowski), with music composed by Ludomir Różycki (1883–1953) and a libretto by Ordon (Stefania Różycka). The work was based on an eighteenth-century Polish legend, and to accentuate the Polish element, Rożycki introduced national dances, such as the polonaise, *krakowiak,* and *oberek,* as well as Polish highland and highwayman dances, which in 1920s Poland were enjoying increasing popularity. The composer likewise employed rhythms of the Viennese waltz and the East, as in Cossack tunes. The work's stark incongruities dismayed critics, who criticized the setting of a polonaise alongside a Cossack dance, an operatic waltz in the depths of a silver mine, and Polish highland dances in a scene portraying a satanic Sabbath. Yet according to Irena Turska, "the composer did not develop more broadly inventions stylistically alien to Polish folk legend, treating them according to an established scheme" (Turska 1959, 83). This conformity is visible particularly with regard to the Jewish and Gypsy treatments: a Jewish dance is introduced in the penultimate scene, in a tavern in Rome, while the Gypsies are included within the Market Square crowd in Cracow, amid peddlers, passersby, students, and teachers. In the urban bustle, the Gypsies dance a typical czardas, composed of a slow *lassan* part (with the cantilena melody line, led by the violas) and the quicker *friska* based upon a single repeated theme.

The theatrical portrayal of a fair or banquet held at a tavern often allowed for the presentation of Gypsy characters in ballets. As elsewhere, Gypsies in such scenarios would be employed to show authenticity amid other representative groups as well as to highlight elements within a national discourse. Such a cheerful scene offered the context for the introduction of Gypsies in the comic Polish ballet *Cagliostro w Warszawie* (Cagliostro in Warsaw), with music by Jan Adam Maklakiewicz and a libretto by Julian Tuwim (1947). Set in Warsaw in 1780, the first scene portrays a folk event—a sort of festival—in the Old Town square, with strongmen, a puppet theater, and Gypsies with bears, even as Gypsies appear sporadically elsewhere in the work.

In the Polish ballet tradition, Gypsies were often immortalized in taverns, such as in *Bajka* (Fairytale), with music and libretto by Ludomir Michał Rogowski (1881–1954), which premiered May 4, 1923, in Warsaw. This four-act extravaganza threw together various kinds of beliefs, legends, traditions, and characters: Baba Jaga (a witch), Czarodziej (a wizard), Królewicz (a prince), and Królewna (a princess). These manifold themes are enacted in the merriment of the tavern scene, in which a Gypsy girl revels in performing a dance for the wizard, which in turn spurs the entire crowd's involvement in a whirl of abandon. Fantasy and the exotic govern this dreamlike tableau, allowing for the mélange of styles and archetypes incorporated.

In the work of Stravinsky, who drew on Russian folklore for his ballets and based his librettos on traditional Russian stories and legends, Gypsy characters are also suspended between the worlds of the exotic and their place in national constructs. Gypsies, therefore, appear frequently in his ballets in a naturalistic, although marginalized, way. *Petrushka* (1911)—with a libretto by the composer and Alexandre Benois—is set in Admiralty Square in St. Petersburg during the final days of the 1830 carnival, where the commotion includes townsfolk, children with nannies, street dancers, and a characteristic puppet prop. The fourth scene includes dancing Gypsies. Also appearing are bear trainers, who are more than likely also Gypsies, although their ethnicity goes unspecified. In 1953, another Russian composer Sergei Prokofiev covered similar material in his ballet *The Stone Flower* (originally *The Tale of the Stone Flower*), with a libretto by Mira Mendelssohn. The work tells the story of the search for eternal beauty on the border between a real and symbolic world. In the market scene (scene 3, Act II), Russian Gypsies appear among the noisy crowd, performing their dances.

Gypsy references and characters were likewise easily identifiable in ballets for children, with the formula often rendering Gypsies thieves and kidnappers. Based on the children's story "Porwanie w Tiutiurlistanie" (Kidnapping in Tiutiurlistan), by Wojciech Żukrowski, a ballet of the same title was created in 1967, with music by Jadwiga Szajna-Lewandowska and a libretto by Klara Kmitto. True to convention, Gypsies are presented as witches and dark characters, with a Gypsy kidnapping the princess in one instance. The reproduction of stereotypes, particularly negative ones, in works designed for the youngest audiences, helped propagate simplified views and cement stereotypical imagery.

Manuel de Falla's Gypsy Ballets

The Creation of *El amor brujo*

In 1914, on returning from Paris, Manuel de Falla composed a work that reflected his fascination with the folk music of Spain and began what became known as the Andalusian period in his career. The ballet *El amor brujo* (Love's Sorcery), which premiered April 15, 1915, at Madrid's Lara Theater, was the product of this effort. The ballet's first performers likely came from a single Gypsy family: Pastora Imperio in the role of Candela, her mother, Rosario, as the witch, a brother, Vito Rojas, playing Carmel, and Lucia as Vito's daughter, Maria del Albaicín (Turska 1989, 71–72). These soloists were accompanied by a Sergei Diaghilev dance troupe; Leonid Miasin was choreographer and the music was conducted by José Moreno Ballesteros.

Given the central role of Gypsies in Gregorio Martínez Sierra's (1881–1947) libretto, commentators have freely described the work according to its Gypsy connotations. In 1917, Georges Jean-Aubry called it a one-act *gitanería* (Jean-Aubry 1917, 153). About a decade later, Istel clarified that it was an "Andalusian Gypsy scene" (Istel 1929, 507). Subsequent authors have more often than not referred to *El amor brujo* as simply a Gypsy ballet (Mayer-Serra 1943, 3).

At the root of the ballet's creation was a fascination with Pastora Imperio (1887–1979), the Gypsy flamenco dancer who approached de Falla with the request that, together with the popular writer Gregorio Martínez Sierra, he write a song, or at least a dance, for her (Pahlen 1953, 157). Influenced by this encounter with Andalusian Gypsy culture, and particularly by the impression made by the singing of Imperio's mother, Rosario, known as "La Mejorana," de Falla decided to create a work broad in scope.

Based on a Gypsy legend, the libretto's action occurs at a Gypsy camp over the course of a single night and involves a mere four protagonists, concentrating on the young heroine Candela, whose suspicion that her lover is dead is confirmed by the camp clairvoyant. Another man, Carmelo, is already interested in Candela, and she reciprocates his feelings, but the ghost of the lover, murdered in a fight, does not allow the new lovers to realize their affections. The old Gypsy fortune-teller tries to help them through magic spells, and a ritual dance performed by Candela herself, accompanied by fire, is supposed to have a purifying effect. But these actions fail and the dismal apparition continues to haunt the lovers, preventing their happiness, so they decide to outwit him. At the insistence of the old Gypsy woman, a friend of the unfortunate betrothed, Lucia, who resembles Candela, successfully seduces the dead lover through a dance. Thereafter, Carmelo's first kiss on Candela's lips has magical powers, forever purging the apparition from the heroes' lives.

The clear construction of the libretto, which also references European literary tradition through Shakespearean motifs, allows for a look into the wealth of Andalusian Gypsy folklore, both musically and—even more so—on the level of beliefs and traditions.

The Ballet's Symbolism and Myth

The dramaturgy of de Falla's work plays out on three planes: the literal, the symbolic, and the cultural (with the last of these connected to legends, traditions, and myths). The first level concerns the events presented onstage and within the ballet's contents. The second level, the symbolic, covers universal territory, with youth associated with light, the life force, and beauty. Candela ("candle" in Spanish) and Lucia (*luz* means "light" in Spanish) embody these principles in the ballet. The alluring lover named Carmelo (hinting at sweet delicacies) symbolizes the bliss of physical love. Yet neither the old Gypsy woman (a witch) nor the murky apparition of the murdered Gypsy has a name, a symbolic conceit. They are seen to represent the dark side, or evil powers in a sphere beyond the reach of mortals and therefore eluding classification.

The dances are also assigned symbolic functions. The "Danza ritual del fuego" (Fire Dance), the ballet's centerpiece, invokes fire as a purifying force ensuring renewal and better days ahead. The blaze cuts through the shadows of the night, becoming a symbol of continuity, with the flames indirectly symbolizing love's power. Lucia's dance, performed to seduce the apparition, is likewise a symbol of female sensuality. The sexual energy conveyed through this dance hints correspondingly at the theme of Gypsy playfulness, as linked to Dionysian frivolity.

Alongside these symbolic connotations, the ballet functions on the level of myth, which calls not so much for intellectual discernment as for imagination and experience, and a particular focus on moments of chance. Allegory is preeminent, given that de Falla sought to present a generalized metaphor for Gypsyness rather than real episodes from the life of Andalusian Gypsies. Ballet allowed for a display of the ceremonies, customs, and musical-dance folklore of Spanish Gypsies.

In building this myth, or allegory, de Falla emphasized only certain fragments, and he subjected these fragments to alterations and transformations and sometimes only referenced them allusively. Indispensable to the discussion of *El amor brujo* and to any discussion of myth is the role of ritual, which here concerns the driving out of evil spirits, with the aim of creating a better tomorrow. In particular, the ceremonial elements of fire, dance, and the darkness of night refer to pagan rites, including those of St. John's Night, cultivated, for example, among Slavs. These elements further suggest the perception of Gypsies as barbarian pariahs of European culture, beyond civilization or the Catholic faith. The ballet's corresponding eeriness, particularly in its orchestral parts, was detected by Edgar Istel, who wrote that "the element of weirdness, in particular, was brought out by Falla with an astonishing accuracy of aim, and this, too, in the instrumental coloration" (Istel 1929, 508).

In the ballet, the role of myth influences the treatment of time. The drama, as we saw, plays out over a single night, but the broader period or era is unspecified, as if irrelevant to the myth itself. The resulting time distortion blurs any sense of life beyond the Gypsy camp, making external non-Gypsy events seem insignificant. Further, the focus on events within the Gypsy camp subordinates the problem of historical time. In turn, the force of the ballet's message remains unchanged, regardless of whether the action plays out in present or past, such as—for instance—during the period of increased persecution of Gypsies in Spain. The open nature of time in the work also allows for major questions to be left to interpretation, including why the initial young lover was killed in a fight. Was this a case of aggression against Gypsies or an internal incident? Was it connected with the 1749 actions undertaken in Spain against Gitanos? We have no precise answers. In reference to concepts proposed by Ludwik Bielawski, we can see *El amor brujo* to occupy a realm in which historical time is secondary, or suspended, and in which the annual cycle of time is barely marked—even as the work's contents suggest a fairly warm time of year. The emphasis, instead, is on the present, and even a given moment, as exemplified by the Spanish night (Bielawski 1995, 147–55).

While referring to the phases of myth (from the perspective of the annual cycle of spring, summer, autumn, and winter and the mythical attributes given to each season) as distinguished by Northrop Frye (Frye 1976, 313–14), the ballet may be considered to treat the change in seasons in particular visual ways. The evening may be seen to mark a later period in the cycle, autumn. The ballet begins with the setting sun—thus hinting at death, decay, loneliness—and moves to winter and its darkness, decomposition, and oblivion. Yet the magical rituals may be seen to signal spring or dawn (through hope). And the ballet's resolution, as expressed in the protagonists' happiness and triumph through their union, may be seen to connote summer. The promise of their union—as if *pars pro toto*—is the kiss.

The "Gypsyness" of the Work

References to Gypsyness appear in both the ballet's plot and its music. The plot references derive not only from the surface details within the libretto or the principal roles held by Gypsies but, even more important, from the pre-compositional aim of reflecting the lifestyle of Andalusian Gypsies. The ballet concentrates on neither Gypsy relations with non-Gypsies nor on the history of Gypsy repression in Spain—with this latter motif only distantly alluded to in the killing of Candela's lover in a fight, which precedes the true action of the ballet. Instead, the ballet focuses centrally on Gypsy beliefs and legends—rather than treating them as a sort of embellishment, as the context of nineteenth-century stage works would dictate. The world of the Andalusian Gypsies as approximated onstage abounds with superstitions and prejudices. Flamenco influences, such as the primordial joining of love and death and the perception of an eternal cycle, also permeate the life philosophy put forth in the ballet, with these influences imbuing both the music and the heroes' fates. Also typical of the flamenco vision, the impossibility of fully realizing sensual love constitutes a main theme in the ballet. Indeed, happiness is always just out of the heroes' reach (at least until the conclusion). The fundamental innovation in de Falla's portrayal of Gypsy love was to have it emerge from the feelings of two Gypsy characters, rather than a male Gypsy and female non-Gypsy (as in *Manru*) or a female Gypsy and male non-Gypsy (as in *Carmen*). De Falla's portrayal thus marked a rejection of the prevailing nineteenth- and early twentieth-century interpretation of the concept.

All characters in de Falla's ballet are Gypsies, allowing for an internal portrait of Gypsy society, even as this portrait is necessarily partial—particularly, an examination of love and magic. Nor is sensuality primary to the picture of Gypsy love, as it was in other stage works, with the exception of Lucia's dance. Eroticism is, in a sense, sublimated into the higher goal of seducing the lover's ghost, who ultimately lets go of Candela. Gypsy women, in turn, are not viewed primarily as objects of sexual desire, even as their eroticism functions as a subtext. In this, de Falla again breaks with the day's conventions.

Jealousy, often encountered in flamenco songs, constitutes an important motif in the ballet alongside Gypsy love and is the source of the work's conflict. This jealousy is so powerful as to persist from beyond the grave. Yet true love and the desire for life overcome this supposedly evil force, bringing to mind the adage *amor vincit omnia.*

In de Falla's ballet, Gypsy associations with magic and supernatural powers are reinforced at the musical layer. In the tension-filled scene in which the phantom is being driven away, the strings and trumpets perform their parts *con sordino* (muted). Twelve horn blows in succession, suggesting an echo, bring to mind a clock striking midnight. Further, the gathering of Gypsy women in total darkness at the camp hints at the nocturnal enchantment of such camps and Gypsies' associations with witches and other dark forces.

Reference to the stereotypical connection between Gypsies and impure forces is illustrated in the scene "El circulo magico" (The Magic Circle), recalling the introduction to Shakespeare's *Macbeth* through typical "witch" props: the campfire, the depths of darkness, and especially the cauldron suspended above the fire, with the bubbling potion. Night, the fire, and the echo—as phenomena of nature unsubdued by man—complement the mysterious ritual and are accentuated by the element of the earth: following the fervid dance, Candela falls straight to the ground.

De Falla's work, finally, viewed Gypsy subject matter through the lens of music, with Istel noting in the 1920s that Gypsy content handled through ballet "afforded the composer ample scope for songs, pantomime and dances" (Istel 1929, 508). Through especially condensed samples of Gypsy music, *El amor brujo* draws its inspiration "from the deepest sources of comprehension of human feelings" (Jaenisch 1952, 38). Furthermore, de Falla welcomes the music of Andalusian Gypsies to the canon and heritage of elite European music (Pahlen 1953, 158).

Songs in the Ballet

Mindful of both contemporary trends in ballet and the musical traditions of Andalusian Gypsies, de Falla introduced into *El amor brujo* the human voice (alto or mezzo soprano). The ballet would thus include songs in the flamenco tradition covering the spectrum of human experience, from sorrow to love to hatred to fate and so on. The songs would thus "[overflow] with that fatalistic quality which characterises the songs of *cante jondo*" (Ewen 1968, 263).

The first song, "Cancion del amor dolido" (Song of Suffering Love) resounds following the ballet's lyrical introduction, with its tuplet notation indicating characteristic flamenco rhythm and its subject matter echoing the philosophy of flamenco. After the energetic dance fragment that follows the "Cancion del fuego fatuo" (Song of the Will-o'-the-whisp), the composer, for contrast, includes a calm, lyrical melody of a simple, unrefined design. The use of G sharp as an elevated sixth degree in the key of B minor indicates a minor third interval (between G sharp and B), equal enharmonically to the Gypsy-associated augmented second. Moreover, the scale's upper tetrachord (F sharp, G sharp, A, B) at the beginning of the melody has a construction identical to the lower tetrachord of the Dorian scale often used in the flamenco. In crafting a melody line to resemble that of a flamenco song, de Falla also introduced grace notes into the vocal part, identifiable as a reference to the flamenco technique of "searching" for a sound by implicitly avoiding its instant achievement. The phrase endings, with their melismatics, may be said to intimate Arab techniques associated with flamenco. The song's lyrics, meanwhile, evince the usually ephemeral passion associated with Gypsy love. (In Bizet's "Habanera," Carmen compares Gypsy love to a skittish bird.)

The song about the phantom inserted into the "Danza del juego de amor" (Dance of the Game of Love), with its flamenco-like instrumental accompaniment and rhythm, tells of an evil Gypsy. The fragment, in the 3/8 meter typical for a Spanish *jota*, is performed by two couples—Lucia with the ghost and Candela with Carmelo—and has a three-verse A-B-B structure, with an introduction that is lyrical in character. The instrumental interludes are irregular in length, ranging from a few to more than sixty bars, suggesting their unplanned, improvised character. The song also spontaneously transforms into a dance, with the unpretentiousness of such a shift authenticating its ties to Gypsy flamenco forms. Such efforts are aided by melodies with a narrow range, with the first verse, for example, contained within a fifth.

The Gypsy dimension to the songs is further bolstered by the use of an Andalusian Gypsy dialect (Pahlen 1953, 161, 165). In this dialect, for instance, the ɪconsonant is replaced with an *r*; thus we have, in "Cancion del amor dolido," "*este mardito* [rather than *maldito*] *gitano me farta* [rather than *falta*]." The line translates as "I miss this damned Gypsy." Likewise, in the Gypsy dialect, the masculine article *el* is changed to *er*; we therefore hear, in "Cancion del fuego fatuo," of "*er* fuego fatuo" and "*er* corazon triste." Equally typical for the Andalusian Gypsies was the dropping of the final consonant. In the same song, we hear "corre" instead of "correr" or "arde" instead of "arder." Interjections also punctuate the songs, as in flamenco, such as *ay!*, most often in the melismatic sections.

The Gypsy Dance

Dance (*baile*) in the flamenco lexicon constitutes a natural reference point for ballet. The "Danza del terror" (Dance of Fear), with a clear A-B-A'-B' structure, was more than likely inspired by an old Gypsy dance, recalling the Italian tarantella (Rogalska-Marasińska 2000, 107). The dialogue between the trumpet and oboe is a kind of symbolic banter, with the trumpet expressing the lover-phantom's position and the world of the living carried by the oboe. The persistently repeated motif (initially by the flutes and violins and subsequently by the remaining instruments) based on intervals of seconds and thirds creates the impression of a frenzied dance whirl that engulfs the ballet's heroes.

The culminating moment in the ballet is "Danza ritual del fuego," inspired by a highly popular flamenco song telling of labor at the blacksmith's forge. This type of song was traditionally performed by Gypsies wishing to drive off evil spirits (Rogalska-Marasińska, 2000, 109). Here, the movement of the blacksmith's bellows is suggested by the movement of the major chords in the horn sections, while the rhythmicity of the bellows is conveyed by the piano and cellos. Structurally, static fragments (to suggest mechanical work) are juxtaposed against lively and accelerated fragments, with the latter achieved by replacing quarter-note with eighth-note accompaniment as well as through concentrated repetitions of a single motif.

The twenty-eight-bar instrumental beginning of "Danza del juego de amor" references the Spanish *jota* dance. The characteristic triple division suggested by the 3/8 meter is preserved, although the later shift in accents forces a change to a 3/4 meter.

The part entitled "Pantomime" is based on tango dance rhythms. The melodic-rhythmic scheme is introduced in a fairly atypical 7/8 meter, with woodwinds (flute and bassoon) playing the melody. The flamenco tango was treated in *El amor brujo* as a kind of rite reflecting the deepest states of the human soul and expressing the tragedy of fate, the inevitability of destiny, and the role of love in a man's life. Movement of the body, then, here and in other dances in de Falla's ballet, allows the performers to communicate profound thought and feeling without the use of language.

Gypsy Stylization at the Instrumental Level

A small orchestra accompanied the ballet: two flutes (with one instrumentalist sometimes switching to piccolo), one oboe (in certain fragments, an English horn), two A clarinets, two F horns, two trumpets (with one A trumpeter sometimes switching to a trumpet in B flat), a kettle drum, and a piano, which was treated as a fully legitimate part of the orchestra. The basis of the orchestra was the string quartet, with the first and second violins as well as violas and cellos often possessing independent voices and, in addition, all the string instruments often playing *divisi*, such as in "Cancion del amor dolido." The orchestra's modest makeup allowed de Falla to take advantage of opportunities to evoke color. The composer had a rare aptitude for using his instrumentalists to imitate the sounds of flamenco, in particular the guitar and castanets (Pahlen 1953, 159).

As we have seen with other composers, de Falla used pizzicato in the strings as well as arpeggio in the piano to evoke the guitar, such as in "Cancion del fuego fatuo." Christoforidis cites *El amor brujo* as an example of "masterly imitation of the flamenco guitar in [de Falla's] orchestral scores" (Christoforidis 1999, 265).

Solo parts by wind instruments (oboe, trumpet, and horn) also hold special significance in the ballet, as marked from the very first bars of the "Introduction." De Falla also enlisted the orchestra to depict moods. For example, tremolos in the cello and double bass accompany the Gypsy camp enveloped in darkness and join with the set design to intensify the atmosphere's eeriness and magic.

The Influence of Flamenco

In his work, de Falla brings together various elements of Gypsy culture modeled on flamenco into a coherent unity. Flamenco permeates the entire ballet, subordinating all other elements: "rhythmically, melodically, and consequently harmonically, the work is almost entirely based on the peculiar Spanish Gypsy music" (Istel 1929, 508). Characteristic instantiations of flamenco include melody lines played within melismatics and with frequently repeated, ornamented motifs (both transposed and not), inevitably leading to a significant narrowing of the ambitus. The repetition of sounds and of identical motifs gives the melody a swinging feel. The melody also has a characteristic descending motion, with an important role fulfilled by the augmented second interval.

The composer, however, followed the "truth without authenticity" slogan and did not quote directly from flamenco sources (Machlis 1961, 260). Rather, de Falla's melodic allusions came from a creative appropriation of methods associated with the music of Andalusian Gypsies. This approach would earn high praise from critics, especially given the composer's creative role and considering that he likely did pull melodies from actual folk songs (Ewen 1968, 263).

As earlier sections have shown, references to flamenco in de Falla's ballet came in rich melodic melismatics, use of the augmented second interval, frequent repetitions of phrases or pitches, and grace notes employed in the "search" for the appropriate sound, with an overall swinging and vibratory effect. Supplementary motifs are also supplied by, for example, the oboe in "Cancion de amor dolido," echoing the characteristic vocal *ay!* exclamation.

The ballet's music shows a clear predilection for the triple rhythms typical for flamenco as well as alternation between 3/4 and 6/8 meters, corresponding to question-and-answer figurations. The composer also applied an irregular division of values, beginning with the common triplets and moving to quintuplets and sextuplets. The juxtaposition of regular and irregular divisions introduces, particularly in the vocal sections, a tension suggesting rubato. Irregularity and asymmetry are also achieved through a polyrhythm derived from the concurrence of various rhythmic divisions, such as in the ballet's finale. Further shifts of emphasis include the introduction of vocals on a weak part of the beat, causing a metric dissonance between words and music, such as in "Cancion del fuego fatuo." Finally, accents inserted by the composer into instrumental parts disrupt the rhythmic flow and suggest its spontaneous flamenco-like character.

Dynamic contrasts noted in the score provide yet another means for flamenco references. These dynamic shifts are often intense, such as in "Danza del terror," when in two bars' time, the marking changes from pianissimo to fortissimo. Such changes can be, stereotypically enough, associated with changeability in Gypsies' moods and the passions tormenting their soul.

The spontaneity associated with Gypsy music manifests itself in de Falla's vocal and instrumental parts alike. De Falla marked related stylistic choices explicitly in the score, including in the melodics, harmony, rhythmicity, and, foremost, the articulation. In the context of evoking flamenco guitar through string pizzicato and piano arpeggiation, we also see intentional pauses in the division of chords, marking clearly the flamenco guitar technique known as *rasgueado*. Furthermore, the short, vibrating sounds typical of flamenco guitar performance are achieved through both staccato and pizzicato articulation in, for example, "Cancion del fuego" and "Danza ritual del fuego"—as well as by juxtaposing shorter-value arco string articulations with longer-value pizzicato, with the sonic effect of the latter including pauses.

De Falla used other techniques to intimate broader references considered exotic within European works. These included empty fifths, which suggest both threat and the primitive in "Danza del terror." Particular instruments are also assigned symbolic value, with the lyrical oboe embodying song, the joy of life, and vitality, while the trumpet recalls the ghost and all that is connected with death, sorrow, pain, and anxiety—a role first announced in the "Introduction." Hence, in "Danza del terror," the interaction of oboe and trumpet signals not so much a conversation as the gulf between two worlds—that of the living and the dead.

El Amor Brujo in the Context of Other Early Twentieth-Century Ballets

The librettos of early twentieth-century ballets conceived in a national context often drew on myth, whether Spanish, Russian, Polish, or more broadly Slavic. As a rule, these ballets were devised with the idea of appealing to a large, international public—and they therefore sought to generalize comparatively local source material. This predisposition can be seen in Stravinsky's *The Rite of Spring* (1913), which references ancient Russian material while purporting to represent pan-Slavism. A similar tendency applied to other ballets, such as Karol Szymanowski's *Harnasie*, in which Polishness is symbolized not so much by the Polish highland milieu as by the hermetic highwaymen of the Tatra Mountains who inhabited it. De Falla, for his part, portrays Spanishness through one of its regional cultures—that of Andalusian Gypsies—a choice that had become particularly attractive in the early twentieth century. A group on society's margins and previously denied lead stage roles was thus cast as representative of a nation. The same principle governed Szymanowski's work as well as Aaron Copland's ballets, such as *Rodeo*, in which American cowboys played the lead role. Also shared by these ballets is the referencing of ritual, which touches deeper and more universal themes than betrayed by the onstage events. Stravinsky's ballet, for example, shows the allure of Slavicness by portraying Russian rites, while de Falla makes use of Gypsyness as an immanent attribute of Spanish national culture.

In offering the possibility of a Spanish national music and crafting his own unique style in the process, de Falla was seen to utilize "with great skill" the range of music associated with Spanish Gypsies (Istel, 1929, 509). The ballet's national aspect did not escape the attention of early reviewers. Yet these same commentators omitted to tie this national dimension with the work's Gypsy character. Jean-Aubry, in 1917, simply extolled the ballet as an example of a "national popular scenic form" (Jean-Aubry 1917, 153), while Clyne wrote that it expressed "the Spanish . . . primitive strength" (Clyne 1926, 268).

The only moderate early success of the ballet was tied to its exceptional innovations, which indeed shocked contemporary Spanish audiences (Jean-Aubry 1917, 153). Such innovations included impressionistic orchestration, no doubt influenced by the composer's stay in Paris. Critics looked upon this particular device with reserve, with one common critique, according to Hess, being that the ballet "failed to evoke a truly Spanish atmosphere precisely because of the composer's absorption of 'foreign influences'" (Hess 2001, 531). The work, in turn, was viewed from its premiere through both national and exotic lenses, indicating the exotic connotations of Spanish music and its close affiliations with Arab sources. In 1922, English audiences could read that "The use of the Oriental elements, which have been perpetuated by the gipsies, may be studied in the score of the ballet *El amor brujo*" (no author 1922, 7). Interestingly, other commentaries suggested a comparison between the musical idiom of the Spanish and Hungarian Gypsies (Istel 1929, 509).

The combination of modern techniques and specific references to music by Gypsies drew one particular objection—over whether the popular Gypsy form could reflect the true Spanish soul (Hess 2001, 531). Generally, however, de Falla's ballets have still been seen to "constitute representative positions of Spanish national creativity" (Turska 1989, 360). Such opinions, therefore, appearing on popular materials for theater connoisseurs, at least indirectly link music performed by Gypsies with the concept of nationality in the works of Spanish composers.

Other Ballets by De Falla with Gypsy Associations

Although no future de Falla ballet would match *El amor brujo* in its focus on flamenco motifs, these elements would constitute important additions to what would be widely considered the composer's most representative work, the ballet *El sombrero de tres picos* (The Three-Cornered Hat). Set in an Andalusian province and based on a novella by Pedro Antonio de Alarcón (1833–1891), the ballet's premiere was performed by Sergei Diaghilev's renowned Ballet Russes on July 22, 1919, at the Alhambra Theatre in London, with set design by Pablo Picasso, who also worked on the costumes. The orchestra was conducted by Ernest Ansermet, and the choreographer, Leonid Miasin, also played one of the principal roles—that of the miller. Martínez Sierra, the librettist for *El amor brujo*, also wrote this work's libretto. The ballet was marked by its playful character, enhanced by folk humor that bestowed a burlesque dimension. The targets of the work's biting satire component were the authorities in general, with the mayor character—the proud owner of the three-cornered hat, a past Spanish symbol of high office—coming in for particular ridicule.

The ballet, which tells a widely known tale from nineteenth-century Andalusia and would become a representative of the Spanish musical idiom, was seen to have a "typical Andalusian character" (Istel 1929, 510, 514). One commentator wrote of the ballet lyrically as reflecting "the true Andalusia, Andalusia after all" (Pahlen 1953, 168). And this Andalusian setting forced an association with Gypsy culture, even if the Gypsy motif appears only indirectly. Here, references to flamenco imply not only a tie to Andalusian Gypsies but also an integral component of all Spanish culture. In the view of some, de Falla consciously used flamenco dances, appearing in the ballet's first and second parts, to connote a national designation (Pahlen 1953, 168).

In the first song, elements from flamenco appear, through shouts of *ole!*, the clatter of castanets, and rhythmic clapping (*palmas*). Typical flamenco dances interweave with court dances, with the former signaling informality and naturalness (and involving ordinary people as dancers) and the latter, the contrived menuet associated with court celebrations, indicating formality. Through this contrast, de Falla revealed the ballet to emerge from a Spanish tradition of vitality and joie de vivre.

In "La danza del molinero" (The Miller's Dance), elements associated with flamenco include references to the Phrygian scale and a narrowed ambitus. On a stylistic level, castanets are used, and the guitar is evoked in the orchestra through the now-familiar techniques of arpeggio, staccato, and pizzicato.

From the day of its premiere, *El sombrero de tres picos* was considered a mature work, while its musical success ensured de Falla the status of national composer. The ballet is, however, fairly rarely performed in opera houses outside Spain as a result of problems with its staging, with these difficulties often tied to the flamenco references. (Such difficulties apply even more notably to *El amor brujo*.)

Further, as a guide indicates, "their realization requires a good knowledge of Spanish dance folklore. We therefore note not many such undertakings. . . ." (Turska 1989, 360). Overcoming these very difficulties and mastering such knowledge, we might then surmise, may constitute a key to success in presenting de Falla's ballets.

CHAPTER EIGHT

Gypsy Themes in Vocal Works

As a genre representative for the Romantic era, song naturally absorbed popular motifs. And because Gypsy motifs were seen as being tied to romantic ideals, these motifs entered artistic songs predominantly through the literary texts of poets. This tendency prevailed for composers through the nineteenth century and into the twentieth. Romantic German poets who dealt with Gypsy subject matter, and whose texts were favored by composers, included Johann Wolfgang von Goethe (1749–1832), followed by Joseph von Eichendorff (1788–1857), Emanuel von Geibel (1815–1884), Theodor Storm (1817–1888), and Max Geissler (1868–1945). These Romantics enjoyed esteem particularly within German and Austrian compositional circles.

Yet along with poetic works, composers located source material on the Gypsies' musical idiom from the collections of anonymous folk songs that appeared during the nineteenth century. In France, for instance, these collections were published for amateur musicians of average to advanced skill. And song titles in these collections often included Spanish or Italian references combined with Gypsy references, perhaps reflecting the associations between Gypsies' physical appearance and that of southern Europeans. Meanwhile, Spanish music, thought to be nearly interchangeable with Gypsy music, reached a wider audience thanks to the popularity in Europe of Spanish composers and performers. This Spanish influence was almost certainly the second most important source of Gypsy-related content for artistic songs, next to the German poems.

Throughout the nineteenth century, composers created songs endearingly titled *zingarella,* or artistic songs with Gypsy-related words. Of course, no "prototype" of a Gypsy song by a specific Gypsy group existed, so *zingarella* arose, paradoxically, as a stylization—that is, a song contemplated within a Gypsy template. The earlier-mentioned Spanish-Italian connotations, evident in the very term *zingarella, zingaresca,* or *zingara* were thought to constitute a significant element in creating the notion of the "Gypsy song" within European culture.

With time, certain characteristic features designed to preserve the pretense of folk song simplicity would take shape. These simpler forms prevailed in the early part of the nineteenth century, with greater stylization and musical refinement taking place later on. The changes were expressed in a departure from the initial aim of imitating allegedly genuine Gypsy songs in favor of an artistic reworking of the concept of Gypsyness in music. This trajectory, however, remained closely connected with the development of the Romantic song genre in general.

By the 1880s, composers' interest in the Gypsy song had clearly intensified as a function of several factors boosting the profile of music by both Hungarian and Spanish Gypsies. One such factor was the success of Bizet's *Carmen* while another was the 1881 reissue of Liszt's influential though controversial publication on Gypsy music. (Both works have been explored in detail in earlier chapters.) Other sources of the surge in interest in the artistic song were Johann Strauss's *The Gypsy Baron* and a general increase in the use of Gypsy subject matter in instrumental works.

By the beginning of the twentieth century, Gypsy motifs would dominate operetta output, in general resulting in a trivialization of Gypsy subject matter. This trend naturally was reflected in songs with Gypsy themes. Other lighter forms in the American Tin Pan Alley idiom incorporated superficial, textual-level Gypsy themes, buoyed by the increasing popularity of entertainment music, jazz, and—particularly in Paris—cabaret. German composers themselves adopted some of these leavening tendencies, sometimes treating Gypsy material—hitherto handled with utmost seriousness—in a more lighthearted, pictorial, and even comic way.

Even with these shifts, the earlier practice of drawing on the texts of Romantic poets would persist, although in limited form, with the Gypsy themes having allowed the original poets to impart their more sweeping views on freedom and links with nature. Whatever the source, in the nineteenth and twentieth centuries, Gypsy motifs would be a reservoir of Romantic ideals and would thus be intimately entwined with European songs, both in their artistic and more popular, entertaining manifestations.

Songs of Gypsy Inspiration in the Early Nineteenth Century

The Poetic Trope

Goethe introduced Gypsy subject matter to German Romanticism with his 1784 publication of *Zigeunerlied* (Gypsy Songs), which he had written thirteen years earlier and which served, for example, as the basis for Louis Spohr's

(1784–1859) song of 1809 of the same name. In the song, the lyrics essentially draw associations with devilish powers, although the term *Zigeuner* does not even appear. The stereotypical connection of Gypsies with witches and pagan customs, embellished with a description of raw nature ("Im Nebelgeriesel, im tiefen Schnee, Im wilden Wald, in der Winternacht, Ich hörte der Wölfe Hungergeheul, Ich hörte der Eulen Geschrei") and black magic tropes ("schwarze Katz"), spoke to the imagination of its Romantic recipients.

The romanticized life of the Gypsies, a theme attractive on its own, drew the attention of nineteenth-century song composers. Exceptionally popular among poetic sources were Geibel's *Zigeunerleben* and *Der Zigeunerbube im Norden,* written in 1834–1835 and referencing Gypsies' mystery and ties with nature. Among those to draw from these texts was Johanna Kinkel, née Mockel (1810–1858), for her 1838 collection *Sechs Lieder* (op. 7), in which number 6 is the song "Die Zigeuner." Tapping the poet yet again, Kinkel placed "Der Zigeunerknabe" first in *Der Hidalgo* (op. 8). Geibel's work was employed as well by Karl Gottlieb Reissiger (1798–1859) for the number 2 in his opus 206.

Also based on Geibel's poetry, Robert Schumann (1810–1856) in 1840, his so-called *Liederjahr* (year of the song), published "Zigeunerleben" (op. 29, no. 3, from his *Drei Gedichte nach Emanuel Geibel für mehrstimmigen Chor und Klavier*). This fairly simple, predominantly homophonic song was maintained in E minor (with basic triad chords) and a C (4/4) meter, remaining within the conventions of European song, with internal divisions signaled by new melodic ideas. A quasi-imitation appears in the contrasting fragments with solos of successive voices, starting from the highest (soprano, alto, tenor, and then bass). At this point in the poem, when Geibel discusses the sounds of instruments associated with Gypsies, the composer has an opportunity to enact imitative effects on the musical level—but he does not carry this out. The song's annotation indicating that it can be performed ad libitum—accompanied by two percussion instruments, the triangle and tambourine, both associated with Spanish Gypsies—may be considered its only gesture toward so-called Gypsyness.

In 1849, when writing two songs for voice and piano accompaniment with Gypsy connotations entitled *Zigeunerliedchen* (nos. 7 and 8 out of 29 songs in op. 79), Schumann once again enlisted texts by Geibel. Despite the title's direct reference to Gypsies, the word "Gypsy" only appears in song number 7. In both works, the poet, followed by the composer, treats the references to Gypsy tradition as a pretext for certain romantic tropes, such as the sorrow of life or the beauty of nature. The plainness of the musical compositions reveals itself in their formal structure, narrowed range of musical material, choice of the A minor key, and prevalence of tonic and dominant functions, as well as the arpeggiated piano accompaniment, and the peaceful, measured flow of the melody, utilizing predominantly eighth and sixteenth notes. Musically, Schumann's "Gypsy songs" do not stand out, although their straightforwardness may connote ruralness. More important, this simplicity does set the songs in the stereotypical context in which Gypsies are the uncomplicated children of nature.

Engrossed in poems describing the mysterious and alluring, yet highly idealized, Gypsy lifestyle, composers often reached for conventional depictions. Indeed, the poetic sources did not evoke associations with Gypsy music—however it was understood—and as a consequence did not influence the composers' musical choices.

The *Zingarella* Genre

In the early nineteenth century, as suggested earlier, musical simplicity and a predilection for combining Gypsyness with manifestations of folk-seeming music forms were to dominate the genre's artistic songs, despite their use of poetic texts. This tradition appears to be rooted in the popularity of the *zingarella*, which was freely incorporated—as a work of allegedly Spanish heritage—into the popular collections of songs representing various countries. Such collections of Spanish songs included *Romancero espagnol: Recueil de chants populaires de l'Espagne* (1844), *Petit romancero, choix de vieux chants espagnols* (1878), and *Chants populaires espagnol* (1882). Likewise, the highly popular Spanish tenor and composer Manuel García piqued interest in Spanish songs, giving concerts in Spain as well as in Paris, London, the United States, Mexico, and elsewhere. In his compositions, García introduced characteristic national elements, which he disseminated to an international audience. Spanish songs thus rose to a level of popularity perhaps equaling Italian songs.

In the early nineteenth century, national discourse sought to define the Spanish song, together with the *zingarella* and its Gypsy connotations. Although the term identified a song form tied to Spain, it also referred to an instrument, an idiophone called a *scacciapensieri* and, in Calabria, a *zingara* (Basso 1984, 780). The typical features of the *zingarella* song were the almost-universal initial minor key with a change to major during the course of the piece. Above all, the *zingarella* was characterized by a triple meter (either 3/8 or 3/4, or, less frequently, 6/8), by a relatively quick tempo, the fairly frequent appearance of irregular rhythmic divisions (chiefly tuplets), and syncopation. It usually employed a strophic form, although significant variations occurred (from verse-chorus arrangements through reference to a roundel form, right up to hybrids constituting a fusion with the song form). The *zingarella* was also characterized by a simplicity in melody and piano accompaniment as well as a transparency in texture. Most important at the textual level was direct reference to Gypsies: beautiful young Gypsy women, for instance, or their ability to tell the future. At times, geographical references appeared to Andalusia and Castille, although Spain was less often referred to as the homeland of Gypsies. The *zingarella* form, dating from the late 1700s and lasting through the next century, would peak in popularity in the 1840s, when George Borrow's books on Spanish Gypsies were enjoying their greatest readership. Schumann, we will note, joined the Gypsy crowd around this time, and even though he did not call his songs *zingarellas*, their simplicity and musical specificity and the texts on which they were based placed them in this tradition.

Contrary to what one might expect, *zingarellas* were not anonymous. In this tradition, in 1843, an Italian publisher and poet, as well as lawyer and politician, Guillame Cottrau (1797–1847)—the father of the composer Teodoro Cottrau—included in his collection 24 *Nouvelles mèlodies national es de Naples* for piano and solo vocals various songs citing origins in, for example, Capri or Sorrento. Number 2, "La Zingarella," is described as a "*canzona di Soccavo* [a part of Naples]." Typical of a *zingarella*, the song is in a minor key (F minor) and has a 6/8 meter. In addition, the verse construction, the unusual simplicity of the piano accompaniment (limited to providing harmony), its brevity at twenty-four bars, and the lack of a credited lyricist may all suggest its traditional, rustic character. Composers of Gypsy songs seem to have deliberately erred toward such simplicity. The French composer Louis Jadin (1768–1853) authored just such a typical *zingarella* (titled "La zingarella"), with its manuscript housed at the National Library in Paris (Ms. 5123). Undated, the work appears to also be unfinished (given that it has no lyrics), yet it still possesses characteristic features. In a minor key (C minor), with a 3/8 meter and moderate tempo, it is distinguished by simplicity in melody, harmony (with chiefly dominant references), and form.

Giuseppe Verdi shaped his "La Zingara" (1845) similarly, setting it to a text by S. Manfredo Maggioni (1808–1870), who applied the Gypsies' lack of homeland symbolically to the Italian situation. In its exceptional use of a major key (F major), it nonetheless represents a typical "Gypsy song" of the period by maintaining a triple meter (3/4) and employing arpeggiated triads in the melody line that correspond to the piano accompaniment based on functional chords. The formal construction of the piece makes reference to the ternary A-B-A scheme within the broader framework. Other factors classifying the song as a typical *zingarella* are its musical cohesion, transparent texture, and lightness. While staying true to the tradition, Verdi enriched the vocal part through noticeable, although not numerous, trills and grace notes (drawing attention in particular are the assembled trills in bars 31–32 and 61–62). On the one hand, these ornamentations undoubtedly gave the singer an opportunity to display technical abilities, while on the other they somehow suggested links with the melismatics of the Spanish vocal works from the 1840s.

In underlining the connotations of the *zingarella*, composers sometimes added the adjective *espagnole*, narrowing the reference to the Gypsy song in Spain. Moreover, rich melismatics in the vocal part offered much of the form's charm. Thus, around 1836, the popular Italian composer Saverio Mercadante (1795–1870), likely during a visit to Paris, composed several songs for voice with piano that referred to various nations and geographical areas, with names such as "tyrolian" or "polonaise." Written to words by Crevel de Charlemagne, his "Zingarella espagnole" is also identified as a bolero. The vocal line, with its rich melismatics, imitates the improvisational character of "authentic" Gypsy songs, with trills and dotted rhythms sustaining the impression of irregularity in the vocal line. As if alluding to the Gypsies' purported emotionality, the composer exploited dynamic possibilities, rapidly shifting from forte to piano. A monotonous piano accompaniment based on the triad chords (and enriched with the applied dominant) in D and A minor alludes—especially in the refrains—to the guitar. Other musical parameters, such as the triple meter (3/4), reliance on periodic structure, transparency of texture, and formal simplicity, reinforce the song's conception as a *zingarella*. Furthermore, the song's text conveys a stereotypical image of Gypsies prophesying the future, as clearly highlighted in the chorus: "Allons vite! Que chacun vienne consulter la Bohemienne c'est l'oracle, c'est l'oracle du destin." The song "Chanson d'une Gitana: Romance bolero" (op. 6, 1846), by François Bonoldi, likewise typifies nineteenth-century *zingarella*, with direct Spanish references. Not only does the piece preserve the character of the bolero, but it is set in A minor and 3/4 meter, with a melody constructed predominantly on the triad notes and lyrics that tell of wandering Gypsies with a song on their lips, accompanied by the sound of the tambourine.

Spanish composers would themselves include Gypsy associations in their song titles. Here, again, nonmention of the text's author could suggest its traditional origin. Further authenticating devices included the insertion, in cases, of glossaries defining the Gypsy terms used in the lyrics. One such glossary accompanied Mariano García's 1852 "El Jitano" (for voice with piano). Titled "Nota: Explicacion de algunas expresiones Jitanas," it includes examples such as *brajani* for guitar, *erachi* for night, and *miliyo* for heart.

In the mid-nineteenth century, the *zingarella* would increasingly be influenced by the instrumental miniature. Corresponding changes in the form would include the phasing out of the minor mode and triple meter and the introduction of increasingly lengthy and virtuosic fragments in the piano accompaniment. The connotations of Gypsies with Spain would remain strong, but they would be affected by the popularity of Liszt's book on Hungarian Gypsy music.

The sung *zingarellas* of the later nineteenth century would retain the foundational principles of the genre. In *Soireés italiennes,* the six duets for voice and piano published by Giovanni Bazzoni (1816–1871) in 1868, for example, he included—among others—a song called "La Zingare" to words by Carlo Pepoli. Along with the obvious genre indications of the title, the composition follows an extremely simple structure—A-B-C-A—and employs unrefined harmonics. Voices—soprano and contralto—are relatively independent or led in parallel thirds or sixths. The piece is written in F major—a key used for the *zingarella* but previously more often seen as the relative major to an initial D minor. Additional blurrings of the prototypical *zingarella* include the C meter and the short, virtuosic piano insertions that betray the influence of the instrumental miniature. Further, the use of two voices, rather than the traditional one, marks a departure from the initial scheme, suggesting a move toward greater complexity in the artistic Gypsy song.

The impact of purely instrumental music on *zingarellas* is demonstrated even more emphatically by Pierre Benoit's (1834–1891) *La Zingaresque* (op. 11) of 1869, with words by J. Mellery. Considering that this is one of the composer's two "mazurkas *chantée,*" the 3/4 meter can be interpreted as an indicator of the mazurka form rather than a desire to maintain the *zingarella* tradition. Its key of F major had by then become popular in songs with Gypsy themes. Structurally, *La Zingaresque* begins and ends with the refrain, while the intervening three stanzas (in B flat major) bring about a somewhat mysterious mood. Their internal symmetry is based on two motives: both midway through and at the end of each stanza, the composer suggests ritardando, perhaps alluding to the rubato observed among many Gypsies singers. Arpeggios are introduced to accompany the refrain, possibly mimicking the guitar associated with Spanish Gypsies. More broadly, such arpeggios in the later stage of vocal *zingarella* development may simply indicate the influence of instrumental miniatures, rich in a variety of effects. The words of the song still, rather stereotypically, present familiar images from earlier *zingarellas,* depicting a beautiful, mysterious, black heroine as a Gypsy queen.

The subtitle "bolero" can be found in the unpretentious *zingarella* by Ludovic Benza (d. 1874) titled "La Bohémienne." Composed in a typical form, in 3/4 meter and B flat major (with stanzas in E flat major), the piece is accompanied by stereotypical words by Ali Vial de Sabligny that underline its Spanishness through the use of the proper noun "Gitanos." The refrain portrays carefree Gypsy girls blissfully singing *tra-la-la*. These asemantic words would soon become characteristic for nineteenth-century songs with Gypsy connotations. In *La Gitane et l'oiseau*, a work by Julius Benedict (1804–1885) for voice, piano, and flute to words by André de Badet, *tra-la-la* is also used in the chorus, with the alternative but equally simple *ah-ah* at the song's end.

The *tra-la-la* sung by Gypsies in a carefree chorus would also appear in "Les Bohémiens: Au bord de la Seine" (1869), by Pompée Barbiano Belgiojoso with words in French by M. Adolphe Baralle, devised for bass and baritone with piano accompaniment. As hinted by the chorus refrain, the text reproduces the stereotypical notion of the free, romanticized Gypsy lifestyle and its connection with nature, with dwellings under the stars and a laissez-faire attitude toward everyday problems. Such features as simple harmony, transparent texture, and triple meter suggest a typical *zingarella*, but the structure, consisting of two different stanzas, A and B (with the latter having two variants), alludes to the quasirondo form. In addition, the influence of instrumental miniatures can be felt in the spectacular quality of the introduction and coda and in the short piano interludes.

The scope of the *zingarella*'s impact would be wide. For example, in Poland, Moniuszko composed "Cyganie" (The Gypsies) to a Russian text, which later was translated into Polish by Piotr Maszyński (1855–1934). The song can be classified as having been conceived under the *zingarella*'s influence, even if it isn't a typical example. Here, the Gypsies are portrayed stereotypically as wanderers, unafraid of either poverty or hunger. The composer references the typical *zingarella* through the use of parallel minor and major keys (G minor and G major) and the simplicity of both the piano accompaniment and the melodic line, with this even suggesting popular connotations.

In the later nineteenth century, a new titling convention also emerged, with *la bohémienne* replacing *zingarella* to identify songs with Gypsy affiliations, including, for instance, a vocal composition depicting a Gypsy girl. This shift owed itself largely to the influence of Liszt's book. Correspondingly, the concept of *la gitane* came into broader use. Moreover, *zingara* would slowly disappear, giving way to various forms of *bohémiennes* and *tzigane,* a result of successful operatic treatments of Gypsy culture in its Hungarian guise.

Transformations at the musical, textual, and naming levels would eventually bring the *zingarella* and the poetic tropes observed in the "Gypsy song" closer together, especially among German composers who preferred working with substantive poetry with Gypsy allusions. Embodying this marriage of text and music were four songs for piano and voice by Eduard Lassen to poetry by Geibel, whose *Der Zigeunerbube in Norden* had appeared in French in a 1886 collection. Adhering to *zingarella* simplicity, Lassen repeated a stanza three times without any changes, with each stanza already divided into two parts. Components of the piece uncommon for the *zingarella* include the A flat major key. Also, through a distribution of accents and characteristic rhythm, the song suggests a 6/8 meter despite a stated meter of 3/4. Spanish connotations for the piece, however, are upheld through the subtitle "Tempo di bolero" and its typical rhythms. Optional castanets—ad libitum—and frequent arpeggios in the accompanying piano part, imitating the guitar, bind the work to the Spanish national context and its accompanying Gypsyness and exoticism.

In another work by Lassen set to words by Geibel, "Au son du Tamburine (Die Musikantin)," the tambourine directly signals associations with Spanish Gypsies. Another song by Lassen, "La fille de Bohéme (Die Zigeunerin)," set to a poem by Storm, relates Gypsy dancing with the jingling of the tambourine. Thus, references to instruments linked with Gypsies commonly appeared at the textual layer and also sometimes entered the music itself, often in the form of an optional, handheld percussion instrument. Relatedly, W. Moreau's *zingarella* for solo voices and three-part choir with piano accompaniment entitled "La Bohemiénne" (with lyrics by Jeunes Gilles), from the *Collection de chansonnettes jeunes avec pour filles parliament* (1887), is characterized by a simple structure and triple 3/4 meter, with a triangle played in the refrain. The composer noted, tellingly, that in the absence of a triangle, the hitting of the table would be sufficient, as if suggesting the spontaneity and naturalness of Gypsy music-making.

Songs Inspired by Gypsy Culture in the Later Nineteenth Century

In 1880s, driven by the German edition of Liszt's book and the popularity of Strauss's operettas connected with Gypsy motifs, the focus for song composers shifted to the Central and Eastern European Gypsy scene. In searching for idealized images, they turned once again to German Romantic poets, with one notable figure being Georg Friedrich Daumer (1800–1875), whose text would accompany a song by George Henschel (1850–1934), "Zigeuner Standchen" (op. 20). Around 1863, the Austrian composer Anton Bruckner (1824–1896) also seems to have composed a song on Gypsy material, "Zigeuner-Waldlied," although this piece, in 3/4 meter, has not survived.

Among tendencies affecting the "Gypsy song" of the later nineteenth century were references to the musical nature of Gypsies. Song titles referred to "Gypsy melodies" or "Gypsy songs," and the texts—and, at times, the music itself—provided similar references. In addition, more and more song cycles on Gypsy topics appeared.

Antonin Dvořak's *Zigeunermelodien*

Over a few days in January 1880, the Czech composer Antonín Dvořak (1841–1904) wrote seven songs entitled *Zigeunermelodien* (Gypsy Melodies) (op. 55). The songs, officially dated to February 1880, were set to seven corresponding poems by the Czech poet Adolf Heyduk (1835–1923), from a collection of 1859. These poems were initially written in German and, thus, the first edition of *Zigeunermelodien*, published by the Berlin-based Simrock in summer 1880, contained only the German versions. But the poet translated the texts into Czech at the composer's request and, as a result, later editions also contained the Czech versions, as well as an English translation by Natalia Macfarren. The Czech versions differed only slightly from Heyduk's original, with Dvořak himself quite probably instigating and authorizing any changes (Šourek 1987, x).

The content of the songs concentrates on motifs stereotypically associated with the Gypsy way of life: singing (nos. 1, 2, 4, and 6), dancing (nos. 2 and 5), sorrow (nos. 3 and 4), affinity with nature (nos. 3 and 7), freedom (nos. 6 and 7), as well as love and eternal wandering (no. 1). Even though the title suggests links with Gypsy culture at both the textual and musical levels, the work, in its technical composition, falls squarely within the European current, with the romantic treatment of Gypsyness encompassing associations and allusions.

The absence of typical nineteenth-century referencing to Gypsy music begins in the melody, where we see no abundance of melismatics, for instance, or recourse to the augmented second interval. On this latter count, the minor third is used often. Although the interval is enharmonically equivalent to an augmented second, it does not have the same effect of stirring up extramusical associations. The absence of the augmented second in the vocal part is compensated for by the increased harmonic activity occurring within the accompaniment layer.

Instead of incorporating typical Gypsy references, the songs' melodies reflect subtlety, naturalism, and simplicity, as chiefly expressed through the use of seconds or the triad notes, along with an absence of ornamentation. The typical melodic figure employed at the start of most songs—falling, then instantly rising—is reenacted as the songs progress, giving the melodies a smooth, almost lulling quality. The simplicity and naturalism of the songs' agogic-rhythmic layer is expressed in a cohesive, uncomplicated form, in which quarter and eighth notes are paired within the framework of an even meter. In song number 6, the composer introduced syncopation and produced a corresponding deviation from the accentuation expected within the meter, disturbing the piece's fluency while suggesting adherence to the text.

Typical instrumentation associated with Gypsy music is achieved through piano techniques that approximate the violin and dulcimer, with the latter instrument being suggested through playing in a low register and rapid movement. The illusion of a quivering tremolo is effected through the quick repetition of two notes an octave apart from each other. The dulcimer's role as a harmonic foundation is suggested through an overwhelming use of arpeggiated chords. Violin, for its part, is imitated only in the seventh song, with the piano taking over for the voice during pauses at the beginning, middle, and end of the piece. The melody played in the piano part, then, employs an irregular division of values full of melismatics and with a narrow ambitus that recalls violin improvisation. In the short section between bars 31 and 39, delicate, staccato articulation in a high register intimates pizzicato violin. Thereafter, the piano moves to a lower register and eschews staccato articulation, with the imitation thus shifting to that of the dulcimer.

The songs in Dvořák's cycle clearly come together to make a logical whole, as borne out in both their sequence and their metric-agogic and tonal arrangement. Slower tempos predominate in the first songs, while faster tempos characterize the later ones. Tonally, functional relations are clearly decipherable in songs 1 and 2, and song 6 is set in D minor, in a subdominant relation to the A minor of song 5—which in turn fulfills a subdominant relation to the E minor of song 3, followed by the dominant B major in song 4. The C minor in the cycle's concluding song, then, appears to destroy the prevailing subdominant referencing. Yet overall, the use of minor keys, with the exception of the song 4 centerpiece, suggests the melancholy of Gypsy music and points to precompositional tonal arrangement.

Dvořák's "Gypsy" cycle, in a discreet, almost imperceptible way, references techniques stereotypically associated with Gypsy culture within the European compositional field. The only direct, clear-cut link to Gypsy music-making is in song 2, when the vocal *ay!* signals the traditions of Spanish Gypsies.

Hugo Wolf's "Die Zigeunerin"

The Austrian composer Hugo Wolf (1860–1903), influenced by Schumann, likewise preferred to enlist texts by the earlier poets Goethe, Eichendorff, and

Heinrich Heine. Based on a poem by Eichendorf is his 1886–1888 "Gypsy song" for voice with piano, entitled "Die Zigeunerin."

Set at a crossroads in a forest on a starless night, the poem's words evoke romantic longing and a wait for one's beloved and the mood suggests Goethe's *Zigeunerlied* of 1771. Structurally, Wolf enacts a modified version of the typical A-B-A song form through a chorus based on *la-la* following the beginning and ending sections and based on *ha-ha* after the middle section—with this latter gesture particularly echoing Goethe. Although the absence of a key signature suggests A minor, the rich chromaticism in the accompaniment blurs its initial key. Meanwhile, the vocal melody is unaltered throughout the piece and, in delicately lulling fashion, includes a perverse, falling diminished fourth (C–G sharp). From a purely musical perspective, Wolf's piece—owing to the minor key, 6/8 meter, and simple (quasichoral) structure—displays features typical for an early nineteenth-century *zingarella*. However, the song's chromatic richness, illustrative accompaniment, and application of characteristic musical gestures (e.g., in the chorus after the first section, with the tuplet motif suggesting the melismatics of Gypsy song) separate it from the *zingarella* tradition and place it in the "higher" category of contemporary songs using poetic texts with references to Gypsyness in order to convey universal emotions.

Johannes Brahms's "Gypsy" Cycle

Brahms's song cycle *Zigeunerlieder* (Gypsy Songs) signaled his continued interest in Hungarian music. To begin with, he had acquainted himself with *Ungarischer Volkslieder*, a collection of twenty-five songs with piano accompaniment published by Márk Rózsavölgyi in Budapest (Reimann 1903, 81) and edited by Zoltán Nagy, with translations into the German by Brahms's close Viennese friend, Hugo Conrat. Brahms was so fond of these texts that in summer 1887 he composed music for seven of them, although he hardly drew from the primary melodies proposed by Nagy. The songs were published as opus 103, while later (1888–1891) he wrote music to an additional four of Conrat's texts, setting them as numbers 3, 4, 5, and 6 ("Himmel strahlt so Helle," "Rote Rosenknospen," "Brennessel steht am Wegesrand," and "Liebe Schwalbe") of opus 112. According to Malcolm MacDonald, these four songs constitute "a kind of appendix to op. 103" (MacDonald 1993, 352). This latter cycle, however, unlike opus 103, would never be referred to as "Gypsy."

The songs of opus 103 were originally intended for a vocal quartet (soprano, alto, tenor, and bass) with piano accompaniment. The leading role went to the tenor, while the remaining voices usually joined in during the group parts (e.g., nos. 1, 3, 6, 7, and 9). As an alternative, the melody was led by the soprano (nos. 3 and 4), although several songs were performed homophonically by the whole group (e.g., nos. 2, 5, and 9). The only exceptions to this rule were songs 8 and 10: in part A of song 8, a simple imitation (tenor, then alto, followed by soprano) was introduced, while song 10 was based on the principle of opposing female and male voices. When Brahms later arranged the cycle for solo voice with piano, he left out the songs (the original nos. 8–10) in which the allocation of voices was essential.

Undoubtedly, practical considerations persuaded Brahms to create new arrangements for eight songs (nos. 1–7 and 11) from opus 103. Eberhard Creuzburg described this undertaking as a conscious move by the composer to make the songs easier to perform and to popularize them within a broader repertoire—for the concert hall and the home alike (Creuzburg 1954, 76).

Brahms's opus 103 premiered in Vienna, with Brahms himself unexpectedly providing the piano accompaniment (May 1905, 35; quoted in Erhardt 1984, 260–61). The positive reception for the songs was captured rather humorously in a comment by the composer's friend, the surgeon Carl Theodor Billroth, who in criticizing the composer's *Double Concerto in A Minor* (op. 102) in a letter to Eduard Hanslick, wrote, "If the *Zigeunerlieder* had not been composed later, one might almost believe it was all up with our Johannes!" (MacDonald 1993, 321).

In utilizing what may be described as quasi-Gypsy motifs, Brahms in fact composed a cycle of songs aimed at exalting love. To start with, romantic effects are produced through the suggestive evening imagery, such as a starless night, glittering moon, rustling wind, blazing red clouds, the quiet murmuring of the Rimava River. Such details of setting belonged to a framework in which the joy of seeing one's beloved is juxtaposed with the pain of separation. The symbols of love—the red roses (song no. 6)—foretell passionate shared promises between the lovers (song no. 7). The songs' Gypsyness, meanwhile, is indicated by a Gypsy fiddler and a young lover. The cry in the first song announces the Gypsy element with particular explicitness: "Hey, Gypsy! Play a tune on your fiddle about an unfaithful maid. Let the strings sob to the sounds of lament and wistfulness, until hot tears flow down my cheek." Song number 5, meanwhile, tells of a young man whose swarthy complexion suggests Gypsy roots, particularly in the context of the czardas he performs along with a Gypsy band.

Given this backdrop, in which the Gypsy element serves as a device for examining love more universally, inflections of Gypsyness nonetheless color the songs. For example, the Gypsy temperament justifies outbursts of passion and the more ambivalent states of sorrow and melancholy, along with impetuosity and unbridled joy. The dance described in song 5 both symbolizes this love and substitutes allusively for the physical joining between a man and a woman.

Whereas textual references to a romanticized vision of Gypsyness are visible, musical references are less so. One such musical reference suggests Gypsy musicians' improvisatory leanings through the construction of a melody based on phrase repetition. The simple melody is rooted mainly in an inclination toward use of only two intervals—a semitone and a perfect fourth—with the appearance of these intervals at vital parts of the songs enhancing the cycle's coherence. Also bridging the songs is the similar melodic shaping of the first and last selections through the same semitone formula.

The dotted rhythms appearing in almost all songs also subtly bring forth associations with Gypsyness (see, for example, song no. 1: bars 1–5 etc.; song no. 2: bars 1, 3, 4, 5, etc.; song no. 4: bars 10, 14, 18, 21; song no. 6: bars 20, 22, 27, 28; song no. 8: bars 2, 3, 4, 10, 11, 12, etc.). Indeed, these dotted figures constitute half of all the cycle's rhythmic figures, making them an identifying trait of the work.

Like Dvořák, Brahms used the common technique of alluding to the dulcimer in the piano accompaniment to establish Gypsy associations. In song 5, the text of which refers to the dulcimer accompanying the czardas, Brahms modeled chords on dulcimer technique. These arpeggiated chords, matched with the explicit Gypsy-related text, may well imply that other songs (e.g., 1, 4, and 6) employing an identical piano technique were also intended to evoke Gypsy associations. Tellingly, Brahms had previously sought to create a similar effect, such as in his "Variations on a Hungarian Song" in D major (op. 21, no. 2), which was invariably aimed at preserving the Hungarian (or Hungarian Gypsy) national perspective through the presentation of dulcimers.

Rhythmic and metric components also ensured the coherence of the cycle, which was maintained all the way through at a quick, vigorous tempo with a 2/4 meter, which hinted at the czardas and thus the music-making tradition of Hungarian Gypsies.

The title of Brahms's opus 103 has meant that the cycle has always been written about with awareness of potential Gypsy connotations. Heinrich Reimann, for example, who was Brahms's biographer, reflected that the songs came about as a result of the composer's legitimate understanding of the art of Gypsy music but claimed that they were far from simply being copies. He insisted that, "the meaning of this exciting wild music is preserved, but all the rest has been idealized in a superbly beautiful and convenient way" (Reimann 1903, 82). In the mid-twentieth century, Creuzberg described the songs as being typically Gypsy in their force, rhythm, and sound: "In these songs there lives genuine Gypsy music; forceful, lively, vibrant, and highly appealing, these songs always exert a strong influence" (Creuzburg 1954, 76). MacDonald, meanwhile, emphasizes the connections of opus 103 with Gypsy music in clear yet unconvincing fashion. He notes, for example, the evocation of the dulcimer in the piano, but he only explains such instances vaguely according to "exotic harmonies." MacDonald does, though, arrive at meaningful conclusions regarding the now artistically mature Brahms's return to Gypsy subject matter. The songs from opus 103, he writes, constitute "further testimony to the extraordinary fascination and fertilizing effect of gypsy music on [Brahms's] musical language." One motive for Brahms, although not the sole defining motive, according to MacDonald, was likely the popularity of the *Hungarian Dances* as well as the earlier song cycle *Liebeslieder* (MacDonald 1993, 353). References to the exotic, which always found a willing audience, may well have encouraged Brahms to take up this subject matter.

The Transformation of the "Gypsy Song" in the Twentieth Century

In the twentieth century, poetic texts continued to be used for songs alluding conventionally to Gyspy subjects but aimed at reaching more universal themes or moods. More particularly, the introduction of Gypsy characters served as a pretext for showing motifs such as love and betrayal. Gypsies were also personified as eternal wanderers molded by the vicissitudes of fortune. All this confirmed the persistence of a romanticized, stereotypical vision of Gypsyness in music.

The degree to which "Gypsy song" became conventionalized is exemplified in "Les Tziganes" of 1894, by Georges Hüe (1858–1948), with a text by Edouard Guinand (1838–unknown). The work's choral arrangement, to begin with—for sopranos I and II, tenor, and basses with piano accompaniment—constituted a rarity within artistic Gypsy song. But the song's formal and other remaining musical features, such as its A minor key, 3/4 meter, and verse arrangement, show its affinity to the *zingarella*. Also recalling the typical *zingarella* is the text, which is based on a merry *tra-la-la*. And in the singing by the basses, a pure fifth appears, a consonance that is often associated in nineteenth-century contexts with primitive music (Scott 2003, 155–78). A Gypsy-associated effect in the choir is further realized through other common methods, including numerous grace notes in the vocal parts and imitation of the dulcimer in the piano part.

In writing artistic songs with Gypsy material, composers often turned to the same German poets as did their forebears. Thus, Joseph Marx (1882–1964) wrote "Zigeuner" (1911) to a poem by Geissler that begins with the words "Mein brauner Liebster, sage mir" ("My brown beloved, tell me"). Meanwhile, Othmar Schoeck (1886–1957) composed "Die Drei Zigeuner" (op. 24a; 1914) to words by Nikolaus Lenau (1802–1850), whose work had already been used by Liszt for a song in 1860. Intended for voice with piano, Schoeck's song conveys the natural rhythm of the poem, although it does not maintain its scheme of repetition. The melody falls and rises, giving it a swinging quality. The piano, initially doubling the melody, eventually separates itself to a small degree and presents individual solo rhythms (e.g., bars 38 and 41). Only in the song's final fragment does Schoeck use an augmented second interval (E flat–F sharp), which he repeats four times in close proximity, as if emphasizing the tie to Gypsy music.

In 1923, the composer and pianist Ferruccio Busoni (1866–1924) published a song to a poem by Goethe used by earlier composers, designating his "Zigeuner Lied" (op. 55, no. 2) for baritone with piano accompaniment. The song's form, four verses with chorus, would issue from the poem's structure. Furthermore, given its reference to the darkness of night and supernatural powers of a devilish provenance, Goethe's poem seems almost to have encouraged musical figures such as the quickly performed sixteenth notes by the baritone on the word "Kreis" or the tritone leap from C to F sharp, associated with *diabolus in musica*, when spells are discussed. Busoni's song has a brisk pace, is harmonically advanced, and has a variable C and 4/6 meter, thus entering the tradition of a broad, romanticized understanding of Gypsyness as colored with distant, and sometimes terrifying, enchantment.

Even anonymous texts on Gypsies, as long as they complied with stereotypical conceptions, were chosen by twentieth-century composers. For example, "Zigeunermusik" (1914), by Arnold Mendelssohn (1855–1933), was written to an unknown poet's work titled "Fliegende Blattern." Nor is an author credited with "Gitane: Esquisse d'Espagne," adapted for voice with piano (1927) by the French composer Gustave Samazeuilh (1877–1967).

In a 3/4 meter and three key signatures suggesting F sharp minor, the song far exceeds the principles of functional harmony, basing itself on an unusually varied piano accompaniment that creates an impressionistic background in the style of Debussy. The vocal part is characterized, though, by richness in rhythm, expressed through the employment of irregular divisions as well as syncopation. The huge number of musical ideas—from chromatization to repetition to the introduction of grace notes—contributes to the shaping of a melody that suggests an improvised nature. Such an impression is fully maintained throughout the composed form, and it is further upheld when breaking the piece into small sections of fewer than twenty bars and accounting for variable conducting of the vocal part or changes in the accompaniment. This, combined with the title's Spanish referencing, can be seen as an attempt to convey the performance of *cante jondo*. This exceptional song is consequently a rare example in which inspiration from Andalusian Gypsies is combined with an impressionistic style.

Leoš Janaček's *The Diary of One Who Disappeared*

Exceptional among Gypsy songs of the early twentieth century is Leoš Janaček's (1854–1928) cycle *Zápisník zmizelého* (The Diary of One Who Disappeared) of 1919—a work for voices and piano accompaniment, written to (allegedly) anonymous lyrics. While continuing the tradition of combining Gypsy songs into cycles and treating the content as a pretext for composing songs about love (and other subjects), Janaček also handled the Gypsy theme from a deeply personal perspective.

In July 1917, the composer met, while vacationing in the spa town of Luhačovice, Kamila Stösslová, the wife of David Stössl, an antique dealer from Lvov, although they may first have met two years earlier (Vogel 1983, 293). Initially, the acquaintance between Janaček and Stösslová was rather prosaic, but in time the composer, at least, would develop deep feelings for this woman, who was almost forty years his junior—and poorly educated, at that. Stösslová, who had two children, was to become the composer's muse for the almost twelve years up to his death. Their relationship is documented in more than seven hundred letters (Tyrell 2001, 773).

The years of Janaček's acquaintance with Kamila would constitute the most productive period in his life. She would inspire such works as *Káťa Kabanová* (1921), *Příhody lišky Bystroušky* (The Cunning Little Vixen) (1923), and *Věc Makropulos* (The Makropulos Affair) (1923–1925), while indirectly her figure was to infuse all his compositions of this period. Distance from Kamila seemed to spur Janaček's creativity and intensify his feelings for her, as reflected in the pieces' subject matter. (Kamila lived in Pisek, while Janaček lived in Brno.)

One of the first Kamila-inspired compositions was the song cycle *The Diary of One Who Disappeared*, with the composer beginning work on this shortly after their first meeting. On the surface level, the story is of the love of a boy for a Gypsy girl, as expressed over twenty-two pieces. The songs about the tormented love of a simple, country boy for a Gypsy maiden can be read as a reflection of the morally ambivalent position in which Janaček found himself. Clear parallels may be deduced between the real and imaginary heroes: the fictional name Janek, in Czech, is a diminutive for Jeníček or Janíček, a surely uncanny echo of Janáček. But physically, Kamila, a Czech Jew with brown curls, dark eyes, and of average height, could well have resembled a Gypsy. Even the 1935 memoirs of the composer's wife, Zdenka Janáčkova, acknowledge Kamila as having won her husband's heart through her "cheerfulness, laughter, temperament, Gypsy-like appearance and buxom body. . . ." (Janáčková 1998, 162). Janáček affectionately called Kamila his "little Gypsy," and in a 1924 letter he admitted that Kamila and the Gypsy girl were one and the same figure; he even complained about not being able to change the Gypsy girl's name to Kamila (Paige 2003, 86). Another of the composer's unfulfilled wishes was to include an image of Kamila on the cover of the song's first print edition, in 1921. The Gypsy heroine in Janáček's songs remained, however, always associated with Kamila, with the literary romance, as the basis for the cycle, mirroring the composer's own mental and emotional state.

For *The Diary of One Who Disappeared,* Janáček used poems published anonymously in the May 14 and 21, 1916, Sunday editions of Brno's *Lidové noviny* (People's News). In seeking to highlight the poems' supposed folk origins, the editorial board titled the segment "From the Pen of a Self-Taught [or Amateur] Writer." Suspicions held, however, that the author of the verses was the quite literate journalist Jan Misárek—although the actual author was later revealed to be the Moravian poet and novelist Josef Kalda. For its part, the editorial board helped fuel the speculation by appending detective-story-like commentary to the poems, such as the following:

> In a mountain village of eastern Moravia, in a mysterious way, there once
> disappeared J. D., an honest and hardworking young man, his parents'
> only hope. At the start, thoughts turned to misfortune or crime. Only after
> a few days was a note found revealing the mystery of the disappearance.
> This contained a few short verses, which were soon forgotten about, for
> at the beginning no one considered that these could constitute the key to
> this mysterious puzzle—as they were seen as simply a notation of folk and
> country songs. Only a court investigation was to reveal their true content.
> As a result of their moving and sincere tone, they are worthy of publication.
> (Vogel 1983, 295–96)

The twenty-three poems in the cycle were written in the Wallachian Romany dialect, emphasizing their link to Gypsies. The fourteenth verse contained only dashes—and no words. In the narrative related by the cycle, the "honest and hardworking" J. D., or Janek, meets a delightful Gypsy girl, Zefka, and tries but fails to resist her charms. Janek and Zefka engage in a passionate affair that involves nightly meetings and ultimately results in her giving birth to a son. This development prompts Janek to leave his family home and join the Gypsies, thereby explaining his sudden disappearance.

The stereotypical image of Gypsyness propagated in *The Diary of One Who Disappeared* is most notable in its portrayal of Gypsy love. Although a stereotype, the Gypsy love narrative can have a complex arc, with Janek's initial aversion rooted in his anti-Gypsy prejudices ultimately being overtaken by obsession with Zefka. Gypsy love is therefore linked to negative emotions, a portrayal that persists toward the end of the cycle when Janek commits vile deeds in Zefka's name, deeds that beg questions about who betrayed whom, and who persuaded whom to sin. Despite Janek's committing of these acts, he continues to be portrayed as "innocent" and "pure," while Zefka remains the temptress. As for the moment of consummation, this clearly comes in poem 14, as expressed in the page awash with dashes and all it implies. Yet, in another trope of Gypsy love, Janek's desire is fully satisfied in this act of consummation, and he senses the loss of something precious, whether of his virginity or his soul. In turn, ridden by guilt toward his parents—the embodiments of village society and the collective consciousness—as well as remorse and shame, Janek yearns to keep his relationship a secret. Encapsulating his sense of guilt and the inevitability of fate are his words "He who goes astray, let him suffer for his deeds" (song 11: bars 14–18), corresponding with the warning that "what is meant for someone cannot be avoided" (song 3: bars 26–32; song 18: bars 1–5).

Gypsies are also portrayed in these poems as a wandering people ("without aim") whose only caregiver is nature itself. The forest location of Janek and Zefka's tryst points to nature's preeminence, as does the scene in song 11 when Zefka pads the lovers' bed with grass and stones. More ominously, Gypsies are presented as thieves, with the camp's location close to the village facilitating their petty theft. In song 16, Janek expresses the view that Gypsies would be unworthy of being his parents by marriage—were he to wed Zefka. The skin color of the Romany is raised in song 10. All in all, the Gypsies are depicted as a collective unworthy of recognition that arouses anxiety and fear in both Janek and all the villagers.

The discrepancy of twenty-three poems versus twenty-two songs can be explained by the joining of verses 10 and 11 by Janáček into a single Zefka song. Designed for (tenor) voice with piano accompaniment, the cycle also incudes an alto (Zefka, in songs 9, 10, and 11) and three female voices (two sopranos and an alto) that appear only in song 10. These three voices serve as a sort of

Greek chorus, expressing the boy's feelings and desires; in staging, it is often suggested they be located offstage to ensure a subdued effect. From a dramatic standpoint, song 10 is decisive as a tale of Gypsy fate, in that this is where Janek succumbs—not yet in a physical sense but in his self-admission to liking and understanding the Gypsy world represented by Zefka.

Alongside the literary Gypsy motifs, musical references to Gypsy material in the cycle are rarer and barely discernible, on both the melodic and rhythmic levels. For example, we must wait until bars 37–43 of song 22 to hear an example of the telltale augmented second interval (E flat–F sharp). Here the interval is used along with Zefka's words "with son," as if to emphasize the rightful belonging of the couple's child to Gypsy society.

On this count, a minor third interval does appear frequently in the melody (see, e.g., song 10: bars 3, 4, 29, 30, and 33; song 11: bars 3 and 4), with its harmonic match to the augmented second but nonspecific function. To tag the word "Gypsy" or "Gypsy woman," Janáček sometimes introduced a triple repetition of a single pitch followed by the interval of the second (see song 1: bar 4) or, alternatively, a double repetition of a pitch and the second (e.g., song 10: bar 5; song 12: bar 13; song 16: bars 4, 6, and 7). The number of repetitions of this motif and the size of the last interval are modified elsewhere (e.g., song 10: bar 5; song 11: bar 24). Since the repetition of certain pitches is characteristic of the whole cycle, it also appears without any connection to the word "Gypsy" (such as in song 1 between bars 2 and 15; song 2, e.g., in bars 6 and 8). This almost obsessive repetition of the characteristic motif could perhaps be linked indirectly to the improvisatory character of music performed by the Romany, in which repetition is a frequent technique. The overall construction of the songs based on direct repetition of motifs, or changes only in individual notes, supports this hypothesis. And in the songs' broader structures, motifs are arranged according to a hierarchy of phrases, all pointing to the dominance of one motif. The forms, then, can be classed according to type A-A (e.g., song 10), A-B-A-C (e.g., song 3), A-B (e.g., song 4), and A-B-C-B-C (e.g., song 6), although the cycle also contains through-composed songs (e.g., no. 5). And while the repetitions may suggest practices in Romany music-making, Janáček does not even attempt to imitate instruments associated with Gypsies as did other composers of the nineteenth and early twentieth centuries.

Yet other suggestive links to stereotypical notions of Gypsies may be identified, such as in the songs' allusion to simple rural beauty, as derived from the lyrics' allegedly folk origins. The songs are also fairly short in duration, lasting from seventeen bars (song 4) to eighty-four (song 10). In character, the melodics resemble those of a recitative. By preserving in the vocal parts the metric and rhythmic schemes of the verse, the composer achieved a fairly conventional sound, despite—as John Tyrell writes—the cycle's deep-rooted dramatism (Tyrell 2001, 778). And for all the songs' apparent simplicity, they are characterized by "a fatalism and lyrical intoxication" (Vogel 1983, 301). The cycle is thus often interpreted as the "reflection of a young man" (Saremba 2003, 886) immersed in the romantic currents of the fin-de-siècle. In the text, then—although not so much in Janáček's musical treatment—the Gypsy heroine constitutes no more than a symbol of another world, one uninhibited by convention.

The Twentieth-Century Gypsy Song

In the twentieth century, the tendency to trivialize Gypsy subject matter within songs owed both to the influence of Viennese operetta and the expansion of popular music. Particularly in the early part of the century, the Gypsy theme was visible in collections of folk and popular songs, as well as in lighter forms. Also continued, though rarer, were sentimental portrayals of Gypsies set to romantic texts, a mode that included songs for children. At the popular and more "serious" levels alike, Gypsyness was rendered in extremely conventionalized ways, in both texts (e.g., the mixing of the designations *bohémienne* and *zingara* or *tzigane*) and music (the mixing of Hungarian and Spanish references).

In crafting so-called Gypsy songs, creators often drew from earlier works. Before the turn of the century, for example, in 1887, the melody "La dame enlevée par les Tsiganes," from volume III of *Chanson populaires*, contained English words supposedly taken from the London edition of *A Selection of the Most Favourite Scot Songs* of 1790. Indeed, the same melody accompanied a different set of words in a ballad consisting of twenty-three verses published in London in the 1847 collection *The Minstrelsy of the English Border*, edited by Frederick Sheldon. On the German scene, a small collection from the 1920s, *Elsassischer Liederkranz*, included a popular "Zigeunerlied," reproducing the stereotype of the merry life of a Gypsy ("Lustig ist's Zigeunerleben"). Song composers also reworked folk songs to include Gypsy figures, such as in 1934 when Alexander Moyzes published *Dvanast' lud'ovych piesní zo Šariša* (op. 9), in which he included the song "Bili še cigáni . . . ," which was based on a popular melody and supported by a simple piano accompaniment.

The twelfth volume of *Music and Art* (1919) showed composers' inclination to emphasize the age of popular songs associated with Gypsy material. Although this work failed to give sources and translated the lyrics into English, it dated an allegedly traditional song, "The Spanish Gypsy," to the seventeenth century.

Formats for publication and popularization of songs on all subjects, among them Gypsies, included booklets as well as postcard series, embellished by either black-and-white or color drawings. "La Bohémienne," for example, with words beginning "*Je suis bonne Bohémienne*," was written for voice and piano by a Madame C. Leon and suggests a highly amateurish venture. The melody, over 2/4 meter, is accompanied by simple C major, G major, and F major chords, but however simple it was, the score contained mistakes such as a flat notated on only one staff and the construction of certain chords leaving much uncertainty as to their nature.

Use of American popular music to carry forth Gypsy themes became common in the twentieth century. Musically, the songs were often based on a thirty-two-bar Tin Pan Alley structure, with simple functional harmony, and classically sentimental content associated with Gypsy love, dance, and song. Other previously employed techniques included imitation of instruments linked to Gypsies, use of minor keys (often preceded by a major for enhanced contrast and effect), irregular rhythmic divisions (chiefly triples), and, most transparently, suggestive titles.

But the fundamental change in the status of the Gypsy song involved its function as entertainment. For one thing, creators of popular songs were open to fresh and fashionable material, which the Gypsy themes provided. For another, designations of the Gypsy, or bohemian, lifestyle and worldview were consciously coupled with those of artists. As we have seen, confusion surrounded the application of the term *bohème* to not only genuine Romanies or romanticized Gypsies but also artistic types inhabiting cabarets, night clubs, and so on. Thus, the artist was often coidentified with the eternally seeking Gypsy.

The entertainment trend, by the 1930s, would include wind accompaniment based on that for jazz bands, although traditional songs for voice with piano accompaniment persisted. Furthermore, dance rhythms permeated the Gypsy song, both in European versions and those imported from elsewhere.

As in the previous century, the piano was often used to mimic instruments deemed typical for Gypsies. Roger de Moliére in "Roman Tzigane" (1945), a piece written in a Tin Pan Alleyesque style, imitated the violin through tuplets, repetitions, and other gestures in the right hand, while echoing the dulcimer tremolo in the left. The lyricist, Denis Michel, characterized the Gypsy camp in broad, romantic strokes, noting the endless sky, evening, the Gypsy song, and the sound of the guitar. Mixing of Spanish and Hungarian Gypsy references reveals yet another compositional convention, with *tzigane* used in the title and *gitane* appearing in the text, with this Spanish reference especially handy given the mention of the guitar.

Use of a jazz band format presented no impediment to displays of violin virtuosity, aimed, for instance, at enlivening text references to fiddling as a Gypsy practice. On this count, J. Jekyll in his 1938 "Tzigeneria: Boston Tzigane" (to words by Louis Serre) introduced a violin solo rippling with quintuplets and sextuplets and a showing a preference for an augmented second interval, clearly alluding to the tradition of the *prímáses*.

Displaying how nineteenth-century techniques of evoking Gypsyness persisted into the next century, the 1935 song "Les Tziganes: Chanson populaire tzigane," by Michel Levine with words by J. Haël and A. Deguila, includes complex chords in the piano that approximate the dulcimer. Additionally, the vocal part contains syncopated rhythms and the G major introduction is followed, quite typically for such Gypsy songs, by a minor key. The case of "Le chemin de l'Aventure: Bohemienne, ou vastu" of 1944, written by the popular operetta composer Guy Lafarge (1904–1990), with words by Guy Dasso (who also wrote the libretto to Lafarge's 1932 operetta *Marquis de Carabas et Cie*), is similar. The composer suggested "tempo *tzigane*" for this light cabaret song, indicating not so much a designated tempo as a certain arbitrariness in the speeding up and slowing down, reflecting the spontaneity of the Gypsy soul. The composer's notion of Gypsyness is further borne out by the text, the use of the minor key (C minor, contrasted with C major), the frequently introduced tuplets or arpeggio, and the imitation of the guitar in the piano part.

Given the increasing popularity of entertainment songs with Gypsy references, some would be published without even piano accompaniment, instead offering a highlighted melodic line with suggested chords. One such example was "Le Tzigane jouait toujours" (1938), by Casimir Oberfeld and Mitty Goldin, with words by André Hornez and Mitty Goldin.

For all the other influences on the early twentieth-century popular Gypsy song, the greatest was that exerted by dance forms, and in particular the waltz. The Viennese operetta had been chiefly responsible for establishing this connection. In preserving the characteristic waltz accompaniment, composers most often chose a major key (eschewing the minor associated with Gypsies) and led the melodic line diatonically, and occasionally with chromatics. Typical "Gypsy waltzes," with a simple structure conducive to performance by amateurs and entertainers alike, were composed by "Nadyval," who produced, among other pieces, "Les Tziganes chantent," with words by Fred Fisher (1875–1942), and

"Tzigane d'amour," with a text by Henri Dumont. Marie Simone wrote both the music and words to a song entitled "La Tzigane: Valse chantée." And Ch. Pons composed the song-waltz "La Bohémienne" (1934) with words by Jean Sorbier, dealing with a "petite Bohémienne."

The Gypsy waltzes, devised as popular songs, were also composed for voice and instrumental groups. In 1930 under the pseudonym Horatio Nicholls, the English creator of light entertainment songs Lawrence Wright (1888–1964), who wrote many hits in the Tin Pan Alley style—including "Dream of Delight" (1916) and "The Toy Drum Major" (1924)—wrote "Gipsy Melody" to words by Harry Carlton, for voice with a jazz group accompaniment. In this little Tin Pan Alley–style waltz in C minor, the Gypsyness is marked mainly in the title, offering a pretext to unfurl dreams about one's beloved against the so-called Gypsy melody. Louis Unia and J. du Rivaux also used an instrumental group in a waltz with words by a writer with the surname Jancel, entitled "Bohémien d'amour." Here, as in other examples, the terms *bohémien* and *gitan* are used interchangeably, with the typical Gypsyness also coming through in the D minor key, the presence of tuplets, and, above all, the title "Valse gitane."

The foxtrot, associated with the waltz's elegance, would also enter the range of songs covering Gypsy material, as in "The Gipsy" (1945), with music by Billy Reid and words by Stan Bowsher. The lyrics referred superficially to Gypsy subject matter, with the Gypsy woman portrayed as a fortune-teller who is seeking to ensure the faithfulness of a visitor's beloved.

Examples of tango *chanté* also appeared, with one example being "Mosquita muerta: La Bohémienne" of the early 1930s, written for voice and piano accompaniment by José M. Lucchesi, with words by Pippo Racho (in the Spanish version) and Didier Daix (in the French version), based on the typical contrast of G minor and G major. Other songs with Gypsy-tied lyrics employed rumba rhythms, such as Abel Monestes's "Myroska," in the 1940s, for voice and piano accompaniment, with words by Andre Myra that begin "La Bohemiénne et la courtisane c'était Carmen c'était Manon...." The *pasodoble* also wrought its effect on dances accompanied by songs with Gypsy subject matter, such as "Tzigane" (1947), by W. Goulart and C. Carvalhinho, popularized with lyrics in French by Jean Loysel and Rolf Marbot.

The popular turn in the treatment of Gypsy material for songs would affect composers of so-called serious music covering Gypsy motifs—namely, by moving them away from a former inclination toward pathos. Although, for example, the song "Bohémiens" (1913; op. 25), by Théodore Terestchenko (1888–1950), with words from the French Symbolist poet Henri Cazalis (1840–1909), aka

Jean Lahor, possessed a text with stereotypical components such as a Gypsy playing a violin at dusk, the violin part is introduced as an equal partner with the vocal line against the accompanying piano. Typical sentimentalism, as well as the association of Gypsy culture with the violin as a motif often exploited in Viennese operetta, remains a characteristic of the song.

The German inheritors of the romantic *lied* would likewise reevaluate the role of sentimentality in songs incorporating Gypsy motifs. Rudolf Desch (1911–1997), in his "Zigeunerweise" of 1959 for male voices (two tenors and two basses a cappella), used words by Georg Britting (1891–1964) that related Gypsy life in a fairly prosaic way. The evening bonfire, dance, and song were supplanted by the description of the preparation of supper, with the main dish being a staple of the wandering Gypsy—hedgehog. In 1961, Paul Zoll (1907–1978) handled Gypsy material similarly, if somewhat more lightly, in the secular cantata *Mond über dem Zigeunerwagen: Zigeunerlieder für gemischten Chor, Bassbariton, und Klavier.* Comprising ten parts, the work paints a picture of the cycle of Romany daily life: the setting up of camp, the search for food, the military draft, and more moving moments such as love for a girl, the death of a father, and the lulling of a child to sleep. This piece's harmonic simplicity, based on dominant-tonic relationships, the minimalism of its harmonies, the frequent use of the empty fifth interval in the piano accompaniment, and the text's suggestive language and imagery result in a composition that tells of Romany reality with an unpretentious yet captivating naturalism hitherto unseen.

Less frequent attempts would be made to portray Romany reality by incorporating flamenco within the artistic song. One successful such effort was Manuel Infante's 1961 "Canto flamenco" for voice with piano. The piano accompaniment imitates the sound of the guitar, while the vocal part effects frequent halts in the song's flow: a 3/4 meter is maintained in the accompaniment, against a melody conducted in changing meters, with these shifts suggesting the naturalness of the sung utterance, in keeping with the spirit of flamenco.

As for the nineteenth-century tradition of setting songs to poetic texts—to idealized, romanticized effect—this practice would be kept up to a limited extent throughout the twentieth century. Here, however, we see a move beyond German poetic source material. The Slovenian composer Marjan Kozina (1907–1966), for example, used the text of the well-known Serbian poet Jovan Jovanović (1833–1904) for a collection of songs for voice with piano, *Izbrane pesmi* (1964). In this work, next to Chinese and World War II partisan songs, one finds "Cigan," in A minor, with a variable meter of 4/8 and 3/8, as if alluding to the old *zingarella* genre. In 1960, the Russian composer Youry Shaporin

(1887–1966) incorporated within a collection of songs for voice and piano accompaniment (op. 21) the "The Song of the Gypsy Girl," written to a poem by Aleksei Nikolaevich Tolstoi (1817–1875). The Mexican composer Manuel M. Ponce (1886–1948) likewise turned to a Russian source for his *3 poems de Lermontov*, on which "La Bohémienne" for voice with piano, dedicated to his wife, Clema, was the final piece.

Songs written for children and incorporating Gypsy figures offered a new field for referencing and trivialization. Germaine Bontemps (1899–1951), for instance, wrote a simple song "Gitane" to a text by the poet Henry de Madaillan, included in the collection *Paganes* (1962). Similarly, as the first song of his exceptionally simple *Six chansons de theatre* (1954), Darius Milhaud set a song for voice and piano with words by Georges Pitoeff that begins "*La Bohémienne. . . .*" All the songs in the collection, easy enough to be played by children, are based on waltz rhythms and utilize the repetition of a single sound, suggesting almost a recitative. A sung version of Eugénie Brunlet's "La Tzigane" also appears in the collection *Études aimables* (1949), serving a didactic function and offering no extramusical associations with Romany culture.

The range of Gypsy themes and their resonance with other tropes offered a rewarding chest of material for composers of songs beginning in the nineteenth century. And although the heyday of the "Gypsy song" has passed, the form, in trivialized, romanticized, and also increasingly naturalistic ways, continues to inspire creators today.

🌿 🐿 🌿 🐿 🌿

CHAPTER NINE

Gypsy Motifs in Instrumental Works

Across the nineteenth and twentieth centuries, one area in which Gypsy motifs were generally absent was longer-form concert works, a gap that may be attributed to composers' inadequate knowledge of Romany music. Exceptions include Henryk Wieniawski's use of a Gypsy-sounding name (*à la Zingara*) to subtitle the third and final part of his *II Violin Concerto* in D minor (op. 22; first presented in public in 1862 but published in 1879)—with the violin being the link to the Gypsies—a piece that incidentally was dedicated to Sarasate, who so willingly employed Gypsy themes in his compositions. In 1924, Maurice Ravel's orchestral poem "Tzigane"—initially for violin and piano and then for violin and orchestra—alluded to Hungarian Gypsies both in its title and by employing the augmented second interval. Even more strikingly, the piece placed considerable technical demands on the solo violin performer, recalling Gypsy violin virtuosity. The piece starts slowly with an elaborate violin cadence abounding in flageolets, double stops, pizzicato, and other virtuosic effects. The work's subsequent frequent tempo changes recall the czardas, although the composition is sometimes referred to as a rhapsody, a genre associated with Gypsy connotations and also utilized in 1844 by Constantin Julius Becker (1811–1859) in his *Die Zigeuner Rhapsodie* (op. 31).

The modest sampling of orchestral compositions linked to Gypsy material make characteristic use of genres such as capriccio and fantasy. In 1894, for example, Sergei Rachmaninoff (1873–1943) wrote *Caprice bohémien* for orchestra, with the variable moods associated with the title's "capriccio" readily linked to a Gypsy trait. Sergei Prokofiev likewise composed his *Gypsy Fantasy* (op. 127; 1951) in the context of his own ballet *The Stone Flower* (mentioned in chapter 7).

The instrumental miniature, and particularly the piano miniature, peaked as a form in the nineteenth century, as we saw earlier. And this form would be the springboard for many composers to explore Gypsy subject matter. References included geographical nods to Spain, Hungary, and Russia as well as romantic allusions to the figure of the wanderer and, by extension, the artist type as a peripatetic Gypsy, including in piece's titles. The *zingarella,* for its part, developed in a sort of parallel with the miniature, and thus the two forms would influence each other. Two other nineteenth-century trends would eventually affect the development of the miniature on Gypsy themes, with one resulting in "songs without words" and another in compositions set to dance rhythms. Also, musical stage works (mainly opera and, later, operetta) influenced Gypsy instrumental miniatures by infusing them with portrayals of Gypsyness that were conventional within European culture. Finally, the *style brillant* would leave a clear mark on instrumental miniatures with Gypsy connotations.

Early nineteenth-century fascination with Gypsy content gravitated to Spanish culture. Then, for a period in the later nineteenth century, attention drifted toward the Hungarian Gypsy tradition, thanks largely to the publication of Liszt's book as well as the broader musical activity of Hungarian Gypsies across Europe. Such an orientation would be strengthened by the Hungarian content in Viennese operetta, a form that would enjoy great popularity well into the twentieth century. By the later nineteenth and, particularly, the early twentieth century, however, attention would recenter on Gypsy flamenco themes within the national Spanish idiom, a focus reflected in the miniatures of the day.

Early Instrumental Miniatures with Gypsy Connotations

The earliest so-called Gypsy miniatures often quoted opera works that only referred to Gypsies in their titles. In certain harpsichord works dating to the eighteenth century, titles suggested some connection with Gypsy culture through the word *bohémienne.* For example, in the collection *Premier receüil de contradanses et la table par lettre alphabétique et chiffree* (1737), by Jean Leclerc, the title "La Boëmiene" is assigned to number 99 on page 37.

The collection *Morceaux pour clavecin,* by a certain Legrand (a common name among musicians in France at the time) also dates from the eighteenth century (Fuller 2001, 483); on page 5, we see "La Bohémienne: Air italien." As in other selections from the volume, this piece is brief and based mainly on reprises and variations, in G minor with a 2/4 meter, with the melody playing an overriding role. The work—whose harmony changes relatively rarely, moving between the chords of the triad—possesses certain characteristics typical for the *zingarella,* which would not experience its heyday until early in the next century.

Published in the 1760s, Charles-François Clement's *Journals de clavecin* comprised twelve booklets, with one for each month of the year and two suites in each. The subtitle announced these pieces to be *Ariettes des Comedies; Intermedes; et Opera Comiques, qui ont eu le plus de succès*. In July 1764, in *Suite XIII* for violin and harpsichord, the third part was titled "Air de la Bohémienne" (next to "Arietta du bucheron," by Philidor, and "Arietta de La fille mal garde"). In 1755, Clement had already developed this music from the interlude to *La Zingara*, by Rinaldo di Capua, calling the former work simply *La Bohémienne*. The work possesses some traits of the *zingarella*—for instance, its popular key of C minor.

Moving into the nineteenth century, with the *zingarella* form gaining popularity as a mode of exotic discourse about Gypsyness in Spain—complemented by the publication of many books on the topic—composers sought musical paraphrases that imparted Spanish Gypsy "local color." Franz Liszt was among those to transcribe *zingarellas* for piano, and he wrote a bolero entitled "La Zingarella spagnola," based on an 1836 *zingarella* by Saverio Mercadante. Around 1847, Liszt transcribed "Zigeunerpolka d'August Conradi" for piano. Other *zingarellas* arranged for piano include François Bonoldi's "Chanson d'une Gitana: Romance bolero," carried out by Wilhelm Kruger (1820–1883) in 1846 and published as *Fantaisie sur la Gitana de Fr. Bonoldi* (op. 6). Still other examples include Carl Maria von Weber's C major variations on Gypsy songs (*Sieben Variationen über ein Zigeunerlied*; op. 55) of 1817 and the piano virtuoso Sigismond Thalberg's (1812–1871) use of a melody from Julius Benedict's very popular 1840 opera *The Gypsy's Warning* (op. 34) for his *Divertissement*. In the later nineteenth and early twentieth centuries, the themes from Bizet's opera *Carmen* enjoyed special popularity, as attested, among other works, by Sarasate's *La fantasía Carmen* (op. 25), which uses the characteristic ostinato technique, repetition of rhythmic figures, and an arabesque melodic line.

Gypsy Songs without Words

The most widespread Gypsy instrumental miniatures of the nineteenth and early twentieth centuries might be divided into two classes: on the one hand, songs, arias, and chansons, and on the other, dances. Showy works titled fantasy, impromptu, fête, and so forth constituted another important class, with these works often tagged as "souvenirs" from either Spain or Hungary. In some cases, the Gypsy connotation could only be located in the name, with the genre left unspecified, showing the vague inclinations of the composer.

Songs without words that carried specific ties to a country—which might be

Russia, as well as Hungary or Spain—entered a broad cultural current in which Romanies were viewed as somehow representing the nation in which they lived. Titles of these miniatures, nonetheless, handled such referencing arbitrarily. In particular, later nineteenth-century works called *air* or *chanson,* accompanied by the adjective *tzigane,* suggested an attachment to the Gypsy idiom of Hungary, but corresponding musical traits to substantiate this tie would be absent. In the work "Air tzigane" of 1884 for piano solo, by Jules Philipot (1824–1897), certain typical traits of the *zingarella* were preserved (including the segmented structure and key changes), but the performance annotation *alla militaire* perhaps suggested an association with the *verbunkos.* Another composition, "Chanson tzigane: Marceaux de genre" (1907), by J. Dovillez, for piano solo (from *Six pieces pour piano*) represents a return to the features typical for the nineteenth-century *zingarella,* such as a simple ternary structure and oscillation between the minor key (G minor) and the major (E sharp major). But no elements bespeak a connection to Gypsy sounds. Another piano miniature recalling a typical *zingarella,* with the title denoting a "song" and written by the British composer and pianist of Czech birth Wilhelm Kuhe (1823–1912), was "Zigeuner Trinklied: Chanson Bohémienne" (op. 138), composed sometime before the composer's death. The piece is written in A-B-A form and, true to the *zingarella* tendency, features the keys D minor and F major.

Likewise, miniature titles indicating an aria (or some variation) did not obligate composers to include actual Gypsy references. "Les Zingari, air de ballet" (1887), by Georges Bachmann (1837–1898), for piano in F major had an unusually simple structure and a highly expressive texture, but the only indication of Gypsy roots lay in the title's indication of the *zingarella.* Meanwhile, the piece "Tziganetta, air de ballet pour piano" (1899), by Paul Rougnon (1846–1934), had a transparent texture, 3/4 meter, and B minor key, within a clear rondo form. The piece was designed to be played at home by amateurs, for whom a taste of the exotic in the title was enough to add interest, even if no authentic musical material attended it.

Composers less often titled their pieces *songs* or *chansons* when referring to Spanish Gypsy culture. But the late nineteenth-century surge of interest in the flamenco of Andalusian Gitanos prompted the composition of instrumental pieces, such as Albert Vizentini's (1841–1906) *Airs espagnols pour piano* (1900), comprising "Bohémienne," along with "Rhapsodie," "Par des mantilles," "Estudiantina," "Les epées," and "Danses finales et jota." Characteristically, the work—composed for an instrumental ensemble but also playable by solo piano—abounds melodically with the augmented second interval.

The work of Russian Romany choirs would also reach Europe, eliciting interest based on its exotic character—although not, overall, based on its specific musical qualities. In 1887, the French music critic Camille Bellaigue (1858–1930) included an account of his trip to Moscow in his *Un siècle de musique francaise*. This account included a discussion of the customs, attire, and musical practices of the Russian Romany. He noted, for instance, how the mainly female Romany choirs were accompanied by guitar. In his work, Bellaigue both emphasized the melancholy and sentimentalism of the Gypsies as well as the need for research to remedy the low understanding of and interest in the subject: "Gypsies, Russians keep the secret of their songs. Science also has not penetrated the divine mystery of this ignorance. For it is essential for research to be undertaken together with understanding" (Bellaigue 1887, 262–67).

In fact, references to Russian Gypsies' singing predated Bellaigue's account, with piano miniatures coming particularly from France beginning in the mid-nineteenth century. The 1861 work *Les Bohémiens* (op. 57) for piano solo, by Jacques Blumenthal (1829–1908), conveys a standard relationship to Russian Gypsy motifs: the title page identifies the work as the transcription of a popular song from "petite Russie," as the territories of Ukraine were then known. The work itself—a virtuoso rondo in E sharp major—is based on the contrast of the refrain's cantilena melody and the choral-like fragment in G minor.

Also bearing the title "Air Bohémien Russe" (Tziganes) (op. 30; 1882) is N. de Wolkoff's *morceau characteristique* for piano. Yet despite the title's suggestion of a connection to Russian Gypsies, the piece inclines itself toward the *zingarella*—through the B minor key and clearly segmented internal structure—as well as toward a typical czardas.

Gypsy Dance Miniatures

As in other instrumental miniatures, miniatures incorporating dance often had titles making reference to a country with which Romanies were strongly affiliated. Practically speaking, such miniatures were notable for being intended for average or more advanced amateur instrumentalists with aspirations to virtuosity. Eventually, certain dances became favored in this form. The waltz, preferred early, eventually gave way to marches and polkas and, at the beginning of the twentieth century, the representative form was considered the czardas. Musically, in the nineteenth and early twentieth centuries, the *zingarella* would be a musical model for the artistic dance miniature. Composers, however—when writing "Gypsy dances"—often named these pieces generically, as a dance in the style of the *zingarella*.

The Waltz

Beginning in the early nineteenth century, certain waltz titles carried references to Gypsy culture. And waltz miniatures, with these intriguing titles, were written to ensure the virtuosic effects of *style brillant*. Such compositions include, for example, Laurent Batta's *grande valse brillante* for piano solo "La Bohémienne" (ca. 1844), a miniature of a mosaic structure in E sharp major dedicated to the Paris-based Polish pianist and composer Edward Wolff. Somewhat later, Rafaël de Aceves (1837–1876) incorporated within his *Danses d'Espagne* (op. 65) for piano a simple waltz entitled "Bohémienne," with an interesting structure referring to an allegro sonata. His *Folie Gitane* (op. 60) is also a waltz, in E sharp major. Despite the clear allusions to Spanish Gypsies in these titles, the musical material does not uphold such references. Moreover, the composer's loose conception of Gypsy tradition is borne out in his interchangeable use of the words *gitane* and *bohémienne*.

The influence of the virtuoso style on Gypsy waltzes is also visible in Melchior Mocker's *La zingarella: Danse Bohéme pour piano* (op. 10) of 1853, the mosaic structure of which allows the performer to show off his or her abilities. The composition is characterized by a simple melody but one with typical traits for a virtuosic miniature, such as octave passages in the left hand and numerous tuplets and sextuplets.

The success of the Viennese operetta, and its simultaneous references to the waltz form and Gypsy themes, would likewise have an effect on the dance miniature. The form, whose titles often included *tzigane* or *tziganerie*, is typified by M. Fiorelli's "Rêve de Tzigane" of 1904 for piano, with a two-part structure expanded by a coda. At around the same time, Michel Barthon composed a waltz for piano, *Tziganerie*, which he dedicated to Gaston Paulin, who, for his part, authored a waltz titled *Tzigania* (op. 143; 1911), with the latter being an unpretentious piece for string quintet to be performed at home.

In the 1920s, the waltz form would undergo a renaissance, particularly in French circles in the form of the waltz *musette*, as a result of the development in Paris of entertainment music.

March

Marches making reference to the tradition of Gypsy music-making became particularly popular around the 1860s. These were works for solo piano, most commonly in minor keys (although internally employing the contrast of minor and major keys), at a 2/4 or alla breve meter with a clearly segmented (e.g., ternary) structure. Included within these works is Ernest Reyer's (1823–1909)

Marsche tzigane of 1869, displaying an A-B-A structure, in C minor but with A sharp major appearing in the middle part. This march has versions for small orchestra as well as piano.

Some Gypsy marches were written as a sort of travel memoir following a visit to Hungary. One such example is the 1860s march for piano by Désiré Magnus (1828–1883) entitled *Tziganes marche: Souvenir de Hongrie*. The work oscillates between minor and major keys (the initial B minor is quickly transformed into B major) in a way characteristic for artistic Gypsy compositions and also uses frequent dotted rhythms. In the twelve-bar introduction, the composer also employs an empty fifth, linked within the European musical tradition with primitive exoticism (Scott 2003, 155–78, and Dahlhaus 1989, 305). In the same "memoir" tradition, Alfred Lebeau created a march for piano entitled *Tzigane Marsch: Ronde Bohéme* (op. 119) with the annotation *Impression de voyage*. Contrary to the title's implication, the piece is not written in rondo, but in ternary, form. Within this framework, however, each section persistently repeats the five motifs. The work makes reference to neither the *zingarella* nor *verbunkos* tradition, constituting rather a fairly easy exercise for amateur pianists, filled with octave passages and cadence formulas.

Polka

We have already seen the reference to Liszt's 1847 transcription of August Conradi's "Zigeunerpolka," but the true surge in the dance form's popularity, and Gypsy associations with it, came later in the century. In particular, composers of parlor music enthusiastically published polkas for musicians of average skill. A. de Jeziorski, for instance, wrote many polkas titled "Hedwiga" or "Lech" (both Polish names), and in 1881 he published "La Zigeuna: Polka pour piano," a typically flashy miniature of ternary structure, in F major and 2/4 meter, with a transparent texture. Similarly, Emile Waldteufel (1837–1915), who enjoyed a far-reaching reputation as a composer of dances, titled his polka from the collection *Danses célèbres pour piano* (1889) "Les Bohémiens."

The designation *bohémienne* tagged to polka might have held Czech as well as Gypsy associations, and it was more or less up to the interpreter to decide which. The ambiguity can be observed, for example, in Filippo Lea's "La Bohémienne: Nouvelle danse" of 1908, a simple, straightforward piece for piano aimed at providing instruction on polka performance, with figures described by Eduard Schiano, a professor of dance.

Polkas intermixed with the (equally popular) mazurka also contained references to Gypsies in their titles, such as Magnus's polka-mazurka "La Zingara"

(1860) and Eugène Stoerkel's "Chanson tzigane" (1890) for piano solo, which bears the subtitle "Susanne: Polka mazurka."

Czardas

The czardas, broadly associated with Hungarian Gypsies in nineteenth-century Europe and popularized by Liszt and by Strauss's *Die Fledermaus*, also appeared in instrumental miniature form. In the early twentieth century, Vittorio Monti's (1868–1922) rendition for violin and piano would garner particular acclaim. The structure of the form would be divided into slower (*lassan*) and faster (*friska*) sections, as follows: A: *lassan*, B-C: *friska*, D-E: *episode* (which was slower), C-B-C: *friska*. The minor key in the introductory section allowed for the frequent use of the augmented second interval in the melody line, initially introduced in the low register of the violin. In the accompanying piano part, arpeggiated chords imitate the dulcimer. The composer also introduced a characteristic rhythm with an irregular division of values (sixteenth tuplets), syncopation, as well as numerous grace notes.

The czardas was especially popular in early twentieth-century literature for amateurs, and its structure and other components typically conformed to common notions of Gypsy music-making. Compositions in this context enabled fairly low-level players to achieve quite striking effects. One typical example is Gustave Michiels's 1908 "Bohéma czardas," which along with the typical structure includes imitation of the violin through a monophonic melody in the right-hand part at a fairly low register as well as a quasivirtuoso cadence. The dulcimer, for its part, is evoked by arpeggiated chords in the left hand and quick two-note repetitions, creating a tremolo effect. Furthermore, the accumulation of the tuplets, the grace notes, and the irregular division of values help create the impression of violin improvisation. Structurally, the piece moves from its E minor introduction, which establishes the piece's idiom in its first bars, to the dance *friska* (in A minor), which is then interrupted by a lyrical fragment (andante) before returning to the joyful *friska*, first in A minor but soon changing to A major.

The popularity of the czardas as an instrumental miniature is borne out by its frequent and visible presence in various roughly turn-of-the-century collections for amateur or semiprofessional piano players. For example, in a collection of mainly dance pieces for piano, *Les musiques bizarre: A l'exposition* (1889), the author, "Benedictus," includes a stylized czardas called "Le Tzigane." In the 1925 *Ce qu'on aime a entendre: Collection de 15 morceaux célèbres publiés* for piano, various czardases are found beside other then-popular dances, including the habanera and intermezzo *americain*. On pages 8–11 of this collection, we encounter the czardas from *Suite tzigane* (1906), by Maurice Gracey (1876–1951), and on pages 24–25, Enrico Toselli's (1883–1926) "Zingaresca" is annotated as a czardas. This latter piece—even as it preserves the same melodic material in both fast and slow sections—does not conform rigorously to the traditional czardas structure. Also, formal components such as the use of F minor for the beginning and ending sections, and F major in the middle, suggest the piece's indirect links (highlighted in the title) to, and the continued pull of, the *zingarella*.

Waltz *Musette, Java*, Rumba, and Others

In the second half of the nineteenth century, artistic references to Gypsy music-making and themes would be transformed and trivialized "by the legions of minor masters" following the fashion (Bellman 1993, 134, 218). This shift simultaneously reflected a pandering to the tastes of bourgeois amateurs, who derived pleasure from Gypsy operettas and their alleged Gypsy music.

Gypsy music, as expressed in early twentieth-century instrumental miniatures, straddled artistic and more utilitarian purposes, such as dance. In this context, the mainly Paris-based renaissance of "Gypsy waltz" in the 1930s and 1940s incorporated a hybrid of waltz rhythms with the *musette* form and a Gypsy-associated title. As for the *musette*, it emerged in the late nineteenth century, incorporating musical elements from migrant peoples, particularly those from rural France and Italy. The compulsory instrument was the accordion. By around the outbreak of World War II, the entertainment industry had identified possibilities in the *musette*, the music of the Parisian poor. Waltz *musettes* thus arose such as Clement Jenner and A. Barthelemo's "Tzingarella" of 1939, for piano, accordion, violin, and alto saxophone. Similarly, Joseph Colombo's 1946 "Zingarella: Valse musette" was written for piano or accordion, with the optional addition of violin and E flat alto saxophone, with a three-part structure and trio. This graceful little waltz has an expressively maintained pulse, against a melody in eighth notes, and is written in a minor key, although such choices were not significant in referencing Gypsy associations. Another representative piece, Louis Ferrari's "Bohémienne valse" of 1945 for piano, accordion, E flat alto saxophone, and violin also remains within established norms, with its three-part structure and characteristic trio, beginning and ending parts in a minor key, and middle part in the parallel major key.

Such works referenced Gypsies in their titles through loosely wielded terms that were deeply rooted in the European tradition, such as *tzigane, zingarella, bohémienne*, or *gitanilla*. Compositions of this type were usually characterized by a schematic structure, maintained in a major key, with harmonic functions spelled out in the published scores.

Also popular during the same period was a fast waltz largely played on the accordion known as a *java*, which likewise employed Gypsy-associated titles. For instance, "Zingarina: Java Variations," by Jean Peyronnin and Gousty Malla reflects the Tin Pan Alley tradition with its regular, temporal structure, uncomplicated harmony, and entertaining character. In the 1950s, the compositional team of Stef Pimack and André Cahard wrote a series of Gypsy waltzes for piano and violin, consisting typically of three (or sometimes four) waltzes and frequently repeated melodic lines. In these simple works, suitable for beginners, the violin plays the melody to piano accompaniment. The first volume was published in 1956 as *Valses de folklore*, which included the parts *Fete a Roustchouk* (with "Melancholie tzigane," "Aube champetre," and "Danse et irresse") and *Tziganes de Craiova* (with "Au crepuscule," "Tristesse d'automne," "Frivole Gitane," and "Festival de joie"). In 1959, they published *Les feux de Temisoara* ("Tziganes au bois," "Fleurs et papillons," and "Amour et feux de joie"), *La Gitane de Nikopoli* ("Le chant du Berger," "Plaines et valées," and "Retour et regrets"), and *Les Bohemiennes de Tchernaia* ("Vagabondage tzigane," "Au clair de lune," and "Danse cosaque"). These titles were notable for displaying Gypsy associations with Romanian society, a relatively rare gesture.

The Gypsy theme also permeated rumba titles in, for example, "Tzigane Rumba" (1946) for piano, by J. R. Baltet and R. Desplanques—an exceptionally simple miniature of a regular recurring structure representative of the popular idiom.

Dances *"alla Zingara"*

In the nineteenth and twentieth centuries, the use of the adjective "Gypsy" in the title of a dance miniature was common, both helping ensure recipients would remember the work and propagating the romantic association of the carefree Gypsies with dance, even if authentic artistic references were absent. In later works, the lack of any such references, even speculative, prompted an abandonment of geographic or genre-based particularizing in favor of highly nonspecific titles, such as "Gypsy dance." Composers, performers, and listeners alike were affected by such names and perhaps stirred to stereotypical musings. Likewise, such naming conventions for home music publications may simply have made pieces easier to identify.

Hence, in forgotten collections such as one by Alfred de Longpérier (undated), next to titles like "Pantalon," "Été," or "Poule," there appears "Les Bohémiens," classified as a quadrille. Similarly, the third part of Schumann's four-part *Sonata for Children* (no. 3), "Zigeunertanz" (1853), is critiqued justifiably as "entirely undistinguished and forgettable" (Bellman 1993, 134) given that the title is the piece's most remarkable trait. Later composers, in their works for children, continued the practice of referencing the "dancing Gypsy." Theodor Blumer's (1881–1964) "Zigeuner mit tanzendem Bär" for flute with piano accompaniment was published in the collection *Aus der Tierwelt*. Devised as a two-part dance, the first part is dominated by a lively flute while the second comes across in a monotonous, clumsy rhythm. Associations of Gypsy culture with dances in the fair tradition would also be conveyed in a 1944 work by Grete von Zieritz (1899–2001) for flute with piano accompaniment, included in the collection *Bilder vom Jahmarkt*. The fourth and final piece, "Zingeunerin," employs the stereotypical augmented second interval (E flat–F sharp).

In Gypsy dances, attempts were made to move beyond the simplicity of the *zingarella* by incorporating virtuosic elements. E. Simonnot's *La Zingara: Saltarelle pour piano* (op. 65) of 1869 thus drew its inspiration from both the *zingarella* (the ternary construction, the arrangement of fragments in the same minor and major keys) and the old Italian folk dance, the *saltarello*.

Other Gypsy dances displayed similar tendencies, such as Charles Lecocq's (1832–1918) *La Zingara: Danse bohémienne pour piano* (op. 9; 1856). Although modeled on a typical *zingarella*—through its A minor (and A major) key and segmented A-B-A-C-B structure (with numerous repetitions)—the work's allegretto tempo and brimming figurative passages lent themselves to spectacular performance.

The degree to which "dance" plus "*zingarella*" signaled Gypsy connotations in a title can be seen in Charles M. Widor's (1844–1937) piece "La Zingarella, danse pour piano" (1924), composed to accompany a dance in his opera *Nerto*, which was written around 1894 but published and performed thirty years later.

Genre Diversity in Miniatures Referencing Gypsy Music

Apart from songs without words and dance miniatures referencing Gypsy themes, a number of other widespread, more specific forms did the same, beginning with the capriccio, impromptu, fantasy, and souvenir. In most such cases, the "Gypsy" part in the title functioned as a kind of self-consent for dispensing with genre discipline, as justified by a social construct defining a "Gypsy way" of music-making. This Gypsy way was viewed as "untameable," but at the same time it was a widely understood component of European culture. The exotic, as we saw earlier, offered a common lens for viewing Gypsy traditions, along with the Hungarian, Spanish, and occasionally Russian national contexts. Moreover, the arbitrary and uninhibited use of terms such as *tzigane, zinagare, gitane,* and *bohémienne* revealed the generally loose treatment of the so-called Gypsy question.

Capriccio

The name *capriccio,* as appended to a miniature, gave the composer license to make frequent changes within a piece and its sections. Through the "Gypsy capriccio," composers could craft pieces of a quasi-improvisational character, while alluding to similar practices among the Gypsies as well as their virtuosic manner of performance.

For example, the 1862 capriccio (*caprice caracteristique*) "La Gitanilla" by the European-educated American composer Louis M. Gottschalk (1829–1869) clearly refers, through the title, to the exotic. Gottschalk enthusiastically wrote works of this type, including making reference to his own Creole roots in the miniature "Bamboula." A capriccio in G minor has a ternary structure and varied moods, with the light, almost aphoristic A section set against a melodious B fragment of a dance character and followed by the colorful C section. Thus, we see how the name *capriccio* could be used to show contrasting effects of mood as linked to the impetuous and changeable Gypsy soul. Around the same time, in 1863, Joseph Joachim Raff (1822–1882), a pupil and admirer of Liszt, wrote a capriccio for piano evoking Spanish and Gypsy associations, *La Gitana: Dance espagnol, caprice* (op. 110).

Other composers to take advantage of the leniency of the capriccio included Maurice Viot, whose 1922 miniature for violin and piano also incorporated the *zingarella* (infused with more recent Hungarian associations) in its title, "Zingara: Caprice hongrois." From the old *zingarella* form, there remained only the refrain, while Hungarian sentiments were reflected in the use of syncopation, tuplets, and so forth. The title, in any case, is the only truly noteworthy component of this piece.

Sometimes, a Gypsy-sounding capriccio title referred instead to artistic bohemia. This may well have been the case with pianist and composer Eugène Ketterer's (1831–1879) *caprice de concert* for solo piano, "Bohéma" (1875). Indeed, the work makes no nods to widespread nineteenth-century notions on the subject of Gypsy music.

The Fantasy

A similar arbitrariness may be seen in the treatment of Gypsy subject matter in works under the category *fantasy.* In the late nineteenth century, Regina

Beretta published the miniature "Zingara: Fantaisie" for piano, which through its movement from D minor to D major hinted at the czardas, while the structure (with short themes taking on the role of refrains) suggested the influence of the *zingarella*. Meanwhile, Dave Rubinoff's "Gipsy Fantasy" of 1938 for violin and piano directly links itself to the czardas through the contrast in tempo and the arrangements (cantabile in *lassan*, figurative in *friska*). The piece also provides a wide berth for violin expression, through its many double stops and quick passages as well as lyrical melodies. The Gypsy title may thus be read as referring equally to the virtuosic tradition of the *prímás*es.

Impromptu

Late nineteenth-century works with Gypsy-sounding titles and labeled *impromptu* were typically related directly to the czardas. For example, Marie de Verginy's "Tzigane: Impromptu pour piano" (1887) is principally distinguished for its contrast in tempos, but it also enacts piano emulations of the dulcimer through arpeggiated chords and the characteristic repetition of two pitches in a very quick tempo. At the rhythmic level, the composer introduced frequent syncopation, grace notes, and tuplets, allowing for the possibility of rubato.

Souvenir

The souvenir, unique in that it was based on popular nineteenth-century travel experiences, reflected the role of Romany people as perceived intermediaries of, particularly, Hungarian (see *tzigane* in titles) and Spanish national culture. For example, Alfred Michel's piano composition "Souvenir tziganes" of 1881 makes clear reference to the czardas, while Leo Streabbog's 1901 "La Gitana: Souvenir d'Espagne" for piano clearly points to Spanish associations. This latter miniature is a delicate piece for beginning or intermediate players and makes a veiled, hardly perceptible reference to the *zingarella* tradition.

Other Miniatures with Gypsy Titles

Still other instrumental miniatures making Gypsy associations have no genre designation at all. Program titles, then, serve the distinguishing role of marking Gypsyness.

The first group of such pieces is distinguished by the substantial presence of the term *zingarella* (and variants), even as this term would lose currency in the later nineteenth century. The 1880s, for example, would include Cecile Chaminade's (1857–1944) "Zingara" (op. 27, no. 2; 1883–1885) for piano, which harbored a distant connection to the traditions of a sung *zingarella*, through the A minor and A major keys (along with E major) as well as the use of a limited number of (just two) musical ideas. This work, with its simple character and striking effects, fits among other miniatures of the later nineteenth century that were written for semiprofessional or even amateur performers. A distant link to the *zingarella* is also displayed in André Renner's 1901 work for piano, *Bohémienne* (op. 3); a connection can also be found in André Gédalge's (1856–1926) never-published work for piano, "Bohémienne" (1887), preserved in manuscript form at the National Library in Paris (Ms. 14894). Written in D minor and a 2/4 meter, the miniature is based on just two melodic phrases, repeated either unchanged or in a slightly altered form. The almost pointillistic notation emphasizes the piece's highly transparent texture and graphically conveys its monophony.

Alongside references to the *zingarella*, program titles often referred to countries associated with Gypsies, namely Hungary or Spain. Evidence of twentieth-century references to Hungarian Gypsies appears in Théodore Lack's (1864–1921) piano work *Tziganyi* (op. 104) and C. Reichenbach's "Tzigana," with the Hungarian subtitle "Itt ringatták bölcsöm." This latter work references Gypsy tradition merely through the author's suggestion for a slowing in tempo every few bars, hinting at emotive Gypsy musicianship. Benjamin Godard's (1849–1895) miniature for piano "Tziganka" (op. 134) of 1895 would make no such references to Gypsy music at all. Instead, it was aimed at a virtuosic effect, utilizing the whole keyboard, with passages running up and down, octave doublings, and mixtures of thirds and sixths.

Charles René introduced "Les Bohémiens" to his 1893 piano suite *Le voyageur*, employing empty fifths as well as suggesting (two) monophonic virtuoso cadences, as if styled for violin, alluding to perceived Hungarian Gypsy violin virtuosity. Gypsy titles, more broadly, could thus signal a piece's virtuosity, as in Monti's "Zingaresca" (1912) for violin with piano accompaniment, a work marked by repetitions, numerous changes in key and tempo, and—foremost— the exemplary violin part, which teems with double stops, quick passages, harmonic flageolet tones, complicated rhythms, and tuplets. Other such spectacular miniatures of the period include Fritz Seitz's (1848–1918) "Zigeuner Kommen" (op. 16, no. 4) for violin with piano, which was devised as a czardas and preserved its characteristic form. In 1878, Sarasate, despite his Spanish origin, had himself invoked the czardas by composing *Zigeunerweisen* (op. 20) for violin and piano, or for violin and orchestra. Sarasate's violin part presents arabesque melodic lines and abounds in virtuoso effects, from pizzicato to double stops to flageolets.

Spanish Gypsy references in instrumental miniatures were generally less frequent than references to Hungarian Gypsies. And, interestingly, the authors of such pieces were more often than not Spaniards, perhaps treating such a title choice as a statement of self-identification. Federico Mompou, influenced by Erik Satie and the French Impressionists, incorporated two pieces, "Gitane I" and "Gitane II," into one of his most impressionistic works, *Suburbis* (1916–1917) for solo piano. In "Gitane I," the central function is fulfilled by repeated empty fifths in the low register to mark the beginning of the piece's four sections (in A-B-B-A structure). Meanwhile, "Gitane II" has a three-part A-B-A structure and the empty fifth consonance appears only once, serving as a link to "Gitane I." Mompou had previously, in 1914, written a related piece, "Gitano," which he entered into the collection for solo piano titled *Impressions intimes* (1910–1914). The piece's ternary structure and the presence of the empty fifth heralded the later pair.

In the early twentieth century, miniature treatments of Spanish Gypsy material (without a particular genre) would shift toward lighter forms, mirroring broader trends and encouraged by the entertainment industry. In 1934, for example, José Sentis's elaborate miniature "Flamenca seguidilla" betrays a link to Gypsyness, and particularly *cante jondo*, through the narrow ambitus of its melody. The composer reinforced this link to flamenco by adding castanets for performance.

Altogether, instrumental miniatures without a specific genre but with title-level links to Gypsyness, such as *tzigane, bohémienne,* or *zingara* in the Hungarian milieu, were quite successful. So successful were some that they were reproduced with other names that, in this context, cannot be treated merely as translations. For example, J. Mulder's simple early twentieth-century piece for piano was popular enough to be revived a half century later under many names: as "Petite Bohémienne," or "Little Gypsy Girl," and also as "Gitanilla" and "Zigeunermädchen."

The National Aspect of Instrumental Miniatures Associated with the Gypsy Topos

During the nineteenth century, in particular, titling a composition "Hungarian" or "Spanish" could suggest Gypsy innuendos. Referencing to cultural or musical material associated with those countries' so-called Gypsy culture and music was indeed rare, but these pieces nonetheless constituted genres associated with Gypsyness, such as marches, dances, and rhapsodies. Given no direct reference to Gypsies in the title (e.g., *tzigane, bohemienne, gitane*), deciphering such associations depended on the listener's cultural competence, knowledge, and openness to the possibility. Sometimes, though, it was the composer who left room for speculation, conceiving what may have resembled compositions *à clef.*

Hungarian Influences

In the nineteenth century, European professional musicians produced music that made the link between Hungarianness and Gypsyness almost inseparable, with titles of such works intermixing adjectives of both groups. From this perspective, Gypsy-associated works conceived in the eighteenth century were also seen to have implications for the evolution of the Hungarian character. Jonathan Bellman, noting a few distinctive musical traits of these pieces that carried a taste of the exotic, has grouped them within the *style hongrois*, a classification aimed, as it seems, at emphasizing Hungarian rather than Gypsy connotations. This was the case despite the *hongrois*'s evocation of musical performances by Hungarian Gypsies, aided by stereotypical social conceptions, literary portrayals, and imagery (e.g., paintings) associated with Gypsies. Hungarian coloring sometimes interpreted as Gypsy can be detected in the work of non-Hungarian composers such as Carl Ditters von Dittersdorf (1739–1799) and Johann Nepomuk Hummel (1778–1837), who remained within European compositional conventions when handling this material.

In writing music in the *style hongrois*, composers used "Hungarian" titles and often borrowed exotic gestures from the existing Turkish-influenced style annotated *alla turca*. According to Bellman, the *style hongrois* was based on imitation (particularly in the piano) of instruments associated with the *Zigeunerkapellen*, on specific rhythms, on melodic emphasis of the augmented second, and on nonfunctional harmonies employed for color (Bellman 1993, 121).

Composers picked and chose from the *style hongrois*, with certain gestures invariably becoming more popular than others and with musical context playing a de facto role. In the instrumental miniature of European salons, for example, *style brillant* prevailed, encouraging certain compositional choices. And Spanish-associated Gypsy sources offered an alternative to Hungarian sources for composers seeking to engage the exotic.

The preeminent inspiration for the *style hongrois*, however, was Liszt and, particularly, his *Hungarian Rhapsodies*. Following these works, miniatures labeled "Hungarian" appeared on a mass level—although their association with Gypsyness remains open to speculation (Bellman 1993, 196). Indeed, in their structure, pieces inspired by Liszt are characterized by a simple czardas arrangement, including the internal division between *lassan* and *friska*. The composers also made use of dance melodies derived chiefly from the traditional *verbunkos* and czardas, or from pieces passing as folk or the works of nineteenth-century Hungarian composers.

Other traits associated with the *style hongrois* included a certain harmonic freedom, numerous enharmonic modulations, and semitonic shifts, which may likewise have evoked Gypsy music (Malvinni 2004, 105). Similarly, it may be claimed that Liszt used the piano to imitate instruments associated with Hungarian Gypsies. Yet the cantilena melodies played usually in a medium or low register characterized Liszt's piano output in general, in which he "transferred the melody from the highest voice to the medium, which allowed for its description from top to bottom with the utilization of all the registers" (Chomiński, Chomińska-Wilkowska 1990, vol. 2, 109).

All the same, Liszt's *Hungarian Rhapsodies* undoubtedly linked themselves to Gypsy music-making, or the "Gypsy style," through their virtuosic character, which in turn conveyed the intense emotional expressiveness and improvisatory characteristics associated with Gypsies and their music. Piano virtuosity, of course, was attached to much of Liszt's oeuvre, not only those pieces labeled "Hungarian."

According to Klara Hamburger, Liszt had indeed incorporated Gypsy features into works also *not* marked Hungarian. Therefore, she argues, the use of Gypsy elements should be interpreted as an attempt to create an original style, separate from general European trends. Also, among Hungarian composers, "this national idiom (rather past its prime time by the second half of the 19th century) had become almost de rigeuer, no one at the time used it as successfully as Liszt. In point of fact, Liszt himself more or less exhausted its potential" (Hamburger 1997, 240). Similarly, Shay Loya recently distanced himself from the term *style hongrois* (and its national Hungarian connotation) and introduced the term *verbunkos idiom*, referring both to the "Gypsy tradition" and other traits of Liszt's compositional output (Loya 2011).

Over time, debates would persist on the Hungarian/Gypsy dimension of the *Hungarian Rhapsodies*. In the 1960s, the French musicologist Claude Rostand claimed that the melodies were de facto Gypsy even as, paradoxically, Liszt himself did not know this (Malvinni 2004, 91). The contemporary researcher Malvinni clarified that Liszt considered the Hungarian milieu an incubator for Gypsy music. Certain Hungarian musicologists—for example, Sárosi—have meanwhile persisted in the view that the *Hungarian Rhapsodies* were derived from Hungarian sources, while Bellman has concentrated on showing the "intensely personal language" of the works (Bellman 1993, 199). Before him, Ujfalussy had suggested that "the shallow sentimental lyricism of the popular folk art-songs" was inadequate for expressing the spirit of the age. Liszt, for his part, in seeking to create a Hungarian national music, preserved "the main features of the musical idiom common to the various social strata of his age, that is to say the popular music that was everywhere in evidence, though in an increasingly weakened version, and [injected] into it a concentrated national music worthy of his own conceptions" (Ujfalussy 1971, 58).

Whatever his sources or intentions, Liszt's work spurred compositional interest in Hungarian and, correspondingly, Gypsy themes. Brahms, for example, composed his *Hungarian Dances* from 1852 to 1869. These twenty-one stylized dance miniatures followed the contemporary trend and were initially written for four hands (although nos. 1, 3, and 10 were also orchestrated). Aimed at perpetuating an idealized image of Gypsyness, the series of technically simple, yet remarkably striking, pieces was destined for performance before concert audiences. Brahms himself incorporated the dances into his own concert programs, such as in Cracow on February 1, 1880 (Erhardt 1984, 217).

The pseudovirtuoso style of the *Hungarian Dances* manifests itself in the frequent use of agogic nuances, dynamic turns, and rhythmic shifts of emphasis, as well as extended, arpeggiated chords, and fairly simple passages that are actually a challenge to play given the fast tempo. Such runs correspond with amplified sound, enhanced by the octave doubling of the melody, while the figurations allow movement to create a saturating effect. And whereas the composition's transparent texture suggests salon miniatures, virtuosity inheres in the use of the instrument's entire range, including leaps and an increased number of resonant sounds. For all these qualities, typical features of Brahms's piano style also permeate the *Hungarian Dances*, including a full sound, a predilection for dark hues, frequent third and sixth doublings, as well as full chords.

Conveying emotion in the *Hungarian Dances* are both harmonic and melodic components as well as simulated sounds typical for a Gypsy orchestra. The alleged Gypsy themes emerge from various sources, mainly Hungarian composers, some of them previously exploited by Liszt. Brahms rarely, however, cited a melody in its entirety, choosing instead shorter fragments, which he combined and modified to create a sense of authenticity and an impression of a refined and fantastic Gypsy world (Malvinni 2004, 83). More specifically, Brahms used the augmented second, such as in "Dance" number 5 in the upper tetrachord (A, B flat, C sharp, D) and the lower tetrachord (D, E flat, F sharp, G) of the scale on which the piece is based. Formally, the *Hungarian Dances* duplicates the ternary scheme, as do many stylized dances, while also referencing the czardas through a contrast in tempos.

Rooted in the tradition of the *verbunkos*, march music would stir the imagination of non-Hungarian composers, with Liszt again a central catalyst, thanks to his *Heroischer Marsch in ungarischem Stil* (1840), *Ungarischer Sturmmarsch* (1843), and *Marche Hongroise* (1844), as well as his role, beginning in 1839, in popularizing the *Rákóczi March* across Europe. For his part, Hector Berlioz combined this famed march with the orchestral dramatic work *La damnation de Faust* (op. 24). The Hungarian march tradition would be continued by, among others, Sydney Smith (*Marche Hongrois*, op. 166) and Hermann Adolf Wollenhaupt (*Marche Hongroise*, op. 66).

More broadly, Hungarian composers took part in the joint referencing of Hungarian and Gypsy material. Examples include works by the Hungarian virtuoso violinist Jenő Hubay (1858–1937), including "Ungarischen Zigeunerlied" (op. 57, no. 6) and "Szenen aus der Csarda" for violin and piano (or violin and orchestra). Outside Hungary's borders, many later nineteenth-century collections would include such miniatures by Hungarian composers, helping mold a conventionalized image of Hungarian music across Europe. For example, *10 Chansons hongroises du repertoire des Tziganes* (ca. 1885), by Elemér Szentirmay, contained simple pieces developed as both songs and purely instrumental miniatures for piano. A collection, *Repertoire des Tziganes*, published in Paris in 1878 contained nineteen works for piano—mainly songs, polkas, czardases, and marches—with "Gypsy" and "Hungarian" used synonymously in their titles. The marches were marked either *tzigane* or *à la hongroise*, the songs either Hungarian (*hongroise*), souvenir, or *des Tziganes*. When surnames were omitted for the Hungarian composers of miniatures, this may have indicated joint Hungarian-Gypsy intent.

Spanish Associations

As compared to the Hungarian context, Gypsy allusions in works with Spain in the title were relatively rare and came initially from composers outside the country. And, particularly in the early twentieth century, instrumental compositions by Spanish composers referenced Gypsy associations in a rather vague, speculative way.

In the nineteenth century, visitors to Spain, who recognized its perceived status as an exotic European outpost, included composers, and Russian composers in particular sought to absorb the musical influences of Iberia. For example, Mikhail Glinka (1804–1857) spent two years in Spain between June 1845 and August 1847, and thus composed his two *Spanish Overtures*. Nikolai

Rimsky-Korsakov (1844–1908) likewise composed his *Spanish Caprice* (1887), a work considered "exceptional and worthy of amazement as an interpretation of the Spanish soul by a Slav" (Corredor 1955, 227). The composition has a multipart structure and, owing to its technical demands, is sometimes called a suite or an orchestral etude. *Spanish Caprice* is a superb example of the unequivocal way in which Spanishness was associated with Gypsyness. The first and third movements, based on the Spanish folk dance with its characteristic melody and accompaniment and with a clear rhythm and simple harmony, are both entitled "Alborada." As Anatol Solovcov writes, "We almost see the crowd of youths, we hear the gay shouting and the patter of the dancers" (Solovcov 1989, 90). Following the lyrical "Variazioni" and the second "Alborada," there occurs the "Gypsy Scene and Dance" based on two dance melodies, which seem to allude to Gypsy music-making by commencing in cadences. Gypsy subject matter is also referenced in the final fandango, through the introduction of an additional three dance melodies (one of these recalling a waltz) and the intense quoting of material from the previous movements.

Russian interest in Spanish Gypsy material was complemented by that of French composers, rooted in Bizet's *Carmen* and the habanera with which the heroine is associated. As we saw in an earlier chapter, Chabrier, Ravel, and Debussy all composed habaneras. Spanish composers, picking up on the form, typically used it as an embellishment of their compositional styles rather than a manifestation of national conviction. Earlier, we saw how Sarasate incorporated a habanera within his *Spanish Dances* of the late 1870s and early 1880s; other links to an exotic conceptualization of Spain in his works include *Caprice basque* (op. 24), *Romanza andaluza* (op. 22), and *Zapateo* (op. 23), with all of these written for violin with piano accompaniment. The verdict, however, could be harsh for Spanish composers who sought to exoticize their country through a "Spanish style." One example was Edouard Lalo (1823–1892), whose *Spanish Symphony* (op. 21), dedicated to Sarasate, was seen as a "false imitation."

Felipe Pedrell, whose influence on reinterpreting Spain's musical culture was elaborated earlier, would leave much of the task of composition to his illustrious pupils de Falla, Albéniz, Amadeo Vives, and Joaquín Turina. The instrumental works written by these composers would incorporate Gypsy inspiration into the ideal of a national music. Thus, their compositions titled "Spanish" included allusions to Gypsy culture as an integral element of a larger unity.

Albéniz's titles, for example, included the orchestral *Rapsodia española* (op. 70; 1887), the piano *Suite española* (op. 47; 1886), *2 danses espagñoles* (op. 164; 1890), *España* (op. 165; 1890), *Serenata española* (op. 181; 1891), and *Chants d'Es-*

pagne (op. 232; 1897). The composer was inspired by the "serene" flamenco variant knows as *cante chico* but avoided direct references to folk music. From flamenco, the composer adopted a predilection for dance as well as specific rhythms, among them complex rhythms. In piano cycles, he introduced typical dances connected with Gypsyness through the flamenco tradition: number 3 of *Española* (op. 165) is a malaguena, a synthesis of Spanish and Gypsy folklore; tango appears in two of the *Danses espagñoles* (op. 164); *Cantos de España* (op. 232) includes a seguidilla. Melodically, Albéniz's work inclines toward rich melismatics and ornamentation. Noting one of the composer's multiple uses of flamenco, Zofia Helman writes, "Many of Albéniz's new texture tricks resulted from imitation of the guitar" (Helman, 1979, 26).

Stylized flamenco also penetrated Albéniz's piano collection *Iberia* (1905–1909). Here, the composer musically painted the Spanish landscape, recalling typical Andalusian songs (the *polo*) and referencing old Spanish traditions (the celebration of Corpus Christi through pompous processions). The work also includes concrete references, through subtitles, to the Mediterranean port of Almería, the old-town Madrid district of Lavapies, as well as to Málaga and Jerez, with this last city, along with Albaicín, known for its sizable Gypsy population. "Triana," one of the cycle's most popular pieces, references Seville's "Gypsy quarter." This piece is written in the triple meter typical for flamenco and abounds in tuplets (as well as sextuplets), as set against the regular division of values and other rhythmic nuances involving, for instance, the introduction of additional accents and application of short pauses. The impression of improvisation—the immanent feature of flamenco—is also suggested through the formal division into smaller, irregularly repeated sections of varied dimensions. More particularly, the piano technique of breaking up the tuplet so that the first note is played by the left hand and the remaining two are played by the right evokes flamenco guitar.

Some of Albéniz's unfinished works were to be completed by Enrique Granados, a talented pianist and a student of Pedrell's who was consumed by the idea of creating a Spanish national music. His efforts would bear fruit in the popular *Danza española* op. 37 (1892–1900), and Granados would be hailed as "the most authentic creator. Granados never drew from folklore sources; his subject matters constitute, admittedly, an extremely characteristic reflection of the folk soul, yet they are a direct, personal creation" (Corredor 1955, 223). The incidental employment of folk melodies or a dance rhythm gave the effect of sparing stylization, helping crystallize Granados's original musical language.

A later composer to incorporate Gypsy influences was Joaquín Rodrigo

(1901–1999), who chiefly wrote for the guitar, employing a manner of performance typical for flamenco and its forms. For example, in the first movement of his 1939 *Concierto de Aranjuez*, "Allegro con spirit," he introduced elements of fandango (e.g., the move between 6/8 and 3/4 meter) while basing the "Adagio" on a melody derived from *saeta*, with the English horn imitating the nasal, tension-filled *canto jondo*. The composer was conscious of the prevailing stereotype of Spain within European musical culture and complained of its Gypsy-associated conventionalization through "a few clichés of picturesque Andalusia" (Corredor 1955, 226).

Considered an eminent representative of a Spanish national music, de Falla drew on "the style of the Gitano," including in his instrumental works titled "Spanish" (Corredor 1955, 225). For example, in the piano work *Cuatro piezas españoles* (1907), movement titles include "Aragonesa," "Cubana," "Montanesa," and "Andaluza." Discussions of the cycle often recall that especially the picturesque "Andaluza" arouses associations with the Gypsy-Spanish milieu. Pahlen, for example, writes: "We are deep in Andalusia, in the Gypsy part of the town" (Pahlen 1953, 129).

Whereas critics and listeners alike sometimes miss the implication of Gypsyness in the Spanish references of such works, commentary regarding works *without* Spanish references in the title often reveals such an awareness. For example, according to Hess, de Falla's *Fantasia beatica* is "a farewell to *cante jondo*" (Hess, 2001, 531). Its structure, based on the ranking of motifs of various lengths, may recall the guitar accompaniment used in flamenco, whereby the specific melodic-rhythmic sections (*falsetas*) appear in a seemingly random sequence as if depending on the volition of the guitarist. Additionally, the melodics suggest a connection to the melismatics encountered in flamenco, and the use of an augmented second establishes the classic link to Gypsy music. However, without either awareness of the attributes commonly ascribed to Gypsy music or a certain knowledge of the history of the Gitanos in Spain, such interpretations would be difficult to undertake.

ᚵ ᚷᚵ ᚵ ᚷᚵ ᚵ

Epilogue

Over centuries, fascination with Gypsy culture would manifest itself in Europe multifariously: both in everyday life, such as in sayings adopted by many languages, and in academic research and influences within the fine arts. Music has often been foremost in these discussions as a means of understanding Romany society, and Romany music would be interpreted and reinterpreted based on diverse geographic, political, and sociological factors.

An analysis of academic and popular texts brings forth a complicated picture, according to which so-called Gypsy music is interpreted as either affiliated with European culture or—quite the opposite—considered an example of extra-European, exotic influences. Hence, the two models proposed in the book—assimilative and nonassimilative—reveal the heterogeneous ways in which the question of Gypsy music has been comprehended in European culture from the end of the eighteenth century to the beginning of the twentieth century (and, in some cases, beyond).

Within the assimilative model, authors have underlined the link between the music played by the Romanies inhabiting a given country and the country's artistic and popular music. The harnessing of the "Gypsy music" concept in the discourse on national symbolism, and the appropriation of this musical culture for the promotion of national self-identity, has concerned first and foremost Hungary and Spain, with both countries having large concentrations of Romany inhabitants. In nineteenth-century Hungary, confusion arose over the character of national music based on a misapprehension that popular Gypsy bands, one, conveyed authentic Romany music and, two, were composed of mainly Romany members, rather than Hungarians. Franz Liszt further promoted the confusion in his famous book on the subject. European works employing the word *tzigane* (and variations) would thus be linked to Hungarian national sentiments. At the same time, those who designated their works Hungarian believed they were employing—allegedly original—Gypsy inspirations that were, in their opinion, indispensable to Hungarian national identity. In a similar way, though on a lesser scale, the French word *gitane* or other references to Andalusian (or Spanish) inspirations suggested the accretion of Spanishness and Gypsyness.

The nonassimilative model assumed a distancing in relation to the musical culture of the Romany, often treating them in the light of the exotic and its discourse. Gypsy music and culture were presented in the context of rising nineteenth-century Orientalism, with the Romany's Indian origins and perceived ties between European Gypsy and Arab music contributing to the viewpoint. The concept of Gypsy music would also be incorporated into racial discourse, a discussion linked most closely to Jewish music. Thus, comparisons between Gypsy and Jewish identity often led to a racial overtone in discussions of Gypsy music.

The assimilative and nonassimilative models of discourse on Gypsy music, as expressed by writers and composers alike, would leave a profound mark on musical works themselves. Composers would create works that not only adhered to one or the other model but that actively supported it. Sometimes composers' stances even shifted over the course of their careers.

In the nineteenth and early twentieth centuries, not only were terms such as "Gypsy" and "Hungarian" and "Gypsy" and "Andalusian" liberally intermixed in works' titles, but librettos and song texts often propagated notions of Gypsy exoticism and other perceived ethnic traits. The ambivalent relationship to Gypsy culture—somewhere between fascination and fear, acceptance and condemnation, assimilation and separateness—manifested itself in the huge number of works dealing with or referring to Gypsy motifs (through titles or accompanying illustrations). Stage works such as operas, operettas, vaudevilles, and ballets reinforced broadly understood notions about Gypsy musicians and music through a thematic "pentalogue" encompassing passionate Gypsy love, Gypsy freedom, Gypsy links with magic, and the affinity of Gypsies with nature and evil. The incorporation of such concepts both endowed stage works with an Oriental hue and often underlined the stereotypical, morally ambiguous position of Gypsy protagonists.

The conventionalized depictions of Gypsy music and Gypsies, who were often portrayed as dancing and carefree wanderers, contributed to superstitions regarding the Romany within European culture. Such portrayals applied to nonstage works and songs as well, including through texts depicting Gypsies in stereotypical situations. In instrumental miniatures, this typecasting role was served by titles and accompanying illustrations, vignettes, and other additions.

In stage and nonstage works alike, composers drew on techniques of the era to reference Gypsy themes. Their compositions for the most part, owing to the absence of source works or research into music-making within Romany communities, would remain uninfluenced by actual Romany musical practices. Yet European composers eagerly employed techniques considered within European culture to be determinants of Gypsyness, including the augmented second interval, syncopated rhythms, the slowing and quickening tempos of the czardas, violin and clarinet virtuosity, and various Eastern inspirations. Formally, genre types such as the rhapsody, capriccio, or fantasy allowed composers to emphasize the improvisational tendencies of Gypsy musicians.

The popularity of Gypsy music, which collectively had a uniform nature, reflected a desire for both lyrical-sentimental melodies and lively rhythms that encouraged dancing. Such entertainment forms were peddled by the Central European Gypsy bands known as *Zigeunerkapellen,* whose playful, feel-good music was quite separate from the ambitious art presented in concert halls and opera theaters. All the same, the virtuosity displayed in these groups, mainly on violin and improvisatory in nature, would draw comparisons to that by onstage artists and fuel the expanding myth of the Gypsy musician. This myth would include the conception of the Gypsy musician as a romantic trope to be reckoned with in discussions of national art—and the related topics of exoticism and race. This musician was viewed as an alienated artist, eternally wandering, finding solace only in music, and traveling all over Europe with a song on his lips. Thus, this figure became tied to the romantic artist more broadly. As the twentieth century dawned, the Gypsy motif would only be exploited further in the service of both artistic expression and entertainment, with hardly a nod to anything resembling Romany musical traditions. This notion of Gypsies as merely a source of entertainment was indeed well rooted in European soil.

In the early twentieth century, when the "avant-garde or kitsch" slogan reigned, scholars felt little need to explore belittled entertainment forms such as Gypsy music. Yet together with the post–World War II collapse of the ideology of progress and the increased appreciation for popular culture, interest grew sharply in the broader range of musical idioms. An analysis of the role of the Gypsy musician and Gypsy music—within broader discussions of music's functioning in culture—fills a gap in the existing picture of music within European culture. The division into assimilative and nonassimilative types further refines this picture.

Research Perspectives

Gypsy inspirations within European culture constitute the subject of multidimensional research, concentrating particularly on the written literature that employs Gypsy motifs. Present-day considerations of the nineteenth-century national fascination with Gypsy subject matter include works by Deborah Epstein Nord (2006), Stefani Kugler (2004), and Karl Hölz (2002). These works point not only to the interest in the problem but also to its academic potential.

The present work situates itself within this current by taking a musicological approach to the European fascination with the culture of Romanies in the nineteenth and early twentieth centuries. In my library research, I have unearthed a wealth of untouched source material on musical inspiration derived from the Gypsy. The findings cited in this book, chosen on the basis of their representativeness for European discourse on the subject from the late eighteenth to the early twentieth century, both contribute to present research and offer a methodological model for future researchers, for whom more discoveries remain to be made.

Alongside published scores, available sources in library collections include manuscripts with Gypsy connotations (in titles, genres, or—in stage works— hidden in librettos). Opportunities for further research on European artistic works informed by Gypsy culture also open up when one shifts the period under consideration. The year range covered by this book, which was guided by methodological considerations, by no means forecloses the possibility of future research, with contemporary Romany music constituting a ripe area for study. In particular, Romany music in Russia underwent substantial developments around the turn of the last century.

The research perspectives in relation to the mutual relationship between Gypsy culture and professional music might also be expanded to incorporate Russian cultural circles. Over centuries, Russian Romanies have played both artistic and popular music, but this subject has rarely elicited academic attention. Along with scholars of music, students of the history and customs of Russian Romanies might well benefit from examining this subject area (Demeter and Bessonov 2000).

The musicological study of Gypsy motifs in the European musical tradition also deserves a comparative treatment against other art forms inspired by Gypsy culture, particularly literature and the fine arts. This comparative study could also entail a broader, transatlantic look at the function of musical culture in the creation or fixing of stereotypes and their role in the stigmatization of the Romany within European culture versus that of the African American in the United States.

❧ ⁊ ❧ ⁊ ❧

Bibliography

Text Sources

Ábrányi, Kornél. 1900. *A magyar zene a 19—ik században* [Hungarian Music of the Nineteenth Century]. Budapest: Pannonia nyomda.

Adamski, Jerzy. 1986. *Obrona teatru dramatycznego* [In Defense of Dramatic Theater]. Cracow: Wydawnictwo Literackie.

Adler, Laure. 1999. *Życie codzienne w domach publicznych w latach, 1830–1930* [in the original French: *Vie quotidienne dans les maisons closes, 1830–1930*]. Translated by Renata Wilgosiewicz-Skutecka. Poznań: Wydawnictwo Moderski i S-ka.

Altenburg, Detlef. 1986. "Liszts Idee eines ungarischen Nationalepos in Tönen." *Studia Musicologica Academiae Scientarum Hungaricae* 28: 213–23.

Angermüller, Rudolph. 1976. "Zigeuner und Ziegeunerisches in der Oper des 19. Jahrhunderts." In *Die 'Couleur locale' in der Oper des 19. Jahrhunderts*, edited by Heinz Becker, 131–159. Regensburg: Gustav Bosse.

Antonietto, Alain. 1994. Histoire de la musique tsigane instrumentale d'Europe central." *Etudes tsiganes* 3: 104–33.

Apel, Willi. 1974. "Gypsy music." In *Harvard Dictionary of Music*, edited by Willi Apel, 364. Cambridge, Mass.: Belknap Press of Harvard University Press.

Arnold, Ben. 1998. "Liszt as Reader, Intellectual, and Musician." In *Liszt and His World: Proceedings of the International Liszt Conference Held at Virginia Polytechnic Institute and State University, 20–23 May 1993,* edited by Michael Saffle, 37–60. Stuyvesant, NY: Pendragon Press.

Awosusi, Anita. 1996–1998. *Die Musik der Sinti und Roma.* Heidelberg: Dokumentations und Kulturzentrum Deutscher Sinti und Roma.

Babral, Henryk. 1991. *Postword to Królowa przedmieścia Konstanty Krumłowski* [The Queen of the Suburbs, with Libretto by Konstanty Krumłowski]. Cracow: Wydawnictwo Secesja.

Bachórz, Józef. 2004. "Miejsce Polski w cywilizacji europejskiej według Józefa Ignacego Kraszewskiego" [The Place of Poland within European Civilization as Seen by Józef Ignacy Kraszewski]. In *Obrazy kultury polskiej w twórczości Józefa Ignacego Kraszewskiego* [Images of Polish Culture in the Oeuvre of Józef Ignacy

Kraszewski], edited by Barbara Czwórnóg-Jadczak, 11–26. Lublin: Wydawnictwo Uniwersytetu Marii Curie–Skłodowskiej.

Baily, John. 1994. "Music and the Afghan National Identity." In *Ethnicity, Identity and Music: The Musical Construction of Place,* edited by Martin Stokes, 45–60. Oxford: Berg Publishers.

Balacon, Maira. 2005. "*Style Hongrois* Features in Brahms's *Hungarian Dances:* A Musical Construction of a Fictionalized Gypsy *Other,*" PhD diss., University of Cincinnati.

Bartók, Béla 1958. *Béla Bartók: Eigene Schriften und die Erinnerungen der Freunde,* edited by Willi Reich. Basel: Benno Schwabe & Co. Verlag.

Bartók, Béla. 1972. *Weg und Werk: Schriften und Briefe,* edited by Bence Szabolcsi. Budapest: Corvina Verlag.

———. 1992. *Béla Bartók's Essays,* edited by Benjamin Suchoff. Lincoln: University of Nebraska Press.

Basso, Alberto. 1984. "Scacciapensieri." In Vol. 4 of *Dizionario enciclopedico universal della musica e dei musicisti.* Turin: Utet.

Baumann, Max Peter. 2000. "Roma in Spiegelbild europäischer Kunstmusik." In *Music, language and literature of the Roma and Sinti,* edited by Max Peter Baumann, 393–443. Berlin: VWB.

Beaumont, Cyril W. 1951. *Complete Book of Ballets.* London: Putnam.

Beckerman, Michael. 2001. "Music; Pushing Gypsiness, Roma or Otherwise." *New York Times,* April 1.

Becket Williams, Christopher. 1923. "Some Notes on Hungarian Gipsy Music." *The Musical Times* 64 (962): 269–70.

Bednorz, Adam. 1997. "Od mitu do rzeczywistości: Rozważania wokół głównego motywu "Chaty za wsią," J. I. Kraszewskiego" [From Myth to Reality: Reflections on the Main Motif of *The Cottage beyond the Village,* by J. I. Kraszewski], *Dialog-Pheniben* 1: 71–77.

Bellaigue, Camille. 1887. *Un siècle de musique francaise.* Paris: Libraire Ch. Delagrave.

Bellman, Jonathan. 1991. "Toward a Lexicon for the *Style Hongrois.*" *The Journal of Musicology* 9 (2): 214–37.

———. 1993. *The "Style Hongrois" in the Music of Western Europe.* Boston: Northeastern University Press.

Berlioz, Hector. 1978. *Correspondance Générale III: September 1842–1850* (nos. 776–1367), edited by Pierre Citron. Paris: Flammarion.

Bertha, Alexandre M. 1878. "Musique hongroise et les Tsiganes." *Revue des deux mondes* (28): 909–20.

Bie, Oskar. 1920. *Die Oper.* Berlin: S. Fischer Verlag.

Bielawski, Ludwik. 1999. *Tradycje ludowe w kulturze muzycznej* [Folk Traditions in Musical Culture]. Warsaw: Instytut Sztuki PAN.

Bielawski, Ludwik, et al. 1995. *Oskar Kolberg—prekursor antropologii kultury* [Oskar

Kolberg: The Forerunner of Cultural Anthropology]. Warsaw: IS PAN–
Akademia Muzyczna.

Bobrownicka, Maria. 1995. *Narkotyk mitu: Szkice o świadomości narodowej i kulturowej Słowian zachodnich i południowych* [Narcotic Power of Myths: Studies on National and Cultural Awareness of the West and South Slavs]. Cracow: Universitas.

Bohlman, Philip V. 1987. "The European Discovery of Music in the Islamic World and the 'Non-Western' in 19th-Century Music History." *The Journal of Musicology* 5 (2): 147–63.

Born, Georgina, and David Hesmondhalgh. 2000. "Introduction to Western Music and Its Others: Difference, Representation, and Appropriation in Music," edited by Georgina Born and David Hesmondhalgh, 1–58. Berkeley: University of California Press.

Borrow, George. 1841. *The Zincali.* London: John Murray.

———. 1905. *The Bible in Spain; or, The Journeys, Adventures, and Imprisonment of an Englishman.* London: Boots Publishers.

Brassai, Sámuel. 1860. *Magyar vagy czigány zene? Elmefuttatás Liszt Ferencz "Czigányokról" írt könyve felett* [Hungarian or Gypsy Music? Reflections on Franz Liszt's Book "on the Gypsies"]. Kolozsvár: Év. Reform—Főtanoda Konyvnyomdája.

Breuer, János. 1995. "Bartók and the Third Reich." *Hungarian Quarterly* 36 (140): 134–40.

Brown, Irving. 1929. *Adventures with Gypsy Songs and Singers in Andalusia and Other Lands.* New York: Harper & Brothers.

———. 1938. "*Don Gypsy*: Review of *Don Gypsy* by Walter Starkie." *The Journal of American Folklore* 51 (200): 206–8.

Brown, Julie. 2000. "Bartók, the Gypsies, and Hybridity in Music." In *Western Music and Its Others: Difference, Representation, and Appropriation in Music,* edited by Georgina Born and David Hesmondhalgh. Berkeley: University of California Press: 119–42.

Brzezińska, Barbara. 1987. *Repertuar polskich tabulatur organowych z pierwszej połowy XVI wieku* [The Repertoire of Polish Lute Tablatures from the First Half of the Sixteenth Century]. Cracow: Polskie Wydawnictwo Muzyczne.

Bücken, Ernst. 1937. *Die Musik der Nationen.* Leipzig: Alfred Kröner Verlag.

Burkot, Stanisław. 2006. "Historia i światopoglądy" [History and Standpoints]. In *Europejskość i rodzimość: Horyzonty twórczości Józefa Ignacego Kraszewskiego* [Europeanism and Polishness: Horizons in the Ouevre of Józef Ignacy Kraszewski], edited by Wiesław Ratajczak and Tomasz Sobieraj, 11–21. Poznań: Wydawnictwo Poznańskiego Towarzystwa Przyjaciół Nauk.

Burnett, James. 1979. *Manuel de Falla and the Spanish Musical Renaissance.* London: Victor Gollancz Ltd.

Castillo, Belén Peréz. 2001. "Spain" (section on nineteenth-century art music). In Vol.

24 of *The New Grove Dictionary of Music and Musicians,* edited by Stanley Sadie. London: MacMillan Publishers Ltd: 128–30.

Cervantes, Miguel de. 1962. "La Gitanilla." *Novelas ejemplares,* 23–90. Garden City, NY: Doubleday & Company Inc.

Charnock, Richard S. 1866. "On the Origin of the Gypsies." *Anthropological Review* 4 (12): 89–96.

Chase, Gilbert. 1959. *The Music of Spain.* New York: Dover Publications, Inc.

Chomiński, Józef M. 1954. Vol. 1 of *Formy muzyczne* [Musical Forms]. Cracow: Polskie Wydawnictwo Muzyczne.

Chomiński, Józef M., and Krystyna Wilkowska-Chomińska. 1989. Vol. 1 of *Historia muzyki* [History of Music]. Cracow: Polskie Wydawnictwo Muzyczne.

———. 1990. Vol. 2 of *Historia muzyki* [History of Music]. Cracow: Polskie Wydawnictwo Muzyczne.

Christoforidis, Michael. 1999. "La guitarra flamenca en la obra y pensamiento de Manuel de Falla." In *Manuel de Falla—Letinite et universalite: Actes du Colloque International tenu en Sorbonne 18–21 novembre 1996,* edited by Louis Jambous, 261–76. Paris: Presses de l'Universite de Paris–Sorbonne.

Clébert, Jean-Paul. 1970. *The Gypsies.* Translated by Charles Duff. Middlesex, UK: Penguin Books.

Clifford, James. 1986. *Writing Culture.* Berkeley: University of California Press.

Clyne, Anthony. 1926. "Spanish Music." *Music & Letters* 7 (3): 265–69.

Collet, Henri. 1947. "La mort de Manuel de Falla." *La revue musicale* 204: 27–28.

Cooper, David. 2001. "Béla Bartók and the Question of Race Purity in Music." In *Musical Constructions of Nationalism: Essays on the History and Ideology of European Musical Culture, 1800–1945,* edited by Harry White and Michael Murphy. Cork: Cork University Press: 16–32.

Corredor, José Maria. 1971. *Rozmowy z Pablo Casalsem: Wspomnienia i sądy Muzyka* [in the original French, Conversations avec Pablo Casals: souvenirs et opinions d'un musicien]. Translated by Jerzy Popiel and Kazimierz Wiłkomirski. Cracow: Polskie Wydawnictwo Muzyczne.

Creuzburg, Eberhard. 1954. *Johannes Brahms: Leben und Werk.* Leipzig: Breitkopf & Härtel Musikverlag.

Crittenden, Camille. 2000. *Johann Strauss and Vienna: Operetta and the Politics of Popular Culture.* Cambridge: Cambridge University Press.

Cunningham, Martin, and Jaume Aiats. 2001. "Spain" (section on characteristics of traditional and popular music). In Vol. 24 of *The New Grove Dictionary of Music and Musicians,* edited by Stanley Sadie, 138–42. London: MacMillan Publishers Ltd.

Czacki, Tadeusz. 1835. *O Cyganach* [On Gypsies]. Cracow: Drukiem D. E. Friedleina.

Czapliński, Lesław. 2003. *W kręgu operowych mitów* [In the Realm of Operatic Myths]. Cracow: Rabid.

Czech, Stan. 1942. *Franz Lehár: Weg und Werk.* Berlin: Werk Verlag GMBH.

Dahlhaus, Carl. 1985. *Between Romanticism and Modernism: Four Studies in the Music of the Later Nineteenth Century.* Berkeley: University of California Press.

————. 1989. *Nineteenth-Century Music.* Translated by J. Bradford Robinson. Berkeley: University of California Press.

Daniłowicz, Ignacy. 1824. *O Cyganach wiadomość historyczna czytana na posiedzeniu publicznem cesarskiego Uniwersytetu Wileńskiego dnia 30 czerwca 1824 roku* [On the Gypsies' Historical Information . . .]. Vilna: W drukarni A. Marcinowskiego.

Davillier, Charles. 1874. *L'Espagne.* Paris: Hachette.

Debrocq, Michel. 1998. "Roby Lakatos: The Nonconformist of the Violin." Text accompanying the CD *Lakatos.* Hamburg: Deutsche Grammophon, PY 900.

De Falla, Manuel. 1922. *El "cante jondo" (canto primitivo andaluz): sus orígenes, sus valores musicales, su influencia en el arte musical europeo.* Granada: Editorial Urania.

De Lafontaine, Henry Cart. 1907–1908. "Spanish Music." *Proceedings of the Musical Association,* thirty-fourth session, 25–45.

Delanty, Gerard. 1999. *Odkrywanie Europy: Idea, tożsamość, rzeczywistość* [in the original English, Inventing Europe: Idea, Identity, Reality]. Translated by Renata Włodek. Cracow: Wydawnictwo Naukowe PWN.

Demeny, János. ed. 1971. *Béla Bartók's Letters.* Translated by Peter Balaban and István Farkas. New York: St. Martin's Press.

Demeter, Nadezhda, and Nikolai Bessonov. 2000. *Istorija tsygan: Novyj vzgljad* [History of the Gypsies: A New Perspective]. Voronezh: IPF "Voronezh."

Desfor Edles, Laura. 2002. *Cultural Sociology in Practice.* London: Blackwell.

De Silva, Tomás Andrade. 1954. *Antología del cante flamenco.* Madrid: Hispavox.

Di Nola, Alfonso M. 2004. *Diabeł* [in the original Italian, Il diavolo]. Translated by Ireneusz Kania. Cracow: Universitas.

Dobos, Ilona. 1981. *Aldozatok.* Budapest: Kozmosz Kiado.

Dobszay, László. 1993. *A History of Hungarian Music.* Budapest: Corvina Press.

Drewniak, Bogusław. 1969. *Kultura w cieniu swastyki* [Culture in the Shadow of the Swastika]. Poznań: Wydawnictwo Poznańskie.

Dufour, F. S. Pierre. 1998. *Historia prostytucji* [in the original French: Histoire de la prostitution]. Translated by Antoni Baniukiewicz. Gdynia: Uraeus.

Duhamel-Amado, Claudie, and Genevieve Brunel-Lobrichon. 2000. *Życie codzienne w czasach trubadurów* [in the original French: Au temps des troubadours XII–XIII siècles]. Translated by Anna Loba. Poznań: Wydawnictwo Moderski i S-ka.

Dziedzic, Maria. 1984. "Miguel Cervantes." In Vol. 2 of *Encyklopedia Muzyczna PWM* [Polskie Wydawnictwo Muzyczne], edited by Elżbieta Dziębowska, 67–70. Cracow: Polskie Wydawnictwo Muzyczne.

Dziekan, Marek M. 1997. "Aš-Šanfara romantyczny: Próba monografii motywu" [Aš-Šanfara: An Attempt at a Monograph of a Motif]. In *Orientalizm romantyczny:*

Arabski romans rycerski (Literatura arabska: Dociekania i prezentacje) [Romantic Orientalism: Arabic Romance Courtship], edited by Marek M. Dziekan, 45–60. Warsaw: Wydawnictwo Akademickie Dialog.

Eichenauer, Richard. 1932. *Musik und Rasse.* Munich: Lehmanns Verlag.

Engel, Carl. 1879. "The Literature of National Music: Treatises." *The Musical Times and Singing Class Circular* 20 (432): 69–72.

———. 1880a. "The Music of the Gipsies (I)." *The Musical Times and Singing Class Circular* 21 (447): 219–22.

———. 1880b. "The Music of the Gipsies (II)." *The Musical Times and Singing Class Circular* 21 (450): 389–91.

Epstein Nord, Deborah. 2006. *Gypsies and the British Imagination, 1807–1930.* New York: Columbia University Press.

Erdely, Stephen. 1983. "Review of Gypsy Music by Bálint Sárosi." *Ethnomusicology* 27 (3): 550–51.

Erhardt, Ludwik. 1984. *Brahms.* Cracow: Polskie Wydawnictwo Muzyczne.

Ewen, David. 1968. *The World of 20th Century Music.* London: Prentice-Hall.

Ficowski, Jerzy. 1953. *Cyganie polscy* [Polish Gypsies]. Warsaw: Państwowy Instytut Wydawniczy.

F. B. 1967 "Zigeunermusik." In *Riemann Musiklexikon,* edited by Hugo Riemann, 1079. Mainz: B. Schott's Söhne.

Ford, Richard. 1846. *Gathering from Spain.* London: John Murray.

Foucault, Michel. 2006. "O innych przestrzeniach: Heterotopie (1967)" [in the original French: "Des espaces autres: Hétérotopies"]. *Kultura popularna* 2: 7–13.

Fraser, Angus. 2005. *Gypsies.* Oxford: Blackwell.

Frey, Stefan. 2005 "Love's own sweet song . . . ," Text accompanying the CD *Der Zigeunerprimasz,* by Emmerich [Imre] Kálmán. CPO 777 058–2.

Frigyesi, Judith. 1994. "Béla Bartók and the Concept of Nation and 'Volk' in Modern Hungary." *The Musical Quarterly* 78 (2): 255–87.

———. 1998. *Béla Bartók and the Turn of the Century.* Berkeley: University of California Press.

———. 2000. "The Verbunkos and Bartók's Modern Style." In *Bartók Perspectives: Man, Composer and Ethnomusicologist,* edited by Elliott Antokoletz, Victoria Fischer, and Benjamin Suchoff, 140–51. Oxford: Oxford University Press.

Frye, Northrop. 1976. "Archetypy literatury" [in the original English: "The Archetypes of Literature"]. In Vol. 2 of *Współczesna teoria badań literackich za granicą* [The Contemporary Foreign Theory of Literary Research], edited by Henryk Markiewicz, 303–21. Cracow: Wydawnictwo Literackie.

Fuks, Marian. 1989. *Muzyka ocalona: Judaica polskie* [Saved Music: Polish Judaica]. Warsaw: Wydawnictwa Radia i Telewizji.

Fuller, David. 2001. "Legrand." Vol. 14 of *The New Grove Dictionary of Music and Musicians,* edited by Stanley Sadie, 483. London: MacMillan Publishers Ltd.

Gabryś, Jerzy. 1961. "'Carmen' G. Bizeta" [*Carmen,* by G. Bizet]. Cracow: Polskie Wydawnictwo Muzyczne.

Gárdonyi, Zoltán. 1983. "Zoltán Kodály über Liszts Hungarismen." *Studia Musicologica Academiae Scientiarum Hungaricae* 25 (fasc. 1/4): 131–34.

Gergely, András, and Zoltán Szász. 1978. *Kiegyezés utan* [After the Compromise]. Budapest: Gondolat Kiado.

Gerson-Kiwi, Edith. 1957. "Béla Bartók: Scholar in Folk Music." *Music & Letters* 38 (2): 149–54.

Gilad, Margalit. 1999. "The Image of the Gypsy in German Christendom." *Patterns of Prejudice* 33 (2): 75–85.

Głuszcz-Zwolińska, Elżbieta. 1988. *Muzyka nadworna ostatnich Jagiellonów* [Music at the Court of the Last Jagiellons]. Cracow: Polskie Wydawnictwo Muzyczne.

González-Caballos Martínez, Fernando. "Two Centuries of Flamenco." Accessed February 9, 2008, from www.flamenco-world.com/magazine/about/200/200 .htm.

Górecka, Beata. 2004. "Między romantyzmem a realizmem—J. I. Kraszewski jako illustrator: Zbiór rysunkowych szkiców artysty do *Wspomnień Wołynia, Polesia i Litwy*" [Between Romanticism and Realism—J. I. Kraszewski as an Illustrator: The Collection of the Artist's Sketches to *Memoirs of Wołyń, Podlasie and Lithuania*]. In *Obrazy kultury polskiej w twórczości Józefa Ignacego Kraszewskiego* [Images of Polish Culture in the Oeuvre of Józef Ignacy Kraszewski], edited by Barbara Czwórnóg-Jadczak, 225–35. Lublin: Wydawnictwo Uniwersytetu Marii Curie–Skłodowskiej.

Grellmann, Heinrich Moritz Gottlieb. 1810. *Histoire des Bohemiens, ou Tableau des Moeurs, usages et coutumes de ce peuple nomade; Suivie de recherches historiques sur leur origine, leur langage et leur premiere apparition en Europe.* Translated from the German 2nd edition. Paris: Chaumerot.

Guenther, Konrad. 1912. *Gerhard Rohlfs: Lebensbild eines Afrikaforschers.* Freiburg im Breisgau: Fehsenfeld.

Gundel, Károly. 1992. *Gundel's Hungarian Cookbook.* Budapest: Corvina.

Günther, Hans. 1929. *Rassenkunde des deutschen Volkes.* Munich: J. F. Lehmann Verlag.

Hamburger, Klara. 1997. "Program and Hungarian Idiom in the Sacred Music of Liszt." In *New Light on Liszt and His Music,* edited by Michael Saffle and James Deaville. Stuyvesant, NY: Pendragon Press: 239–51.

Haraszti, Emile. 1931. "La question tzigane—Hongroise au point de vue de l'histoire de la musique." In *Report from the International Society for Musical Research—First Congress,* Liege, Belgium, September 1–6, 1930.

———. 1947. "Franz Liszt—Author Despite Himself: The History of a Mystification." Translated by John A. Gutman. *The Musical Quarterly* 33: 490–516.

Helman, Alicja. 2003. "W rytmie flamenco, w klimacie duende" [In the Rhythm of Flamenco, in the Spirit of Duende]. In *Complexus Effecutuum: Musicologiae Studia*

Miroslao Perz Septuagenerio Dedicata, edited by Tomasz Jeż, 563–72, Cracow:
    Rabid.

Helman, Zofia. 1979. "Isaac Albéniz." In Vol. 1 of *Encyklopedia Muzyczna PWM,* edited
    by Elżbieta Dziębowska, 24–26. Cracow: Polskie Wydawnictwo Muzyczne.

Hemetek, Ursula. 2003. "Roma, Sinti, Manush, Cale." In Vol. 8 of *Die Musik in*
    Geschichte und Gegenwart, edited by Ludwig Finscher, 443–57. Kassel and Basel:
    Bärenreiter-Verlag.

Hess, Carol A. 2001. "Manuel de Falla." In Vol. 8 of *The New Grove Dictionary of Music*
    and Musicians, edited by Stanley Sadie, 529–35. London: MacMillan Publishers
    Ltd.

Heyer, Hermann. 1967. *Vorwort to "Carmen" [by] Georges Bizet.* Edition Peters, no. 3200.

Hindemith, Paul. 1952. *A Composer's World: Horizons and Limitations.* Cambridge, MA:
    Harvard University Press.

Hofer, Tamás. 1994. "Construction of the 'Folk Cultural Heritage' in Hungary and Rival
    Versions of National Identity." In *Hungarians between "East" and "West": Three*
    Essays on National Myths and Symbols, edited by Tamás Hofer, 27–52. Budapest:
    Museum of Ethnography.

Hooker, Lynn. 2001. "The Political and Cultural Climate in Hungary at the Turn of the
    Twentieth Century." In *The Cambridge Companion to Bartók,* edited by Amanda
    Bayley. Cambridge: Cambridge University Press: 7–23.

Hölz, Karl. 2002. *Zigeuner, Wilde und Exoten: Fremdbilder in der französischen Literatur*
    des 19 Jahrhunderts. Berlin: Erich Schmidt.

Inzega, José. 1888. *Cantos y bailes populares de España.* Madrid: A Romero.

Infante, Blas. 1980. *Orígenes de lo flamenco y secreto del cante jondo.* Seville: Junta de
    Andalucía.

Istel, Edgar. 1926. "Manuel de Falla: A Study." Translated by Theodore Baker. *The*
    Musical Quarterly 12 (4): 497–525.

———. 1929. "Isaac Albéniz." *The Musical Quarterly* 15 (1): 117–48.

Jachimecki, Zdzisław. 1907. *Muzyka w Polsce* [Music in Poland]. Lvov: Nakładem
    Macierzy Polskiej.

Jaenisch, Julio. 1952. *Manuel de Falla und spanische Musik.* Zürich: Atlantis Verlag.

Jančková, Zdenka. 1998. *My Life with Leoš Janáček: The Memoirs of Zdenka Janáčkova.*
    Translated by John Tyrrell. London: Faber & Faber.

Janta, Aleksander. 1982. *A History of Nineteenth Century American-Polish Music.* New
    York: Kościuszko Foundation.

Jarman, A. O. H., and Eldra Jarman. 1991. *The Welsh Gypsies: Children of Abram Wood.*
    Cardiff: University of Wales Press.

Jaspert, Werner. 1939. *Johann Strauss: Sein Leben, sein Werk, seine Zeit.* Berlin:
    Werkverlag BMBH.

Jean-Aubry, Georges. 1917. "Manuel de Falla." *The Musical Times* 890: 151–54.

Jendrusik, Augustyn. 1958. Introduction to *Utwory dramatyczne: Wybór* [Dramatic

Works: Selection], by Franciszek Dionizy Kniaźnin. Warsaw: Państwowy Instytut Wydawniczy.

Kajanova, Yvetta, and Lubica Zaborska. 2007. "Slovak Scene of World Music." *Musicologica Istropolitana* 6: 217–45.

Kantor, Ryszard. 2003. *Poważnie i na niby: Szkice o zabawach i zabawkach* [Seriously and Frivolously: Studies on Games and Toys]. Kielce: MAC Edukacja S.A.

———. 2001. "Flamenco." In Vol. 8 of *The New Grove Dictionary of Music and Musicians,* edited by Stanley Sadie, 920–25. London: MacMillan Publishers Ltd.

Katz, Israel J. 1962. "Toward a Musical Study of the Judeo-Spanish *Romancero.*" *Western Folklore* 21 (2): 83–91.

Kendrick, Donald. 2004. *Gypsies: From the Ganges to the Thames.* Hatfield: University of Hertfordshire Press.

Kertész-Wilkinson, Iren. 2001. "Gypsy Music." In Vol. 10 of *The New Grove Dictionary of Music and Musicians,* edited by Stanley Sadie, 613–20. London: MacMillan Publishers Ltd.

———. 2005. "Nomadisme et musique: Le cas des Tsiganes." In Vol. 3 of *Musiques: Une encyclopedie pour le XXIe siècle,* edited by Jean-Jacques Natiez, 796–822. Actes SUD, Cité de la Musique.

Kilenyi, Edward. 1919. "The Theory of Hungarian Music." *The Musical Quarterly* 5 (1): 20–39.

Kisbán, Eszter. 1994. "From Peasant Dish to National Symbol: An Early Deliberate Example." In *Hungarians between "East" and "West": Three Essays on National Myths and Symbols,* edited by Tamás Hofer, 53–60. Budapest: Museum of Ethnography.

Klich, Edward. 1931. *Cygańszczyzna w "Chacie za wsią" Kraszewskiego* [Gypsyness in *The Cottage beyond the Village,* by J. I. Kraszewski]. Warsaw: PAU.

Klotz, Volker. 2004. *Operette: Porträt und Handbuch einer unerhörten Kunst.* Kassel: Bärenreiter.

Kobbe, Gustave. 1999. *Tout l'opera.* Paris: Robert Laffont.

Kodály, Zoltán. 1960. *Folk Music of Hungary.* London: Barrie and Rockliff.

Kopyś, Tadeusz. 2001. *Kwestia narodowościowa na ziemiach Korony świętego Stefana w latach 1867–1918* [The Issue of Nationality within the Territories of the Crown of St. Stephen in the Years 1867–1918]. Cracow: Promo.

Koválcsik, Katalin. 1990. "On the Historical Folk Music Layers of the Gypsies in Hungary." In *100 Years of Gypsy Studies: Papers from the 10th Annual Meeting of the Gypsy Lore Society,* North American chapter, March 25–27, 1988, edited by Matt T. Salo, 177–92. Cheverly, MD: Gypsy Lore Society.

Kozubek, Lidia. 2001. *Opera "Manru" I. J. Paderewskiego* [The Opera *Manru,* by I. J. Paderewski]. Katowice: Unia.

Kramer, Corinna, and Leo J. Plenckers. 1998. "The Structure of the *Saeta Flamenca:* An Analytical Study of Its Music." *Yearbook for Traditional Music* 30: 102–32.

Křenek, Ernst. 1996. *Exploring Music: Essays by Ernst Krenek*. London: Calder and Boyars.

Krzyżanowski, Julian. 1964. *Historia literatury polskiej* [A History of Polish Literature]. Warsaw: Państwowe Wydawnictwo Naukowe.

Kugler, Stefani. 2004. *Kunst-Zigeuner: Konstruktionen des "Zigeuners" in der deutschen Literatur der ersten Hälfte des 19 Jahrhunderts*. Trier: Wissenschaftlicher Verlag.

Kydryński, Lucjan. 1985. *J. Strauss*. Cracow: Polskie Wydawnictwo Muzyczne.

———. 1984. *Przewodnik operetkowy*. Cracow: Polskie Wydawnictwo Muzyczne.

Lacombe, Hervé. 2000. *Georges Bizet*. Paris: Fayard.

Laster, Arnaud. 2003. "Victor Hugo." In *Dictionnaire de la musique en France au XIXe siècle*, edited by Joël-Marie Fauquet, 597–601. Paris: Fayard.

Leblon, Bernard. 2003. *Gypsies and Flamenco: The Emergence of the Art of Flamenco in Andalusia*. Translated by Sinead ni Shuinear. Hatfield: University of Hertfordshire Press, Gypsy Research Centre.

Legány, Dezső. 1976. *Ferenc Liszt and His Country, 1869–1873*. Budapest: Corvina Kiado.

———. 2001a. "Ferenc Erkel." In Vol. 8 of *The New Grove Dictionary of Music and Musicians*, edited by Stanley Sadie, 295–99. London: MacMillan Publishers Ltd.

———. 2001b. "Hungary: Art Music." In Vol. 11 of *The New Grove Dictionary of Music and Musicians*, edited by Stanley Sadie, 846–53. London: MacMillan Publishers Ltd.

Lemon, Alaina. 1991. "Roma (Gypsies) in the Soviet Union and the Moscow *Teatr Romen*." *Nationalities Papers* 19 (3): 359–72.

Lepenies, Wolf. 1996. *Niebezpieczne powinowactwa z wyboru: Eseje na temat historii nauki* [in the original German, Gefährliche Wahlverwandtschaften: Essays zur Wissenschaftsgeschichte]. Translated by Anna Zeidler-Janiszewska. Warsaw: Oficyna Naukowa.

Liszt, Franz. 1859. *Des Bohémiens et de leur musique en Hongrie*. Paris: Bourdillat.

———. 1883. *Die Zigeuner und Ihre Musik in Ungarn*. Translated by Lina Ramann. Leipzig: Breitkopf und Härtel.

———. 1905. *Briefe*, Vol. 4, edited by La Mara [Marie Lipsius]. Leipzig: Breitkopf & Härtel.

———. 1960. *The Gipsy in Music*. Translated by Edwin Evans. London: William Reeves.

Lorca, Federico García. 1965. Edited and translated by Joan L. Gili. Bungay, Suffolk: Penguin Books.

———. 1987. *Od pierwszych pieśni do słów ostatnich* [From the First Songs to the Last Words]. Edited and translated by Zofia Szleyen. Cracow: Wydawnictwo Literackie.

Lowe, David A. 1996. "Pushkin and *Carmen*." *19th-Century Music* 20 (1): 72–76.

Loya, Shay. 2011. *Liszt's Transcultural Modernism and the Hungarian-Gypsy Tradition*. Rochester: University of Rochester Press.

MacDonald, Malcolm. 1993. *Brahms*. London: J. M. Dent.

Machlis, Joseph. 1961. *Introduction to Contemporary Music*. New York: W. W. Norton.

Madeyska, Danuta. 1997. "Wstęp do Opowieść o Az-Zairze Salimie Abu Lajli al-Muhalhilu: Saga arabska" [Introduction to the Story of Az-Zair Salim Abu Lajla al-Muhalhil: An Arab Saga]. In *Orientalizm romantyczny: Arabski romans rycerski (Literatura arabska: Dociekania i prezentacje)* [Romantic Orientalism: Arabic Romance Courtship], edited by Marek M. Dziekan, 63–66. Warsaw: Wydawnictwo Akademickie Dialog.

Mairena, Antonio, and Ricardo Molina. 1963. *Mundo y formas del cante flamenco*. Madrid: Revista de Occidente.

Malvinni, David. 2004. *The Gypsy Caravan: From Real Roma to Imaginary Gypsies in Western Music and Film*. New York: Routledge.

Manuel de Falla. No author. 1922. London: J. & W. Chester Ltd.

Manuel, Peter. 1998. "Andalusian, Gypsy, and Class Identity." In *Gypsies: An Interdisciplinary Reader*, edited by Diane Tong, 175–97. New York: Garland Publishing Inc.

Manuel, Roland. 1930. *Manuel de Falla*. Paris: Editions "Cahiers d'Art."

Marco, Tomas. 1993. *Spanish Music in the Twentieth Century*. Translated by Cola Franzen. Cambridge, MA: Harvard University Press.

Marín, Francisco Rodríguez. 1929. *El alma de Andalucía en sus mejores coplas, elegidas entre más de veintidos mil*. Madrid: Archivos, 1929.

Matos, Manuel García. 1953. "Folklore en Falla I." *Música* 2 (3–4): 41–68.

———. 1958. *Una historia del cante flamenco*. Madrid: Hispavox.

Mátray, Gábor. 1854. "A magyar zene és a magyar cigányok zenéje" [Hungarian and Hungarian Gypsy Music]. In Vol. 4 of *Magyar és Erdélyország képekben* [Hungary and Transylvania in Illustrations], edited by Ferenc Kubinyi and Imre Vahot. Pest: Emich Gusztáv.

May, Florence. 1905. *The Life of Johannes Brahms*. London: Edward Arnold.

Mayer-Serra, Otto. 1943. "Falla's Musical Nationalism." *The Musical Quarterly* 29 (1): 1–17.

McClary, Susan. 1992. *Georges Bizet: Carmen*. Cambridge: Cambridge University Press.

Mérimée, Prosper. 2001. *Listy z Hiszpanii* [Letters from Spain]. Edited by Leszek Sługocki. Łódź: Oficyna Bibliofilów.

Meyer, Michael. 1975. "The Nazi Musicologist as Myth Maker in the Third Reich." *Journal of Contemporary History* 10 (4): 649–65.

Miles, Elizabeth J., and Loren Chuse. 2000. "Spain." In *Europe*, edited by Ellen Koskoff, 588–603. Vol. 8 of the *Garland Encyclopedia of World Music*. New York: Garland.

Mindlin, Roger. 1965. *Die Zarzuela: Das spanische Singspiel im 19 und 20 Jahrhundert*. Zurich: Atlantis Verlag.

Mirga, Andrzej, and Nicolae Gheorhe. 1997. *Romowie w XXI wieku: Studium polityczne* [The Romany of the Twenty-first Century: A Political Study]. Cracow: Universitas.

Mróz, Lech. 2001. *Dzieje Cyganów—Romów w Rzeczypospolitej XV–XVIII w.* [The History of the Romany-Gypsies in Poland from the Fifteenth to Eighteenth Century]. Warsaw: Wydawnictwo DiG.

Mulcahy, F. David. 1990. "Flamenco Women in the 1880s." In *100 Years of Gypsy Studies: Papers from the 10th Annual Meeting of the Gypsy Lore Society,* North American chapter, March 25–27, 1988, edited by Matt T. Salo, 233–50. Cheverly, MD: Gypsy Lore Society.

Murphy, Michael. 2001. Introduction to *Musical Constructions of Nationalism: Essays on the History and Ideology of European Musical Culture, 1800–1945,* edited by Harry White and Michael Murphy. Cork: Cork University Press.

Myers, Helen. 2001. "Ethnomusicology: Pre-1945." In Vol. 8 of *The New Grove Dictionary of Music and Musicians,* edited by Stanley Sadie, 368–78. London: MacMillan Publishers Ltd.

Narbutt, Teodor. 1830. *Rys historyczny ludu cygańskiego* [A Historical Sketch of the Gypsy People]. Vilna: Nakładem i drukiem A. Marcinowskiego.

Newman, Ernest. 1937. *The Life of Richard Wagner.* Vol. 2. London: Cassell.

Noel, Eugenio. 1913. *Escenas y andanzas de la campaña antiflamenca.* Valencia: F. Sempere.

Nohl, Ludwig. 1879. "Franz Liszt's Writings on Music." *The Musical Times and Singing Class Circular* 20 (440): 513–14.

Noica, Constantin. 1995. *The Cantemir Model in Our Culture; or, Memo to the One-Above regarding the Situation of the Spirit in the Three Romanian Provinces.* Translated by Bogdan Stefanescu. Bucharest: Editura Athena.

Northup, Georg T. 1915. "The Influence of George Borrow upon Prosper Mérimée." *Modern Philology* 13 (3): 143–56.

Olszewska, Maria Jolanta. 2004. "O powieściach ludowych J. I. Kraszewskiego raz jeszcze: Próba lektury w kontekście tragedii ludowej" [On the Peasant Novels of J. I. Kraszewski Once Again: An Attempt at Interpretation within the Context of the Peasant Tragedy]. In *Obrazy kultury polskiej w twórczości Józefa Ignacego Kraszewskiego* [Images of Polish Culture in the Oeuvre of Józef Ignacy Kraszewski], edited by Barbara Czwórnóg-Jadczak, 199–213. Lublin: Wydawnictwo Uniwersytetu Marii Curie-Skłodowskiej.

Opieński, Henryk. 1960. *Ignacy Jan Paderewski.* Cracow: Polskie Wydawnictwo Muzyczne.

Paderewski, Ignacy Jan. 1984. *Pamiętniki* [in the original English: *The Paderewski Memoirs*]. Translated by Wanda Lisowska and Teresa Mogilnicka. Cracow: Polskie Wydawnictwo Muzyczne.

Pahlen, Kurt. 1953. *Manuel de Falla und die Musik in Spanien.* Olten und Freiburg im Breisgau: Verlag Otto Walter.

Paige, Diane. 2003. "Janáček and the Captured Muse." In *Janáček and His World,* edited by Michael Beckerman, 79–98. Princeton, NJ: Princeton University Press.

Pesovár, Ernő. 1987. "Typen und Entstehung des Csárdás." *Studia Musicologica Academiae Scientiarum Hungaricae* 29 (1–4): 137–79.

Philips, Miriam. 1990. "The Trained and the Natural Gypsy Flamenco Dancer." In *100 Years of Gypsy Studies: Papers from the 10th Annual Meeting of the Gypsy Lore Society,* North American chapter, March 25–27, 1988, edited by Matt T. Salo, 267–78. Cheverly, MD: Gypsy Lore Society.

Piotrowski, Michał. 1984. *Autonomiczne wartości muzyki.* Poznań: Wydawnictwo Naukowe Uniwersytetu Adama Mickiewicza.

Pobożniak, Tadeusz. 1972. *Cyganie* [The Gypsies]. Cracow: Polska Akademia Nauk.

Presberg, Charles D. 1998. "Precious Exchanges: The Poetics of Desire, Power, and Reciprocity in Cervantes's 'La Gitanilla.'" *Bulletin of the Cervantes Society of America* 18 (2): 53–73.

Pritchett, Victor Sawdon. 1954. *The Spanish Temper.* New York: Alfred A. Knopf.

Przybyszewski, Stanisław. 1959. Moi współcześni. Vol. 1: Wśród obcych [My Contemporaries. Vol. I: Among Strangers]. Warsaw: Czytelnik.

Quintana, Bertha B., and Lois Gray Floyd. 1972. *¡Que Gitano!* New York: Holt, Rinehart and Winston, Inc.

Raba, Bogusław. 2010. *Między romantyzmem a modernizmem: Twórczość kompozytorska Ignacego Jana Paderewskiego* [Between Romanticism and Modernism: The Ouevre of Ignacy Jan Paderewski]. Wrocław: Wydawnictwo Uniwersytetu Wrocławskiego.

Radano, Ronald, and Philip V. Bohlman. 2000. Introduction to *Music and the Racial Imagination,* edited by Ronald Radano and Philip V. Bohlman, 1–53. Chicago: University of Chicago Press.

Reimann, Heinrich. 1903. *Johannes Brahms.* Berlin: Harmonie.

Ribera, Julian. 1929. *Music in Ancient Arabia and Spain.* California: Stanford University Press.

Ringer, Alexander L. 1965. "On the Question of 'Exoticism' in Nineteenth Century Music." *Studia Musicologica Academiae Hungaricae* 7 (fasc. 1/4): 115–23.

Rogalska-Marasińska, Aneta. 2000. *Magiczny świat flamenco* [The Magical Word of the Flamenco]. Cracow: Impuls.

Roth, Norman. 1995. *Conversos, Inquisition, and the Expulsion of the Jews from Spain.* Madison: University of Wisconsin Press.

Ruiz, Enrique Martinez. 2003. *Zarys dziejów Hiszpanii nowożytnej od końca XV wieku do 1808 roku* [An Outline of Spanish History from the End of the Fifteenth Century to 1808]. Translated by Maciej Forycki. Poznań: Instytut Historii UAM.

Salmen, Walter. 1983. "The Musician in the Middle Ages." In *The Social Status of the Professional Musician from the Middle Ages to the 19th Century,* edited by Walter Salmen. 3–29. New York: Pendragon Press.

Sampson, John. 1932. "The Wood Family." *Journal of the Gypsy Lore Society* 11: 56–71.

Saremba, Meinhard. 2003. "Leoš Janáček." In Vol. 9 of *Musik in Geschichte und Gegenwart,* edited by Ludwig Finscher, 871–97. Kassel: Bärenreiter-Verlag.

Sárosi, Bálint. 1970. "Gypsy Musicians and Hungarian Peasant Music." *Yearbook of the International Music Council* 2: 8–27.

———. 1978. *Gypsy Music.* Translated by Fred Macnicol. Budapest: Corvina Press.

———. 1986. *Folk Music: Hungarian Musical Idiom.* Translated by Marina Steiner. Budapest: Corvina Press.

———. 1987. "Die Klarinette in der Zigeunerkapelle." *Studia Musicologica Academiae Scientiarum Hungaricae* 29: 237–43.

———. 1997. "Hungarian Gypsy Music: Whose Heritage?" *The Hungarian Quarterly* 38 (147): 133–39.

———. 2001. "Hungary: Folk Music." In Vol. 11 of *The New Grove Dictionary of Music and Musicians,* edited by Stanley Sadie, 857–60, 863–67, 868–71. London: MacMillan Publishers Ltd.

———. 2004. "The Golden Age of Gypsy Bands in Hungary." *The Hungarian Quarterly* 45 (173): 153–62.

Schneider, David E. 2006. *Bartók, Hungary, and the Renewal of Tradition: Case Studies in the Intersection of Modernity and Nationality.* Berkeley: University of California Press.

Scott, Derek B. 2003. *From the Erotic to the Demonic: On Critical Musicology.* New York: Oxford University Press.

Silverman, Carol. 1996. "Music and Marginality: Roma (Gypsies) of Bulgaria and Macedonia." In *Returning Culture: Musical Changes in Central and Eastern Europe,* edited by Mark Slobin, 231–53. Durham, NC: Duke University Press.

———. 2000. "Rom (Gypsy) Music." In *Europe,* edited by Ellen Koskoff, 270–93. Vol. 8 of the *Garland Encyclopedia of World Music.* New York: Garland.

Sinclair, Albert Thomas. 1907. "Gypsy and Oriental Music." *The Journal of American Folklore* 20 (76): 16–32.

Skarga, Barbara. 1973. "Czy pozytywizm jest kierunkiem antynarodowym?" [Is Positivism a National Current?]. In *Swojskość i cudzoziemszczyzna w dziejach kultury polskiej* [The Domestic and Foreign in the History of Polish Culture], edited by Zofia Stefanowska, 276–304. Warsaw: Państwowe Wydawnictwo Naukowe.

Sokolewicz, Zofia. 1974. *Wprowadzenie do etnologii* [Introduction to Ethnology]. Warsaw: Państwowe Wydawnictwo Naukowe.

Solovcov, Anatol. 1989. *Rimsky-Korsakov.* Cracow: Polskie Wydawnictwo Muzyczne.

Stanton, Edward F. 1974. "The Poetry of Federico García Lorca and *Cante Jondo.*" *South Atlantic Bulletin* 39: 94–103.

Starkie, Walter. 1935–1936. "The Gipsy in Andalusian Folk-Lore and Folk-Music." *Proceedings of the Musical Association,* sixty-second session: 1–20.

Stęszewski, Jan. 1996. "*Lexikon der Juden in der Musik* z perspektywy współczesnej i polskiej" [*Lexikon der Juden in der Musik* from a Contemporary and Polish Perspective]. In *Muzyka i Totalitaryzm* [Music and Totalitarianism], edited by Maciej Jabłoński and Janina Tatarska, 47–59. Poznań: Ars Nova.

Stewart, Michael. 1997. *The Time of Gypsies*. Boulder, CO: Westview Press.

Stokes, Martin. 1994. Introduction to *Ethnicity, Identity and Music: The Musical Construction of Place*, edited by Martin Stokes, 1–27. Oxford: Berg Publishers.

Stutschewsky, Joachim. 1935. *Mein Weg zur jüdischen Musik*. Vienna: Jibneh-Muskiverlag.

Szabolcsi, Bence. ed. 1997. *Béla Bartók: Studies in Ethnomusicology*, Lincoln: University of Nebraska Press.

Szabolcsi, Bence. 1964. *Béla Bartók. His Life in Pictures*. Budapest: Corvina Press.

———. 1974. *A Concise History of Hungarian Music*. Budapest: Corvina Press.

———. 1989. *Pisma*. Vol.2: *Pisma literackie* [Writings. Vol. 2. Literary Writings], edited by Teresa Chylińska. Cracow: Polskie Wydawnictwo Muzyczne.

———. 1989. *Przewodnik baletowy*. Cracow: Polskie Wydawnictwo Muzyczne.

Szász, Zoltán. 1996. "Inter-Ethnic Relations in the Hungarian Half of the Austro-Hungarian Empire." *Nationalities Papers* 24 (3): 391–408.

Szenic, Stanisław. 1969. *Franciszek Liszt*. Warsaw: Państwowy Instytut Wydawniczy.

Szymanowski, Karol. 1925. "Zagadnienie 'ludowości' w stosunku do muzyki współczesnej (Na marginesie artykułu Beli Bartoka u źródeł muzyki ludowej)" ["Folk" in Relation to Modern Music]. *Muzyka* 10: 9–13.

Ševčíková, Hana. 1992. "The Romani Band Leader Panna Cinková." In *Neznámi Rómovia: Zo života a kultúry Cigánov—Rómov na Slovensku* [Unknown Romanies: From the Life and Culture of Gypsies—Romanies in Slovakia], edited by Arne B. Mann, 117–26. Bratislava: Ister Science Press.

Šourek, Otakar. 1987. Introduction to *Ciganske melodie* (op. 55), by Antonin Dvořak. Prague: Editio Supraphon.

Tari, Lujza. 2012. "The Verbunkos: A Music Genre and Musical Symbol of Hungary." *Bulletin of the Transilvania University of Braşov*, series VIII, 5 (54): 81–86.

Taruskin, Richard. 2001. "Nationalism." In Vol. 17 of *The New Grove Dictionary of Music and Musicians*, edited by Stanley Sadie, 689–706. London: MacMillan Publishers Ltd.

Tcherenkov, Lev, and Stéphane Laederich. 2004. *The Roma, Otherwise Known as Gypsies, Gitanos, Ґυφτοι, Tsiganes, Ţigani, Cingene, Zigeuner, Bohémiens, Tavellers, Fahrende, etc*. Basel: Schwabe.

Tiersot, Julien. 1927. "Bizet and Spanish Music." Translated by Theodore Baker. *The Musical Quarterly* 13 (4): 566–81.

Traubner, Richard. 2003. *Operetta: A Theatrical History*. New York: Routledge.

Treugutt, Stefan. 1973. "Postword." In *Swojskość i cudzoziemszczyzna w dziejach kultury polskiej* [The Domestic and Foreign in the History of Polish Culture], edited by Zofia Stefanowska, 393–96. Warsaw: Państwowe Wydawnictwo Naukowe.

Tuchowski, Andrzej. 1998. "Rasistowskie podstawy narodowosocjalistycznej myśli w muzyce" [The Racist Background of National Socialist Thought in Music]. *Muzyka* 1: 41–64.

Turska, Irena. 1959. *"Pan Twardowski" L. Różyckiego* [Pan Twardowski, by L. Różycki]. Cracow: Polskie Wydawnictwo Muzyczne.

Tyldesley, William. 2003. *Michael William Balfe: His Life and His English Operas.* Aldershot: Ashgate.

Tyrell, John. 2001. "Leoš Janáček." In Vol. 12 of *The New Grove Dictionary of Music and Musicians,* edited by Stanley Sadie, 769–92. London: MacMillan Publishers Ltd.

Ujfalussy, József. 1971. *Béla Bartók.* Translated by Ruth Pataki. Budapest: Corvina Press.

Vechten, Carl van. 1920. *The Music of Spain.* London: Kegan Paul, Trench, Trubner & Co.

Vogel, Jaroslav. 1983. *Janaczek.* Cracow: Polskie Wydawnictwo Muzyczne.

Volland, Anita. 1990. *"Carcelera:* Gitano Prison Songs in the 18th Century." *In 100 Years of Gypsy Studies: Papers from the 10th Annual Meeting of the Gypsy Lore Society,* North American chapter, March 25–27, 1988, edited by Matt T. Salo, 251–66. Cheverly, MD: Gypsy Lore Society.

Wagner, Richard. 1964. *Wagner on Music and Drama.* Translated by A. Ashton Ellis. New York: E. P. Dutton & Co.

Waigand, József. 1970. "Totenklage über Panna Czinka." *Studia Musicologica Academiae Scientiarum Hungaricae* 12: 299–310.

Waldenfels, Bernhard. 2002. *Topografia obcego* [in the German original: *Topographie des Fremden*]. Translated by Janusz Sidorek. Warsaw: Oficyna Naukowa Warszawa.

Waldorff, Jerzy. 1959. "Nie dość czarna Carmen." [Not Enough "Black Carmen"] *Film* 47: 4–5.

Walker, Alan. 1989. *The Weimar Years, 1848–1861.* Vol. 2 of *Franz Liszt.* New York: Alfred A. Knopf.

No author. 1897. "Deserted Her Gypsy Lover: The Princess Chimay [Ward] and Rigo Have a Violent Quarrel." *New York Times,* January 28.

No author. 1916. "Clara Ward Dies in Italy." *New York Times,* December 19.

Washabaugh, William. 1996. *Flamenco: Passion, Politics and Popular Culture.* Oxford: Berg Publishers.

———. 1997. "Flamenco Music and Documentary." *Ethnomusicology* 41 (1): 51–67.

Weber, Alison. 1994. "Pentimento: The Parodic Text of 'La Gitanilla.'" *Hispanic Review* 62 (1): 59–75.

Weber, Eckhard. 2000. *Manuel de Falla und die Idee der Spanischen Nationaloper.* Frankfurt am Main: Peter Lang.

Wechsberg, Joseph. 1999. *Królowie walca:Życie, czasy, i muzyka Straussów* [in the original English: *The Waltz Emperors: The Life and Times and Music of the Strauss Family*]. Translated by Maria Boduszyńska-Borowikowa. Warsaw: Państwowy Instytut Wydawniczy.

Weinzweig, Meira. 1990. "Flamenco Fires: Form as Generated by the Performer-

Audience Relationship." In *100 Years of Gypsy Studies: Papers from the 10th Annual Meeting of the Gypsy Lore Society,* North American chapter, March 25–27, 1988, edited by Matt T. Salo, 223–32. Cheverly, MD: Gypsy Lore Society.

Weissweiler, Eva. 1999. *Ausgemerzt! Das Lexikon der Juden in der Musik und seine mörderischen Folgen.* Cologne: Dittrich Verlag.

Westrup, Jack A. 1995. *Purcell.* Oxford: Oxford University Press.

Willems, Wim. 1997. In *Search of the True Gypsy: From Enlightenment to Final Solution.* London: Frank Cass Publishers.

Williams, Adrian. 2000. *Portrait of Liszt: By Himself and His Contemporaries.* Oxford: Clarendon Press.

Williams, Patrick. 1996. *Les Tsiganes de Hongrie et leurs musiques.* Paris: Cité de la Musique and Arles: Actes Sud, collection Musiques du monde.

Wolff, Larry. 1994. *Inventing Eastern Europe: The Map of Civilization on the Mind of the Enlightenment.* Stanford, CA: Stanford University Press.

Wright, Lesley A. 1978. "New Source for *Carmen.*" *19th Century Music* 2 (1): 61–71.

Zern, Brook. 1990. "The Evolution of the Flamenco Guitar." In *100 Years of Gypsy Studies: Papers from the 10th Annual Meeting of the Gypsy Lore Society,* North American chapter, March 25–27, 1988, edited by Matt T. Salo, 215–21. Cheverly, MD: Gypsy Lore Society.

Zieliński, Władysław K. 1896. "Baśnie cyganów polskich." *Wisła* 10: 117–18.

Scores

Songs

Bazzoni, Giovanni. 1868. "La Zingara" (text: Carlo Pepoli). *Soirées italiennes.* Paris: Leon Escudier.

Becker, Julius. 1896[?]. *Die Zigeuner Rhapsodie in VII Gesängen für Solo-und-Chorstimmen mit Beleitung von 2 Violinen, Viola, Violoncelle, Bass, Flöte, 2 Clarinetten, 2 Fagotten, 4 Hörnern, Guitarre, Pauken, Triangel, und Tambourin oder des Pianoforte* (op. 31). Leipzig: C. F. Peters (2866).

Belgiojoso Pompée, Barbiano. 1869. "Les Bohémiens." *In Trois duos pour baryton ou basse-taille* (text: Adolphe M. Baralle). Paris: Au Ménestrel.

Benoit, Pierre. 1869. *La Zingaresque* (op. 11) (text: J. Mellery). Paris: Schott.

Benza, Ludovic. 1868. *La bohémienne bolero* (text: Ali Vial de Sabligny). Paris: A l'Agence Theatre Lyrique et Musicale, H. C. de Ploosen.

Bonoldi, François. 1845. *Chanson d'une Gitana. Romance bolero* (text: Louis Delâtre). Geneva––Graz: no ed.

Bontemps, Germaine. 1962. *Paganes.* Paris: Les Cahiers Francais.

Bouvat, E., and A. Mario. 1911. *Les Bohémiens.* Paris: Chanson Parisienne.

Brahms, Johannes. 1997. "Zigeunerlieder" (op. 103) (text: Hugo Conrat). *The Complete Liebeslieder and Zigeunerlieder for Four Solo Voices and Piano Accompaniment.* Mineola, NY: Dover Publications, Inc.

Busoni, Ferruccio. 1933. *Zigeunerlied im Nebelgeriesel im tiefen Schnee Ballade für Bariton mit Orchester* (op. 55, no. 2) (text: Johann Wolfgang Goethe). Leipzig: Breitkopf & Härtel.

Cottrau, Guillaume. 1843. "La zingarella." In 24 *Nouvelles mélodies national es* [sic] *de Naples.* Paris: Chez l'Auteur.

Desch, Rudolf. 1976. "Zigeunerweise." In *Rudolf Desch: Eine Dokumentation,* edited by Heinrich Poos. Mainz: B. Schott's Sohne.

Dvořák, Antonín. 1987. *Zigeunermelodien* (op. 55) (text: Adolf Heyduk). Prague: Editio Supraphon.

García, Mariano. 1852. *El Jitano.* Paris: Librería Española y Americana.

Goulart, W., and C. Carvalhinho. 1947. *Tzigane (Cigana),* Brésil: Irmaos Vitale.

Hűe, Georges. 1894. *Les Tziganes* (text: Edouard Guinand). Paris: Alphonse Leduc.

Jadin, Louis, *La Zingarella,* Bibliothèque Nationale de France, Paris, Ms. 5123.

Janaček, Leoš. 1984. *Zápisník zmizelého* (anonymous text). Prague: Editio Supraphon.

Jekyll, J., *Tziganeria* (text: Louis Serre). Paris: Crescendo, 1938.

Kozina, Marjan. 1964. "Cigan" (text: Jovan Jovanović). In *Izbrane pesmi.* Lubyána: Notografiral Franc Leder.

Lafarge, Guy. 1944. *Le chemin de l'aventure* (text: Guy Dassoa). Paris: Etoile.

Lambotti, Lucien. 1935. "Le Tsigane dans la lune." *Mélodie avec acc. de piano.* Paris: Alphonse Leduc.

Lassen, Edouard. 1886a. "Au son du tambourin" [Die Musikantin] (text: Emanuel Geibel). *Lieder et Duetti.* Paris: Henri Heugel.

———. 1886b. "La fille de Bohéme" [Die Zigeunerin] (text: Theodor Storm). *Lieder et Duetti.* Paris: Henri Heugel.

———. 1886c. "Ma douce Espagne" [Zigeunerbub im Norden] (text: Emanuel Geibel). *Lieder et Duetti.* Paris: Henri Heugel.

Liszt, Franz. 1907–1936. "Die drei Zigeuner" (text: Nikolaus Lenau). *Musikalische Werke.* Series VII, Vol. 3. Leipzig: Breitkopf & Härtel.

Mercadante, Saverio. 1836. "Zingarella espagnole." *Le retour desire.* Paris: A. Cotelle, 1836.

Michel, Fred. N.d. "Le Tzigane dans la lune." *Dix melodie pour chant et piano.* Paris: Editions Maurice Senart.

Milhaud, Darius. 1954. "La Bohémienne la main." *Six chansons de theatre.* Paris: Heugel & Cie.

Moliére, Roger de. 1945. *Roman Tzigane* (text: Denis Michel). Paris: Comptoir General de Musique Françoise et Etrangere.

Monestes, Abel. 1946. *Myroska* (text: Andre Myra). Paris: La Gasconne.

Moniuszko, Stanisław. 1971 "Cyganie" (anonymous text). In *Dzieła wszystkie.* Seria A. Pieśni IV. Cracow: Polskie Wydawnictwo Muzyczne.

Moreau, W. 1887. "La Bohémienne." *Collection de chansonnettes avec parlé pour jeunes filles.* Paris: Rene Haton.

Moyzes, Alexander. 1934. "Bili še cigáni." *Dvanast' lud'ovych piesni zo Šariša.* Prague: Hudebni matice umelecke besady.

Nicholls, Horatio. 1930. *Gipsy Melody* (text: Harry Carlton). Paris: Lawrence Wright.

Ponce, Manuel M. 1951. "La Bohémienne." *3 poems de Lermontov.* Argentina: Mendoza.

Reid, Billy. 1945. *The Gipsy.* Paris: Editions Musicales Peter Maurice.

Samazeuilh, Gustave. 1928. *Gitane: Esquisse d'Espagne.* Paris: Alphonse Leduc.

Schoeck, Othmar. N.d. "Die drei Zigeuner" (text: Nikolaus Lenau). In *Lieder nach Gedichten von Lenau, Hebbel, Dehmel und Spitteler,* Edition Breitkopf, no. 5027a.

Schumann, Robert. N.d. "Zigeunerleben" (op. 29) (text: Emmanuel Geibel). In *Gesänge für gemischten Chor,* no. 9559. Leipzig: Edition Peters.

———. N.d. "Zigeunerliedchen" (op. 79, nos. 7 and 8). In *Sämtliche Lieder.* Leipzig: Edition Peters, no. 2242.

Shaporin, Youry. 1960. Desiat romansov: Na stikhi sovetskikh poetov (op. 21) *(Ten Romances to Words by Soviet Poets).* Moscow: Sowiecki Kompozytor.

Simone, Marie. N.d. *La Tzigane: Valse chantée.* Bordeaux: Propriete de l'autor.

Szentirmay, Elemertol. Ca. 1855. *10 chansons hongroises du repertoire des Tziganes.* Budapest: Harmonia.

Terestchenko, Théodore. 1913. *Bohémiens.* Paris: J. Hamelle.

Unia, Louis, and J. du Rivaux. N.d. *Bohémien d'amour.* Paris: Editions Jancel.

Verdi, Giuseppe. "La Zingara" (text: Manfredo Maggioni). *Reccolta di melodie.* Paris: Leon Escudier.

Wolf, Hugo. N.d. "Die Zigeunerin." *Gedichte von J. von Eichendorff.* Edition Peters, no. 9246.

Wolkoff, N. de. 1882. *Air Bohémien Russe* (*Tziganes*) (op. 30). Paris: Delanchy.

Zoll, Paul. 1961. *Mond über dem Zigeunerwagen.* Munich: Verlag F. E. C. Leuckart.

Instrumental Compositions

FOR PIANO (OR *CLAVECIN*)

Aceves, Rafaël de. 1901. "Bohémienne" (op. 65 no. 6). *Danses d'Espagne.* Paris: Henry Lemoine.

———. 1904. "Folie Gitane" (op. 60, no. 5). *Danses d'Espagne.* Paris: Henry Lemoine.

Bachmann, Georges. 1887. *Les Zingari: Air de ballet.* Paris: Brandus et Cie.

Baltet, Jean-Raymond, and R. Desplanques. 1946. *Tzigane rumba.* Paris: Editiones Musicales Imperia.

Bartalus, Étienne. 1878. "Chanson hongroise." *Repertoire des Tziganes.* Paris: Aux bureaux du Journal de Musique.

Barthon, Michel. 1906. *Tziganerie pour piano.* Paris: G. Hamelle.

Batta, Laurent. 1844. *La Bohémienne: 1er grande valse originale pour piano.* Paris: Bernard Lutte.

Benedictus. 1889. "Le Tzigane." *Les musiques bizarre: A l'exposition.* Paris: G. Hartmann et Cie.

Beretta, Regina. 1887. *Zingara: Fantaisie pour piano.* Paris: Brandus et Cie.

Bermalty, P. 1901. *Tzigana: Valse pour piano* (op. 3). Paris: Hachette.

Blumenthal, Jacques. 1861. *Les Bohémiens: Chanson populaires Russes* (op. 57). Paris: Alexandre Grus.

Brahms, Johannes. 1963. *Ungarische Tänze.* Budapest: Edition Musica.

Chaminade, Cecile. N.d. *Zingara* (op. 27, no. 2). Breslau: Jules Hainauer.

Clement, Charles-François 1764. "La Bohémienne." *Journal de clavecin: Composé sur Ariettes des Comedies; Intermedies; et Opera Comiques, qui ont eu le plus de succès, Par Mr. Clement.* Paris: Grave par Mme. Leclair.

Colombo, Joseph. 1946. *Zingarella: Valse musette.* Paris: Martin-Cayla.

Dovillez, J. 1907. "Chanson Tzigane: Morceaux de genre." *Six pieces pour piano.* Paris: Herbert Strasser.

Fiorelli, M. 1904. *Rêve de Tzigane.* Paris: Alphonse Leduc.

Goddard, Benjamin. 1895. *Tziganka: Bohémienne Russe pour piano.* Paris: J. Hamelle.

Gottschalk, Louis M. 1907. *La Gitanilla.* Paris: Hachette.

Gracey, Maurice. 1925. *Suite tzigane no. 3, "Czardas"* [1906]. *Ce qu'on Aime a entendre: Collection de 15 morceaux célèbres publiés (pour piano).* Paris: Editions Smyth.

Jeziorski, A. de. 1881. *La Zigeuna: Polka pour piano.* Paris: Joly Imp.

Ketterer, Eugène. 1875. *Bohema caprice de concert.* Paris: Leon Grus.

Kruger, Wilhelm. 1846. *Fantaisie sur la Gitana de Fr. Bonoldi.* Paris: Pacini.

Kuhe, Wilhelm. N.d. "Zigeuner Trinklied: Chanson Bohémienne" (op. 138). *Recueil des pieces modern es [sic]et classiques pour piano.* Kieff: I. Tchokoloff.

Lack, Theodore. 1886. *Tziganyi* (op. 104). Paris: Henri Heugel.

Lea, Filippo. 1908. *La Bohémienne: Nouvelle danse.* Nice: Delrieu Freres.

Lebeau, Alfred. 1872. *Tzigane Marsch: Ronde Bohéme* (op. 119). Paris: Leon Grus.

Leclerc, Jean. Ca. 1725. "La Boëmiene." *Premier receüil de contradanses et la table par lettre alphabetique et chiffrée.* Paris: Bibliotheque National de France, Paris, Ms. 6675.

Lecocq, Charles. 1856. *La Zingara: Danse bohémienne pour piano* (op. 9). Paris: E. Girod.

Liszt, Franz. 1843. *Ungarischer Sturmmarsch.* Berlin: Schlesinger.

———. 1972. *Hungarian Rhapsodies.* Budapest: Editio Musica.

———. 2002. "La zingarella spagnuola," from "Soirées italiennes." *Six amusements pour piano sur des motifs des Mercadante.* Budapest: Editio Music.

Longperier, Alfred de. N.d. *Les Bohémiens: Quadrille pour le piano a quatre mains.* Paris: Au Bureau du Journal des Pianistes.

Magnus, Désiré. 1868. *Tziganes marche: Souvenir de Hongrie.* Paris: G. Brandus et S. Dufour.

Michel, Alfred. 1881. *Souvenir tziganes.* Paris: Ed. Delanchy.

Michiels, Gustave. 1908. *Bohema czardas.* Paris: A. Rouart & Cie.

Mocker, Melchior. 1853. *La zingarella: Danse boheme pour piano* (op. 10). Paris: Etienne Challiot.

Mompou, Federico. 1921. "Gitano." *Impressions intimes.* Bilbao: Union Musicales Espanola.

———. 1922a. "Gitane I." *Suburbis.* Paris: Editions Maurice Senart.

———. 1922b. "Gitane II." *Suburbis.* Paris: Editions Maurice Senart.

Peyronnin, Jean, and Gousty Malla. 1942. *Zingarina: Java variations.* Paris: Parnasse-Edition.

Philipot, Jules. 1884. *Air tzigane* (op. 133). Paris: Leon Grus.

René, Charles. 1893. "Les Bohémiens." *Le Voyageur.* Paris: A. Quinzard.

Renner, André. 1901. *Bohémienne* (op. 3). Paris: F. Durdilly.

Reyer, Louis-Etienne Ernest. 1869. *Marsche tzigane.* Paris: Choudens.

Rougnon, Paul. 1899. *Tziganetta: Air de ballet pour piano.* Paris: Gaston Gross.

Simonnot, E. 1969. *La Zingara: Saltarelle pour piano* (op. 65). Paris: E. Chatot Editeur.

Smith, Sydney. N.d. *Marche Hongrois* (op. 166). London: Ashdown and Parry, no. 12778.

Stoerkel, Eugène. 1890. *Chanson tzigane.* Paris: G. Ondet.

Streabbog, Louis. 1901. *La Gitana: Souvenir d'Espagne.* Paris: Benoit.

Toselli, Enrico. 1925. "Zingaresca/Czardas." *Ce qu'on aime a entendre: Collection de 15 morceaux célèbres publiés.* Paris: Editions Smyth.

Verginy, Marie de. 1887. *Tzigane: Impromptu pour piano.* Paris: A. O'Kelly.

Vizentini, Albert. 1900. "Bohémienne." *Airs espagnols pour piano.* Paris: Paul Dupont.

Waldteufel, Emile. 1889. *Les Bohémiens.* Paris: Durand & Schoenwerk.

Widor, Charles Maria. 1924. *La zingarella: Danse pour piano.* Paris: Heugel.

Wollenhaupt, Hermann Adolf. N.d. *Marche Hongroise* (op. 66). Moscow: A. Gutheil.

FOR VIOLIN AND PIANO

Monti, Vittorio. 1912. *Zingaresca.* Paris: G. Ricordi et Cie.

———. 2002. *Czardasz na skrzypce i fortepian.* Cracow: Polskie Wydawnictwo Muzyczne.

Pimack, Stef, and André Cahard. 1956. "Tziganes de Craiova." *Valses de folklore.* Paris: Editions Fernard Grave.

———. 1959. "La Gitane de Nikopoli." *Valses de folklore.* Paris: Editions Fernard Grave.

Rubinoff, Dave. 1938. "Gipsy Fantasy." Paris: Editions Salabert.

Sarasate, Pablo. 1883. *Carmen: Fantaisie de concert pour violon avec accompagniment de piano* (op. 25). Paris: Choudens Editeur.

———. 1895. *Zigeunerweisen* (op. 20). New York: Carl Fischer.

Viot, Maurice. 1922. "Zingara: Caprice hongrois." Paris: Jules Raux.

FOR INSTRUMENTAL ENSEMBLE

Ferrari, Louis. 1945. *Bohémienne valse.* Paris: Editions Continental.

Jenner, Clement, and A. Barthelemo. 1939. *Tzingarella: Valse musettte.* Paris: Petit Duc.

Lucchesi, José M. 1941. *Les Tziganes de Budapest.* Paris: Henry Lemoine.

Michel, Fred. 1924. *Le Tzigane amoureaux.* Paris: Maurice Senart.

Paulin, Gaston. 1911. *Tzigania* (op. 143). Paris: Henry Lemoine et Cie, Éditeurs.

FOR ORCHESTRA

Ravel, Maurice. 1924. *Tzigane* (op. 25). Paris: Durand & Cie.

Wieniawski, Henryk. 1976. "Allegro con fuoco" (à la Zingara), from *II Violin Concerto in D minor* (op. 22). In Vol. 3 of *Dzieła wszystkie.* Cracow: Polskie Wydawnictwo Muzyczne.

Stage Works

SCORES

Bizet, Georges. 1967. *Carmen*. Leipzig: Edition Peters.

De Falla, Manuel. 1961. *El amor brujo*. Moscow: Casa de Ediciones Musicales de Estado.

Di Capua, Rinaldo. 1753. *La Bohémienne: Intermedie en deaux actes*. Bibliotheque Nationale de France, Paris, Ms. 188D.

García, Manuel. *El Jitano por amor*. Bibliothèque Nationale de France, Paris, Ms. 8364 and Ms. 8365.

Lully, Jean-Baptiste. 1720. *Le carneval mascarade mise en musique*. Paris: De l'Imprimerie de J-B-Christophe Ballard.

Moniuszko, Stanisław. 1952. *Gypsy Dance from Opera "Jawnuta."* Cracow: Polskie Wydawnictwo Muzyczne.

Paderewski, Ignacy Jan. 1901. *Manru*. Berlin: Ed. Bote & G. Bock.

Strauss, Johann. 1968. *Die Fledermaus*. Leipzig: Edition Peters, no. 9778.

Stravinsky, Igor. 1952. *The Fairy's Kiss*. London: Boosey & Hawkes.

———. 1965. *Petrouchka*. London: Boosey & Hawkes.

Thomas, Ambroise. N.d. *Mignon*. Paris: Heugel et Cie.

Weber, Carl Maria von. 1986. "Overture to Preciosa." *Great Overtures in Full Score*, by Carl Maria von Weber. New York: Dover Publications, Inc.

Ziehrer, Carl Michael. 1898. *Der schöne Rigo: Operette in 2 Acten*. Leipzig: Josef Weinberger.

PIANO EXTRACTS

Balfe, Michael William. 1870. *La Zingara*. Paris: E. Gerard et Cie.

Donizetti, Gaetano. 1855. *La Zingara*. Paris: Schonenberger.

Herbert, Victor. 1898. *The Fortune Teller*. New York: M. Witmark & Sons.

Kálmán, Emmerich. 1924. *Gräfin Mariza*. Vienna: W. Karczag.

Lehár, Franz. 1908. *Zigeunerliebe*. Vienna: W. Karczag & C. Wallner.

Noskowski, Zygmunt. 1902. "Gypsy Song" from *Święto ognia* (text: Marian Prażmowski). Cracow: S. A. Krzyżanowski.

Strauss, Johann. N.d. *Zigeunerbaron*. Brussels: Verlag von Aug. Granz.

LIBRETTOS

Champsaur, Félicien. 1887. *Les Bohemiens*. Paris: E. Dentu & Cie.

Krumłowski, Konstanty. 1931. *Piękny Rigo* (with music by Józef Marek). Cracow: Nakładem księgarni "Wiedza i Sztuka."

Lehár, Franz. 1910. *Cygańska miłość* [Gypsy Love]. Polish translation by A. Kitschman and L. Śliwiński. Warsaw: A. Thiell.

Index